ISLAMIC MYTHS AND MEMORIES

T0353055

To the memory of Joseph Kostiner

Islamic Myths and Memories

Mediators of Globalization

Edited by

ITZCHAK WEISMANN
Haifa University, Israel

MARK SEDGWICK
Aarhus University, Denmark

ULRIKA MÅRTENSSON
Norwegian University of Science and Technology,
Trondheim, Norway

Routledge
Taylor & Francis Group

LONDON AND NEW YORK

First published 2014 by Ashgate Publishing

Published 2016 by Routledge
2 Park Square, Milton Park, Abingdon, Oxfordshire OX14 4RN
711 Third Avenue, New York, NY 10017, USA

First issued in paperback 2016

Routledge is an imprint of the Taylor & Francis Group, an informa business

British Library Cataloguing in Publication Data
A catalogue record for this book is available from the British Library.

The Library of Congress has cataloged the printed edition as follows:
Islamic myths and memories : mediators of globalization / edited by Itzchak Weismann, Mark Sedgwick and Ulrika Mårtensson.
    p. cm.
    Includes bibliographical references and index.
    ISBN 978-1-4724-1149-5 (hardcover) –
1. Globalization–Religious aspects–Islam. 2. Islam–Historiography. 3. Islamic sociology. I. Weismann, Itzchak. II. Sedgwick, Mark J. III. Mårtensson, Ulrika.
    BP190.5.G56I85 2014
    297.2'7–dc23

                                                                                2013051040

ISBN 13: 978-1-138-24598-3 (pbk)
ISBN 13: 978-1-4724-1149-5 (hbk)

Contents

List of Figures and Tables

Figures

Tables

Notes on Contributors

Gerd Marie Ådna is an associate professor at the School of Mission and Theology in Stavanger, Norway, where she teaches Religious Studies. She works on Islam, rituals, and the pedagogics and didactics of religion. Her doctoral thesis, "O Son of the Two Sacrifices: Muhammad and the Formation of Sacrifice in Early Islam," was defended at the University of Bergen in 2007.

Shosh Ben-Ari is a senior lecturer in Middle East History and Arabic and Islamic Literature at the University of Haifa, Israel. Her PhD, on Abraham in Islamic literature, was awarded by Tel Aviv University in 2003. As well as publishing on Abraham, she has researched historical periodicity and the evolution of language in Ibn Khaldun's *al-Muqaddima*, and the transition from nomad to sedentary life (acculturation) in the Arab world and its reflection in social and cultural life. She also researches Islamic preaching and preachers' adaptation to globalization.

Nimrod Luz is a senior lecturer at the Department of Sociology and Anthropology at the Western Galilee College, Israel. His areas of research include the relationship between culture, politics, and the built environment, focusing mostly on the Middle East and the Muslim world. He explored urbanism in the premodern Middle East and published several monographs on minority communities in Israel as well as numerous articles in Middle Eastern and geographical journals. He has held several research posts in Indiana University South Bend and the Max Planck Institute in Berlin. His latest project, "Enchanted Places in the Margins," focuses on the politics of sacred places among Palestinian communities in Israel.

Ulrika Mårtensson is a professor at the Norwegian University of Science and Technology, Trondheim, Norway, where she teaches Religious Studies, including religion and globalization. Her main work focuses on relations between social institutions and Islam in medieval and contemporary contexts. Her recent works include *Tabari* (2009, in the series Makers of Islamic Civilization), and she has recently co-edited *Fundamentalism in the Modern World* (2 volumes,

I.B. Tauris 2011) and a special issue of the *Journal of the Economic and Social History of the Orient*, "Challenging Culturalism: 'Materialist' Approaches to Islamic History" (also 2011).

Anne Birgitta Nilsen is associate professor at Oslo and Akershus University College of Applied Sciences, Norway. She is by training a sociolinguist with a specialization in Arabic and Middle Eastern studies. Rhetoric, discourse analysis, translation studies and intercultural communication are among her research interests. Her recent publications include "Verbal and visual hate speech" (2012, in Norwegian), "Osama bin Laden – the hero and the demon" (2012, in Norwegian), "The visual rhetoric of Osama bin Laden" (2013, in Norwegian).

Martin Riexinger is associate professor of Arab and Islamic Studies at Aarhus University, Denmark. His MA is from Tübingen, his PhD from Freiburg im Breisgau, with a dissertation on *Ṣanāʾullāh Amritsarī (1868–1948) und die Ahl-i Ḥadīs im Punjab unter britischer Herrschaft*, and his Habilitation from Göttingen, with *Die verinnerlichte Schöpfungsordnung: Weltbild und normative Konzepte in den Werken Said Nursis (gest. 1960) und der Nur Cemaati*. Riexinger works on Islam from the eighteenth century to the present, and in particular on the reception of modern science.

Mark Sedgwick is professor of Arab and Islamic Studies at Aarhus University, Denmark. He previously taught for many years at the American University in Cairo, Egypt. He is by training a historian, and works primarily on Sufism, Islam and modernity, Islam in Europe, and terrorism. His books include *Muhammad Abduh: A Biography* (2009), *Saints and Sons: The Making and Remaking of the Rashidi Ahmadi Sufi Order, 1799–2000* (2005), and *Against the Modern World: Traditionalism and the Secret Intellectual History of the Twentieth Century* (2004).

Uriya Shavit is a senior lecturer at the department for Arab and Islamic Studies and the Program for Religious Studies at Tel Aviv University, Israel. His recent books include *My Enemy, My Mentor: Arab Islamist and Liberal Discourses on the Zionist Movement and Israel* (with Ofir Winter, 2013, in Hebrew), *The New Imagined Community: Global Media and the Construction of National and Muslim Identities of Migrants* (2009), and *The War of Democracy: Arabs and the West since the End of the Cold War* (2007, in Hebrew), also a new book, *Islamism and The West* (2013).

Xiaofei Tu is lecturer in the Department of Foreign Languages, Literatures, and Cultures at Appalachian State University, USA. As well as working on Islam in China, he has worked on the philosophy of the Chinese New Confucian thinkers, and the Japanese Kyoto School philosophers. His most recent book is *In the Face of a Brave New World* (2008).

Itzchak Weismann is professor of Middle Eastern History and head of the Jewish-Arab Center at the University of Haifa, Israel. He has also held research posts at St Anthony's College, Oxford and at Princeton University. He works on Islamic movements, Sufism, the preaching of Islam, modern Syria, and Islam in the Indian subcontinent. His books include *The Naqshbandiyya: Orthodoxy and Activism in a Worldwide Sufi Tradition* (2007) and *Taste of Modernity: Sufism, Salafiyya, and Arabism in Late Ottoman Damascus* (2001).

Introduction:

Islamic Myths and Memories Facing the Challenge of Globalization

Itzchak Weismann, Mark Sedgwick and Ulrika Mårtensson

"To be born again," sang Gibreel Farishta tumbling from the heavens, "first you have to die ... To land upon the bosomy earth, first one needs to fly ..." Out of thin air: a big bang, followed by falling stars. A universal beginning, a miniature echo of the birth of time ... the jumbo jet Bostan, Flight AI-420, blew apart without warning, high above the great, beautiful, snow-white, illuminated city, Mahagonny, Babylon, Alphaville.[1]

So begins a powerful postmodern myth of globalization that spans Muhammad's jahiliyya and today's cosmopolitan London: immigration, the big city, and the unavoidable accompaniment: terrorism. Salman Rushdie's *Satanic Verses* features as its heroes Gibreel Farishta, the angel Gabriel who doubles as a Bollywood superstar, and Saladin Chamcha, the satanic anti-hero Salah al-Din who tries but fails to be British. In their interactions in heaven and on earth both are beyond reality and imagination, good and evil, past and present, East and West.

The present wave of Islamic resurgence coincides with the era of globalization. Radical Islamists perpetuate the religio-national struggles begun at the height of modernity by the Muslim Brothers and Jama'at-i Islami against colonial powers and indigenous secularized governments; but, operating from globally marginalized Muslim countries or from Western diaspora enclaves, Osama Bin Laden and the Jihadi-Salafis also transcend their forebears in an apocalyptic fight against worldwide unbelief.[2] At the other end of the scale, liberal Islamic intellectuals, many of them living in North America or Western Europe, are reiterating the modernist quest of Muhammad 'Abduh and Sayyid Ahmad Khan to accommodate the West; yet, at the same time today's modernists substitute for their predecessors' apologetics a new confidence in a shared worldwide

---

[1]   Salman Rushdie, *The Satanic Verses* (London: Viking, 1988).

[2]   Bernard Rougier (ed.), *Que'st-ce que le Salafisme?* (Paris: Presses Universitaires de France, 2008); Roel Meijer (ed.), *Global Salafism: Islam's New Religious Movement* (London, Hurst & Co., 2009).

destiny.[3] From yet another angle, localized Muslim masses in the shantytowns of underdeveloped Muslim-majority countries or in the banlieues of the big cities in the West, once thought to be festering in their place, are now seen claiming their rights and freedoms, whether in the popular uprisings of the so-called Arab Spring or in demanding recognition as citizens on equal terms with the non-Muslim majorities in the West.

The media is an indispensable component of these popular uprisings as well as of the contemporary Islamic resurgence. From Imam Khomeini's smuggled cassette tapes of his sermons during the Islamic revolution in Iran, to Osama Bin Laden's provocative declarations of unbounded jihad against America and its allies on al-Jazeera, to Yusuf al-Qaradawi's moderated Wasatiyya tendency on the same channel, to Tariq Ramadan's appearances in the Western media calling for intercivilizational dialogue, to Shaykh Nazim's online spiritual advice to virtual disciples, to 'Amr Khalid's "New Preaching," Muslim men of religion of all colors and shades have made full use of the new informational technology to promote their various causes. The veteran Arab Afghans' easy shift between arenas of conflict in Bosnia, Chechnya, Somalia, Kashmir, and the Philippines, the spectacle of 9/11 in New York and Washington, and internationally financed "start-up" terrorist acts from Madrid and London to Casablanca and Bali, and the jihadi da'wa (call to Islam) on the internet, all indicate that radical Islam fully participates in the current compression of the world.[4]

Myth and Memory

The literature on Islam and globalization is vast and rapidly growing.[5] There is also a wide variety of studies on the place of the mass media in the contemporary Islamic resurgence.[6] The present book seeks to contribute to this ongoing research

---

[3] John Cooper, Ronald Nettler, and Mohamed Mahmoud (eds), *Islam and Modernity: Muslim Intellectuals Respond* (London: I.B. Tauris, 1998).

[4] Gary R. Bunt, Islam in the Digital Age: E-Jihad, Online Fatwas, and Cyber Islamic Environments (London: Pluto Press, 2003); Mark Sageman, *Understanding Terror Networks* (Philadelphia: University of Pennsylvania Press, 2004).

[5] See for example, Olivier Roy, *Globalized Islam: The Search for a New Ummah* (New York: Columbia University Press, 2004); Peter Mandaville, *Global Political Islam* (London and New York: Routledge, 2007).

[6] Charles Hirschkind, *The Ethical Soundscape: Cassette Sermons and Islamic Counterpublics* (New York: Columbia University Press, 2006); Mohamed Zayani (ed.), *The Al Jazeera Phenomenon: Critical Perspectives on New Arab Media* (Boulder: Paradigm

by focusing on two interrelated theoretical perspectives that constitute a major component in the culture of globalization. These revolve around the concepts of myth and memory. The importance of myths of origins and collective memory has been recognized in the study of Western culture, and perhaps especially in the study of Israel,[7] but until now it has been little used in the study of Islam, and hardly at all in the study of globalized Islam.[8]

Mythological thinking and socio-cultural remembering (and forgetting) have been major mechanisms for the constitution and maintenance of all societies, both premodern and modern. Articulated through religious beliefs,[9] or the imagination of the nation,[10] they secure their communities' attachment to specific times and places. The essays in this collection seek to explore how the annulment of spatial/temporal distances by globalization and the contraction of the world by the new communication technologies underlying it has affected the cherished myths and memories of the Muslim community, and how various contemporary Islamic thinkers and movements have responded to the challenges of globalization by preserving, reviving, reshaping, or transforming these myths and memories altogether.

In the present environment of impersonal market forces, ubiquitous media signs, governmental disengagement, mass consumption, and worship of the here and now, myths may seem redundant and collective memory attenuated. Pierre Nora believes that it was under such circumstances that myth came to be

---

Publishers, 2005); Gary R. Bunt, *iMuslims: Rewiring the House of Islam* (Chapel Hill: The University of North Carolina Press, 2009).

7   See, for example, Yael Zerubavel, *Recovered Roots: Collective Memory and the Making of Israeli National Tradition* (Chicago: University of Chicago Press, 1995).

8   For the use of these concepts for studies of early Islam, see: Jaroslav Stetkevytch, *Muhammad and the Golden Bough: Reconstructing Arabian Myth* (Bloomington, IN: Indiana University Press, 1996); Suzanne Pinckney Stetkevytch, *The Poetics of Islamic Legitimacy: Myth, Gender, and Ceremony in the Classical Arabic Ode* (Bloomington, IN: Indiana University Press, 2002); and Suleiman Ali Mourad, *Early Islam between Myth and History: al-Hasan al-Basri (d. 110H/728CE) and the Formation of His Legacy in Classical Islamic Scholarship* (Leiden: Brill, 2006). Regarding globalized Islam, see Samir Amghar on Salafi political myth in S. Amghar, Amel Boubakeur, and Michaël Emerson (eds), *European Islam: Challenges for Public Policy and Society* (Brussels: Centre for European Policy Studies, 2007), pp. 38–51.

9   Mircea Eliade, *The Myth of Eternal Return: Or, Cosmos and History* (Princeton: Princeton University Press, 1954).

10   Anthony Smith, "National Identity and Myth of Ethnic Descent," in his *Myths and Memories of the Nation* (Oxford: Oxford University Press, 1999); Benedict Anderson, *Imagined Communities: Reflections on the Origins and Spread of Nationalism* (revised ed., London and New York: Verso, 1991), ch. 11.

regarded as merely false belief, while memory resorted to the aid of unceasing cycles of commemorations.[11] We contend that not only are past myths and collective memory very much alive in contemporary localized struggles for identity, but that they are also deployed in the ongoing construction of worldwide networks. For today's Islamic thinkers and activists—as, indeed, for all myth-makers—myths and memories are not mere nostalgia, but rather important tools in the cultural politics of globalization. Myth and memory are constantly deployed, at both global and local levels, in evolving public discourses on religion, society, and politics, in the practical ways in which *da'wa* (Islamic preaching) is reconstructed as the backbone of community and meaning, and in the modes by which jihad is reformulated in the struggle for the sake of the faith community.

The concept of myth usually refers to stories of epic character about gods or (super)human heroes. Such stories are known from the dawn of history, and in modern times their study has been pursued particularly by social anthropologists and students of comparative religion. Most myths deal with the past—creation myths, of the universe or of the ethnie—but some may turn to the future, as with apocalyptic myths. Many of them are also connected to specific places—the center of the world, the place of origin, the site of the end of days.[12] As Emmanuel Sivan notes in his discussion of Arab political myths, their function beyond the recreational aspect is twofold: to provide an explanation for current realities, and to mobilize for action. The first involves locating the present in the historical continuum, the second legitimizes or delegitimizes the existing order.[13]

Islam has its share of myths of origins and hero myths, epic stories about the time, places, and people with whom the deity was present. These of course center on Muhammad, the seal of the prophets (*khatam al-nabiyiin*) and the model (*al-uswa al-hasana*) for all Muslims throughout the ages, and on Mecca and Medina, the sites of his call. Other prophets, righteous men and fighters for the cause of Islam, second him in various localized levels. This is the context of the myth of the Satanic temptation of the Prophet that Salman Rushdie reused with reference to contemporary concerns of Muslims in the West, as Ulrika Mårtensson's contribution to this volume demonstrates, as well as of the retelling of stories of the prophets among Muslim immigrants discussed by Gerd Marie

---

[11]   Pierre Nora (ed.), *Les Lieux de Memoire* (3 vols. Paris: Gallimard, 1984–1992).

[12]   Robert A. Segal, *Myth: A Very Short Introduction* (Oxford: Oxford University Press, 2004); David Leeming, *Myth: A Biography of Belief* (New York: Oxford University Press, 2002).

[13]   Emmanuel Sivan, *Arab Political Myths* (Tel Aviv: Am Oved, 1988), in Hebrew; see also Samir Amghar's analysis of Salafi political myth, note 8 above.

Ådna. In the Muslim majority countries, the lessons of the prophets are taken up and adapted to the concerns of the common people by "new preachers" such as Amru Khaled, analyzed by Shosh Ben Ari. Of special status for the Sunni Muslims are also the Prophet's companions, the collective hero of the pious forefathers (*al-salaf al-salih*), which is the best of generations, while for Shi'is these are the imams, the usurpation of whose power is deplored in the Ashura ritual to this day.

The myth of the Rightly Guided Caliphs, who were responsible for the great conquests of early Islam, and the reenactment of this myth by the Ottomans in the face of the modern European onslaught, inspires not only Bin Laden and the globalized militants of al-Qaeda, but also contemporary Turkish popular culture, as Martin Riexinger's chapter shows. The myth of the *shura*, the council that was formed to choose the third Caliph, frames some liberal Muslims' call for democracy, as well as that of Yusuf al-Qaradawi, as presented by Uriya Shavit. A later myth, which was appropriated for a time by Arab nationalists but has now returned to the Islamic fold, is that of the Crusaders, who had attacked Muslim lands but were ultimately repulsed. The contemporary use made of this myth is discussed in this volume, among others, by Xiaofei Tu in the unusual context of China. The myth of the apocalypse, as Itzchak Weismann shows, has been adjusted to the global cultural economy by the Sufi Shaykh Nazim, who frames it as a response to the globalized Salafi-Wahhabi challenge to Sufism.

More recently a different, depersonalized and profanitized, meaning of myth has been offered and gained ground within the cultural discipline of semiotics. Roland Barthes characterizes "myth today" as an ideology or "speech," in which preexisting signs are appropriated and stripped of their historical context and signification, to be infused with new mystifying conceptual content. This has "the task of giving an historical intention a natural justification and making contingency appear eternal." In this way myths make particular worldviews appear to be unchallengeable because natural or God-given.[14] Capitalizing on these insights, Bruce Lincoln remarks that such mystification may serve not only the bourgeoisie, as Barthes believed, but also other strata of society, and that myths not only reflect, encode, and help replicate established structures, but may also be employed as effective instruments of struggle against them.[15]

Most powerful among the sort of ideological myths observed by Barthes in contemporary Islam are Sayyid Qutb's trans-historical use of the concept of *jahiliyya* (the era of ignorance or barbarity that preceded Islam), through which

---

[14] Roland Barthes, *Mythologies* (Paris: Editions du Seuil, 1957).

[15] Bruce Lincoln, *Discourse and the Construction of Society: Comparative Studies of Myth, Ritual, and Classification* (New York: Oxford University Press, 1989), pp. 5–7.

he conveyed Islamist resistance to Nasser's oppressive regime,[16] and the image of *al-Haram al-Sharif* in Jerusalem found in so many houses across the Muslim world, a visual representation of the Palestinians' plight which Nimrod Luz discusses in relation to the Palestinian minority in Israeli. Such myths on the more mundane level are women's struggle to drive in Saudi Arabia, the *purda* in London, and the American Idol competition in Afghanistan, which point to specifically Islamic tensions between freedom and bondage, equality and hierarchy, individualism and collectivism, tradition and modernity, and the local and the global. Globalized media may transform and globalize these myths, but they have their limits: the global *umma* created through images in the media remains a virtual *umma*.

The concept of memory has likewise two major meanings that span the fault line of the cultural turn of the late twentieth century. One is conveyed through Maurice Halbwachs' seminal term of collective memory, which emphasizes the importance of the social in the process of remembering. He claimed that every social group develops a memory of its past through shared images, stories, and rituals that highlight its unique identity, providing it with a sense of continuity through time and space, and enhancing its solidarity. Modern societies in particular also tend to refashion their past in order to further some present political objective. What society remembers or forgets thus reflects its self image, identity, aspirations, and the course of action it wishes to take.[17] Jan and Aleida Assmann's complementary concept of cultural memory stresses the role of traditions transmitted through the generations in shaping the collective memory. Within it they distinguish between functional memory, which reflects what a society needs, and stored memory, conscious and unconscious, which makes room for the heretical, the subversive, and the disowned.[18]

Like all other peoples, Muslims' remembering and forgetting are shaped between their sociopolitical circumstances and cultural traditions. The predominant Islamic regressive view of history as a process of deterioration from the time of the Prophet to the end of days attunes Muslims' social memory to the distant past. This does not always come at the expense of the more recent past, as Mark Sedgwick's examination of Arab popular historical memory demonstrates. Still, as we have seen, Muslims' collective memory has usually focused on the myths of origins relating to the Prophet and the early generations.

---

[16]   Sayyid Qutb, *Ma'alim fi al-Tariq* (many editions).

[17]   Maurice Halbwachs, *On Collective Memory* (Chicago: The University of Chicago Press, 1992).

[18]   Jan Assmann, *Religion and Cultural Memory: Ten Studies* (Stanford: Stanford University Press, 2006), pp. 1–30.

Islamic fundamentalism, in the basic meaning of a return to the fundamentals of religion, which is the hegemonic discourse in modern Islam, has capitalized on this tendency in its quest to modernize Islam and enhance its place among the nations. This has prompted its proponents to constantly narrow the definition and the acceptable experiences of the early generations (*al-salaf*) that ought to be remembered, and to enlarge the scope of their successors (*al-khalaf*) about whom everything is better forgotten (with the exception of those rare premodern figures who are thought to have followed the same course, most notably Ibn Taymiyya and Ibn Qayyim al-Jawziyya).[19] Ulama, Sufis, and liberal religious intellectuals, each from a different angle, challenge both assumptions. They want to remember their illustrious predecessors in the schools of law, mystic brotherhoods, and Modernist trends, while not forgetting that early Muslims had their share of faults, disagreements, and eventually civil wars.[20]

Eric Hobsbawm and Terence Ranger's notion of the invention of tradition has turned attention to the cultural politics of memory. Hobsbawm and Ranger illustrate the ways in which the past is manipulated to suit present dominant interests. In their view, with the progress of electoral politics new traditions and rituals were deliberately designed through public commemorations, education systems, official records, and the mass media to preserve the primacy of the state and of the dominant sectors of society. Invented memories thus legitimize power through the complementary means of celebration and censorship, that is, the organized forms of remembering and forgetting.[21] As critics point out, however, today not only elites but also other sectors of society are increasingly capable of asserting their own versions of the past. Popular memories, or counter-memories, are constructed from the bottom up by marginalized groups, lower classes, minorities, and opposition movements. Contemporary collective memory thus becomes a permanent process of negotiation between dominant ideologies and alternative popular views of the past.[22]

Like other peoples, Muslims too are engaged in the politics of memory. Among the major invented, or rather reinvented, traditions of the past decades

---

[19] Mona Hassan, "Modern Interpretations and Misinterpretations of a Medieval Scholar: Apprehending the Political Thought of Ibn Taimiyya," in Yossef Rapoport and Shahab Ahmed (eds), *Ibn Taymiyya and His Times* (Karachi: Oxford University Press, 2010), pp. 338–66.

[20] Itzchak Weismann, "Modernity from Within: Islamic Fundamentalism and Sufism," *Der Islam* 86 (2011), pp. 142–70.

[21] Eric Hobsbawm and Terence Ranger (eds), *The Invention of Tradition* (Cambridge: Cambridge University Press, 1983).

[22] Barbara A. Misztal, *Theories of Social Remembering* (Maidenhead and Philadelphia: Open University Press, 2003), pp. 61–74.

we find the commemoration of Husayn's martyrdom in Karbala in post-revolutionary Iran[23] and in Hezbollah strongholds in Lebanon, and the collection of the alms tax (*zakat*) by the state in Ziaulhaq's Pakistan.[24] The revival of the glorious Ottoman past mentioned above served the Turkish opposition Islamic party which has meanwhile overtaken the government to promote the interests of religious-minded Anatolian entrepreneurs at the expense of the state-backed secular elites of Istanbul.[25] The memory of eighteenth-century Wahhabism is negotiated today between the Saudi state, in which it serves as the official creed to legitimize the ruling family, and Islamist and liberal dissent movements, which employ it to further their respective agendas of jihad and democratization.[26]

Myth and memory, as our discussion and examples demonstrate, are closely intertwined. Myths are the origins, heroes, and everyday narratives that a society remembers from its distant, recent, or immediate past. Collective memories are constructed, invented, negotiated, and transformed through such myths by and between elites and popular strata according to the constantly changing circumstances and perceptions of their society. As personified stories and grids, they together constitute important keys for understanding how society views itself in the world, which are the challenges it faces, and what are the directions that its various components strive to follow in order to overcome them. The Prophet's example, the model of the Caliphate or the imams, the legacy of the Arabs, and myriad other cherished myths and memories provide both the symbols and the instruments around which revolve the global cultural politics of contemporary Islamic movements, states, and of Muslim society at large.

Structure of the Book

The individual chapters of this book are arranged in three parts: The Past in the Present, Sacred Places and Persons, and Preaching, New and Old. Each chapter considers one aspect or another of myth and memory in the context of globalization.

---

[23] Haggai Ram, *Myth and Mobilization in Revolutionary Iran: The Use of the Friday Sermon* (Washington DC: American University Press, 1994).

[24] Jamal Malik, *Colonization of Islam: Dissolution of Traditional Institutions in Pakistan* (New Delhi: Manohar, 1996).

[25] See also M. Hakan Yavuz, *Islamic Political Identity in Turkey* (New York: Oxford University Press, 2003), pp. 86–90.

[26] David Commins, *The Wahhabi Mission and Saudi Arabia* (London: I.B. Tauris, 2006), ch. 6.

In the first section, four chapters look at specific memories of the past. Mark Sedgwick reports a study of Arab-Islamic popular historical memory that confirms the importance of the ancient myths and memories covered in other chapters and in other work, but also shows that Arab-Islamic memory of the modern period is fragmented, in that local memories—typically of former national leaders—loom larger than pan-Arab or pan-Islamic ones. Arab historical memory, however, also recognizes global icons such as Hitler that are of Western origin, and in this sense is more globalized than Western historical memory, which does not on the whole register non-Western icons.

Martin Riexinger looks at Turkey's memories of its mythical Ottoman past, showing how religious conservatives such as the Nurcu movement and the writer Sâmiha Ayverdi regard the Ottoman Empire as a holistic utopia, a counter-model of what they see as a grim, materialist Republican present. This is a theme that center-right politicians use to undermine the authority of the Kemalist élite. When it comes to politics, however, the very same politicians advocate a policy of industrialization and urban modernization that has destroyed much of what was left of the Ottoman past.

Although rather less well known than the Ottoman period, the nineteenth-century rebellion of the Sufi Jahrinya brotherhood in China is also a source of myth. Xiaofei Tu looks at how the very widely read Hui (Sinophone Muslim) author Zhang Chengzhi has used the memory of this rebellion in his novels to continue a political stance that in fact differs little from that which he once took as a youthful Red Guard, and also as a vehicle for criticism of a globalization that seems to privilege the power of the non-Chinese as much as it seems to privilege the power of the non-Muslim.

In the concluding chapter of this section, Ulrika Mårtensson challenges the globalized public myth of Salman Rushdie's *Satanic Verses*, arguing that the novel is a commentary on the medieval myth about the Prophet's Satanic temptation found also in Tabari's *History of the Messengers and the Kings*, and for similar purposes: to comment on the bigotry that follows when doubt is banished by certitude, and divine revelation is invoked in quests for power.

The second part of the book, on places and persons, starts with the Haram al-Sharif in Jerusalem. Nimrod Luz looks at the local interests and agendas among Israeli Arabs that result in the production and promotion of specific memories of the Haram, and also shows how the rescaling of the Haram onto a global level functions as a means of resistance to Israeli state authority.

Next comes Shaykh Nazim, founder and leader of the Haqqaniyya, an important globalized Sufi order. Itzchak Weismann shows that, as well as making extensive and effective use of the internet, Nazim's Haqqaniyya has adapted itself to the transnational spiritual market it serves, notably in its emphasis on the myth of the apocalypse, which in part responds to the modern materialist challenge, and is explained through Christian and universal symbols of the millennium as well as in Islamic terms.

Last in this section comes a recent but iconic figure, the late Osama bin Laden. Anne Birgitta Nilsen shows how presentation of bin Laden, first as *mujahid*, then as statesman, and then as other-worldly figure, manufactured a symbol of resistance out of Muslim collective memory. Bin Laden's death in 2011 was, in a sense, anticipated by the last stage of the myth of Bin Laden.

The final part of the book deals with preaching, both new and old. Uriya Shavit looks at Yusuf al-Qaradawi and the relations between his vision, the modern nation-state and postmodern advanced media technologies. Shavit argues that the advanced media technologies associated with globalization have broken the affinity between territorial boundaries and mass media consumption that was at the heart of Benedict Anderson's theory of nationalism, and that Qaradawi has exploited this to the full in order to realize his vision of a global *umma*. His success, however, is limited: the *umma* that results is a virtual one, not a real, viable one.

Shosh Ben-Ari looks at the phenomenon of "the new preachers," typified by 'Amr Khalid. She argues that this alternative to established official preachers appeals to those who suffer oppression and deprivation, just as was the case with alternative preachers at the beginning of Islam, and their stories of the prophets (*Qisas al-anbiya'*). Some media aspects of globalization, then, are not as new as they might appear.

Finally, Gerd Marie Ådna also looks at the stories of the prophets and shows how, for one group of Muslims especially exposed to globalization—immigrants in Europe—these stories belong to two active chains of memory: a main universal religious narrative chain, and a minor national or regional chain. As well as serving as vehicles for the transmission of moral religious truth, stories of the prophets have been merged with childhood memories.

Acknowledgments

The editors of this volume wish to thank the authors of chapters for their tolerance, forbearance, and above all for their cooperation over the sometimes drawn-out process of aligning the focus of individual research efforts and inspirations to produce a book that is more than the sum of its parts. They would also like to thank the Faculty of Humanities and the Globalization Program of the Norwegian University of Science and Technology in Trondheim for recognizing the importance of the topic covered in this book and generously funding the conference at which the individual chapters now contained in this book were first discussed. The volume is dedicated to the memory of the late Professor Joseph Kostiner, who participated in that conference, but did not live to see its outcome.

PART I
The Past in the Present

Chapter 1

Modern and Islamic Icons in Arab-Islamic Popular Historical Memory

Mark Sedgwick

Myth and memory are, as Itzchak Weismann writes in the introduction to this volume, 'constantly deployed, on both global and local levels, in evolving public discourses', providing explanations of reality and sometimes mobilising for action, either for or against a dominant system.[1] Myth and memory are used not only in public discourses, however, but also in private discourses, and in private reactions to public discourses and to actual events. Myth and memory are consumed, or perhaps not consumed, in ways explained by the social processes identified by Maurice Halbwachs, as well as produced, in ways explained for example by Eric Hobsbawm and Terence Ranger.[2] The relationship between public and private uses of myth and memory, between production and consumption, may usefully be understood in terms of a market in myth and memory, just as the production and consumption of religious goods is understood in terms of a market, or 'field', by Pierre Bourdieu.[3]

This chapter focuses on two aspects of the market in myth and memory: the relationship between production and consumption, and the consequences of consumption, understood in terms of popular historical memory. The chapter reports a study of contemporary Arab-Islamic popular historical memory that identified its major and minor 'icons'. This study confirmed the importance of Islamic myths of origin, of the Prophet and the Rightly Guided Caliphs, and the importance of one later myth, that of the period of the Crusades. It also suggested, however, that Arab-Islamic popular historical memory has three elements: a common Islamic element, a common modern element and

---

[1]   Itzchak Weisman, Introduction, p. 1.

[2]   Eric Hobsbawm and Terence Ranger, *The Invention of Tradition* (Cambridge: Cambridge University Press, 1983).

[3]   Pierre Bourdieu, 'Genesis and Structure of the Religious Field', *Comparative Social Research*, 53 (1991), pp. 1–44.

a segmented modern element. While Arab-Islamic popular historical memory is unified with regard to its Islamic element, popular historical memory of the modern period is diverse when it comes to Arab icons. With the single exception of Egypt's President Nasser, the common modern icons of Arab-Islamic popular historical memory are non-Arab: Adolf Hitler, Napoleon Bonaparte, Abraham Lincoln, Mahatma Ghandi, Karl Marx and others. Although it is hard to say what these have in common, they all suggest a preoccupation with liberation.

Finally, the study suggested that the various and diverse modern national Arab icons are more prominent in Arab-Islamic popular historical memory than are the common icons that make up the Islamic element. This raises the question of the extent to which it is possible to speak of one 'Arab-Islamic' popular historical memory, save in relation to its (less prominent) Islamic element.

The Market in Myth and Memory

To understand the market in myth and memory, a distinction must be made between what Halbwachs called 'formal history' and what later scholars have called 'popular historical memory'. Formal history is what is produced, and includes the history that historians are professionally concerned with. Popular historical memory is the consequence of consumption, and includes what historians who teach at universities find in really bad student essays. Teaching history is partly about trying to fill a *tabula rasa*, but it is also a struggle to replace popular historical memory with formal history. As Pierre Nora puts it, somewhat lyrically, 'history is perpetually suspicious of memory, and its true mission is to suppress and destroy it'.[4]

Formal history is not, of course, 'what really happened'. Except at the most basic level of the date of a king's death, formal history is a constructed narrative, and like all constructed narratives it to some extent reflects ideologies and agendas. Formal history, then, is also myth. Sometimes the ideologies and agendas reflected in formal history are those of the individual historian or of an intellectual consensus, and sometimes they are those of a state. The vast differences in narrative between an English history of the conquest of India written in the 1890s and a similar history written in the 1990s above all reflect changes in intellectual consensus. The equally vast differences

---

[4]   Pierre Nora, 'Between Memory and History: Les lieux de mémoire', *Representations*, 26 (Spring 1989), p. 9.

recently noted by Michael Kemper between a Russian history of Dagestan written in 1937 and one written only 16 years later, in 1953, reflected changes in Soviet state ideology.[5] Formal history, then, may be produced by states as well as by historians. A third variety of formal history, which matters more in some times and places than in others, is the formal history incorporated into a religion. This may be understood, as it was by Halbwachs, as *former* formal history: as Halbwachs noted, the essence of many religious ceremonies is commemorative.[6]

The supply of formal history is one of the major sources of popular historical memory. Everyone learns some history at school and during religious instruction, and no one forgets all of it, but school is not the only channel through which formal history is made available for consumption; others include the media, monuments and place names. For the formal history of religion, preaching is also an important channel of distribution.

Formal history, however distributed, is not the only source of popular historical memory, however. That something else intervenes is shown by the distance between formal history and popular historical memory, which can be significant. This was recently demonstrated by a survey testing 5,219 German schoolchildren's knowledge of the former German Democratic Republic (GDR, East Germany, DDR) reported in 2007 by Monika Deutz-Schroeder and Klaus Schroeder. This survey found that 55 per cent of schoolchildren in the eastern part of Berlin thought that Konrad Adenauer had been an East German politician, that only 32 per cent there knew that democratic elections did not take place in the German Democratic Republic, and that more children in Brandenburg (in the former GDR) than in Bavaria (in the former Federal Republic) considered the Stasi to have been 'a normal secret service'.[7]

Deutz-Schroeder and Schroeder, who were not interested in popular historical memory, concluded that the schoolchildren's knowledge of the GDR

---

[5]   Michael Kemper, 'The Changing Images of Jihad Leaders: Shamil and Abd al-Qadir in Daghestani and Algerian Historical Writing', *Nova Religio*, 11/2 (November 2007), p. 40.

[6]   Maurice Halbwachs, *On Collective Memory* (trans. of *Les cadres sociaux de la mémoire*, 1952, and of *La topographie légendaire des évangiles en terre sainte: Etude de mémoire collective*, 1941), ed. Lewis A. Coser (Chicago: University of Chicago Press, 1992), pp. 88, 93. *On Collective Memory* is not to be confused with *The Collective Memory* (New York: Harper & Row, 1980), which is a translation of *La mémoire collective. Ouvrage posthume*, 1950.

[7]   Monika Deutz-Schroeder and Klaus Schroeder, 'Das DDR-Bild von Schülern in Bayern', *Einsichten und Perspektiven: Bayerische Zeitschrift für Politik und Geschichte*, 1 (2008): at http://www.km.bayern.de/blz/eup/01_08/3.asp, accessed 16 February 2014.

was inadequate. In fact, their survey revealed differences in popular historical memory between two segments of the school-age population of Germany, and thus revealed the impact of other factors on the consumption of formal history. These other factors include family history and, perhaps most important of all, the process whereby, in the words of Halbwachs, 'the collective memory [reconstructs] an image of the past which is in accord, in each epoch, with the predominant thoughts of the society'.[8] These two factors may be understood as the most important determinants of demand within the market in myth and memory. 'Ossis' and 'Wessis' remain distinct groups, in a sometimes uncomfortable relationship. A slight majority of eastern Berlin schoolchildren thought that Ossis had nothing to thank Wessis for, a view held by only half of that percentage among Wessi schoolchildren.[9] Given these predominant thoughts, it is hardly surprising that Ossis have a more positive view of their former state than Wessis do, resulting in different patterns of consumption of formal history, and thus in different popular historical memory.

Deutz-Schroeder and Schroeder's survey was unusual. Scholars interested in memory have generally focused not on popular historical memory but on one or another variety of formal history, a focus against which Alon Confino warns in an excellent essay in the *American Historical Review*,[10] drawing attention to the risk of failing to distinguish clearly enough between the production and reception of memory. As he argued, many studies of memory focus on objects – museums and monuments, for example – and then interpret them either in terms of existing understandings of history, making them into mere illustrations of what is already known, or in terms of the understandings of the researcher, not of those who actually encounter the objects in question. Confino argues for paying more attention to how and why the understandings of the general population differ from those intended by the patrons and creators of objects, and to how and why understandings among different segments of a population differ and change. In effect, he was arguing for the study of the consumption of formal history.

One of the pioneers of the study of Arab-Islamic historical memory was Yoram Meital, who examined Egyptian official commemorations of the 1973 October War (known in Israel as the Yom Kippur war). Meital looked at the monument to the Unknown Soldier in Cairo, at the October War Panorama

---

    [8]   Halbwachs, *On Collective Memory*, p. 40.

    [9]   Deutz-Schroeder and Schroeder, 'Das DDR-Bild'.

    [10]   Alon Confino, 'Collective Memory and Cultural History: Problems of Method', *American Historical Review*, 102 (1997), pp. 1386–403.

museum and at a selection of postage stamps.[11] In so doing, he revealed much about how the Egyptian state would *like* the October War to be remembered, i.e. about the formal history produced by the state. This, however, tells us nothing about how Egyptians actually *do* remember the October War, about how they consume formal history, converting it into popular historical memory. Apart from anything else, almost nobody in Cairo ever visits the monument to the Unknown Soldier or the October War panorama, and normal Egyptians pay little attention to postage stamps, if only because the post is much less used as a means of communication than it is in the West.[12] It cannot be assumed that the formal history of the Egyptian state has the impact on Egyptian popular historical memory that the Egyptian state wishes it to have. If a significant gap between formal history and popular historical memory is found in Germany, the gap in Egypt may be expected to be even wider.

As well as gaps between formal history and popular historical memory in terms of content, there are gaps in terms of structure. Formal history, as has been said, generally takes narrative form, though the formal history promoted by a state may be represented in objects. According to Joanne Rappaport, who worked on the popular historical memory of a small Andean community, popular historical memory, in contrast, 'is not made up of carefully woven narratives but of a series of brief and incomplete images, which are never developed in any detail'.[13] This lack of coherent narrative was thought by Antonio Gramsci to be one of the characteristics of 'subaltern thought', which he sees as a 'counter-hegemonic' force.[14] Rappaport may be going too far: while it is certainly true that popular historical memory is not as narrative-based as formal history, it does also contain narratives, or at least narrative fragments. Gramsci may also be going too far: popular historical memory is not *only* popular or subaltern. It is shared, in one form or another, by all who are not professional historians. Even when the latter think of places or periods way beyond their own fields of expertise (let the average historian of the Middle East here reflect on nineteenth-century Siam), popular historical memory

---

[11]   Yoram Meital, 'Sadat's Grave and the Commemoration of the 1973 War in Egypt', in Michael E. Geisler (ed.), *National Symbols, Fractured Identities: Contesting the National Narrative* (Lebanon, NH: Middlebury College Press, 2005), pp. 222–40.

[12]   Comments such as these are based on 20 years' residence in Egypt, from 1987 to 2007.

[13]   Joanne Rappaport, *Cumbe Reborn: Andean Ethnography of History* (Chicago: University of Chicago Press, 1994), p. 6.

[14]   Andrea L. Smith, 'Heteroglossia, "Common Sense", and Social Memory', *American Ethnologist*, 31 (2004), p. 252.

to some extent replaces formal history, though professional historians are naturally more cautious about accepting it. Popular historical memory is not only subaltern, then, even if it is counter-hegemonic in the sense that it is in tension with formal history.

Following Rappaport and Gramsci in modified form, then, we may see popular historical memory as counter-hegemonic and fragmentary, consisting of incomplete images and narrative fragments. Formal history is one source of popular historical memory, but not the only source. Family history is another, and most important of all is probably 'the predominant thoughts of [contemporary] society'.

In the Arab-Islamic market in myth and memory, Islam enjoys a monopoly in producing the formal history of religion, though this is in fact more of an oligopoly, since somewhat different versions of Islam are taught and preached in Egypt, Saudi Arabia and Iraq. The production of formal history of the modern period is, in contrast, segmented: the school system in each Arab state gives priority to the history of that state, an emphasis that is followed by national media and other such channels of distribution. Even the pan-Arab media, it has been suggested, are segmented along national lines.[15] Only when it comes to global formal history, as distributed through such channels as Western movies, do divisions between Arab states cease to matter.

Finding Popular Historical Memory

Relatively little empirical work has been carried out on popular historical memory anywhere, and even less on Arab-Islamic popular historical memory. A search through the full 15 years of the journal *History and Memory* for the term 'Arab', for example, reveals seven articles dealing with Israel, one dealing with Chechnya, and only one dealing with Arabs proper. That one article deals

---

[15]   Yeslam Al-Saggaf, 'The Online Public Sphere in the Arab World: The War in Iraq on the Al Arabiya Website', *Journal of Computer-Mediated Communication*, 12 (2006), pp. 311–34. Al-Saggaf studied comments posted on the pan-Arab Al Arabiya website, and finds that 'the topics about Iraq attracted mainly, albeit not exclusively, Iraqis, and topics about Saudi Arabia, for example, attracted mainly Saudis'. Similarly, Dyala Hamzah questions the existence of one integrated Arab public sphere: 'Is There an Arab Public Sphere? The Palestinian Intifada, a Saudi Fatwa, and the Egyptian Press', in Armando Salvatore and Mark le Vine (eds), *Religion, Social Practice, and Contested Hegemonies: Reconstructing the Public Sphere in Muslim Majority Societies* (New York: Palgrave, 2005), pp. 181–206.

with the production of myth for the consumption of the Lebanese army, i.e. with formal history rather than with popular historical memory.[16]

One exception to the general rule is Smadar Lavie, who carried out ethnological fieldwork among the Sinai Bedouin in the 1980s, but the results of this work are hard to assess, since her account of Bedouin popular historical memory is complicated by her focus on innovative presentation and Zionist historiography.[17] Another example is Wael Ismail's work on the popular historical memory of Cairo's Palestinian diaspora, which identified two major segments: the rich, for whom popular historical memory was close to Palestinian nationalist formal history and performed the identity-related functions that theory predicted, and the poor, who knew little of nationalist formal history, and whose identity was determined largely by multiple experiences of discrimination and hostility, on the part both of the Egyptian state and its representatives, and of ordinary Egyptians.[18] Wael Ismail's work reminds us that collective memory is not always the most important source of identity.

Both Smadar Lavie and Wael Ismail used essentially ethnographic methods, suitable for small and defined groups such as Sinai Bedouin or Cairo Palestinians, but impracticable for larger populations. In theory, the survey approach used in Germany might also be used to investigate Arab-Islamic popular historical memory, but it is hardly practicable – the machinery for large-scale polls does not generally exist in the Arab world, and to the extent that it does exist, a foreign researcher would have great difficulty in gaining access to it.

There are, however, a few non-ethnological studies of popular historical memory which, though not dealing with the Arab world, provide useful methodological models. One was conducted by Wulf Kansteiner, who reviewed the content of German television transmissions from 1963 to 1993, looking at programmes dealing with the issue that interested him, the Nazi period, and then reviewed ratings for the same period. He finds, as he expected, that the less problematic events of the Second World War featured more in German popular historical memory than the more problematic events of the period, but also

---

[16] Oren Barak, 'Commemorating Malikiyya: Political Myth, Multi-ethnic Identity and the Making of the Lebanese Army', *History and Memory*, 13/1 (2001), pp. 60–84.

[17] The Hajj [*sic*], Smadar Lavie and Forest Rouse, 'Notes on the Fantastic Journey of the Hajj, His Anthropologist, and Her American Passport', *American Ethnologist*, 20/2 (May 1993), pp. 363–84. She may have published other work on this that I have not read.

[18] Wael Ismail, 'The Construction of a National Identity in Exile: Palestinians in Egypt'. Unpublished MA thesis, American University in Cairo, 2007.

that this was less true for the generation that had not personally experienced the war than for the generation that had. He also found that the Nazi period featured less in popular historical memory in the 1970s than in the 1960s or 1980s. Although, as Kansteiner recognises, television is only a 'conduit' between formal history and popular historical memory (in the terms used in this chapter, a channel of distribution), it reflects popular historical memory to the extent that television executives are interested in ratings, and so have to read audience interest.[19] Ratings, however, as Kansteiner also concedes, are difficult to interpret: they are affected not simply by an audience's views on the programme in question, but by factors such as what is showing on other channels, and even by what the weather is like.

The second study was conducted by Michael Frisch, a professor of history at the State University of New York at Buffalo, who for eight years started his American history classes by asking students to write down 10 names from American history. Frisch found that the results were so consistent over the years that he concluded that they reflected 'collective cultural mechanisms and structures we need to understand better'. Though he did not use the term popular historical memory, the consistency of his results indicated that he had found a reliable instrument for measuring popular historical memory, at least in terms of name recall, which he saw as a proxy for awareness or an 'icon'.[20] Frisch's term 'icon' will be used here to indicate that which symbolises Rappaport's 'incomplete images' and the narrative fragments that attach to them.

Kansteiner's approach cannot be directly replicated to investigate Arab-Islamic popular historical memory. Arab television archives are less accessible than German ones, and ratings either do not exist or are not reliable. A more fundamental problem is that, until the advent of satellite television, Arab states' monopolies over broadcast media relieved their television producers of any great need to attend to ratings or audience interest. Pre-satellite Arab television may therefore be expected to be further from Arab-Islamic popular historical memory than German television is from German popular historical memory.

---

[19]   Wulf Kansteiner, 'Nazis, Viewers and Statistics: Television History, Television Audience Research and Collective Memory in West Germany', *Journal of Contemporary History*, 39 (2004), p. 577.
[20]   Michael Frisch, 'American History and the Structures of Collective Memory: A Modest Exercise in Empirical Iconography', *Journal of American History*, 75 (1989), p. 1132.

The approach taken by a study which this chapter will now report was therefore to apply Kansteiner's method to the new media, by measuring the volume of internet searches from a selection of Arab countries, using internet search data going back to 2004 that is readily available from Google Insights.[21] This data may be expected to reflect popular historical memory fairly accurately, since people generally search for what they are interested in, and people can only be interested in what they are aware of. Search terms, in other words, may be understood as icons of popular historical memory. In the West, internet search volumes also reflect school history projects, but project-based teaching methods are not yet much used in the Arab world. Internet searches also reflect the impact of movies and of current events as reported in the media, but this does not contaminate the data, since the immediate cause of the search is still interest, not obligation.

Frisch's method was used as a starting point for establishing the list of terms for which search data would be measured. Students at the American University in Cairo were asked to list their top ten names from history, without being told why[22] (the limitations inherent in using only one country are discussed below). Internet search volume was then measured for historical names on the resulting list.[23] Internet search data, of course, only indicates the popular historical memory of that section of society that uses the internet. Even in Europe, internet penetration is still less than 50 per cent in most countries.[24] In the Arab world, only the United Arab Emirates (UAE) reaches European levels, while outside the Gulf Cooperation Council (GCC: the UAE and Saudi Arabia plus the other oil statelets) penetration varies between around 10 per cent (in Syria and Egypt) and a mere 1.5 per cent in Yemen.[25] These statistics probably underestimate Arab internet penetration by underestimating users per internet connection, but even so, penetration is clearly low. Search data, then, reflects not the popular historical memory of the entire Arab population, but

---

[21]   See at http://www.google.com/insights/search.

[22]   Fifty-six students, in late 2008.

[23]   Data was measured on 9 July 2009 using 'Google Insights for search' (at http://www.google.com/insights). Searches using both Arabic and Latin script were measured together.

[24]   'Internet Usage in Europe', *Internet World Stats*, at http://www.internetworldstats.com/stats4.htm, accessed 9 November 2008.

[25]   'Internet Usage Statistics for Africa', *Internet World Stats*, at http://www.internetworldstats.com/stats1.htm, accessed 9 November 2008; 'Internet Usage in the Middle East', *Internet World Stats*, at http://www.internetworldstats.com/stats5.htm, accessed 9 November 2008.

that of the computer literate section of it.[26] There are, however, advantages to this. Popular historical memory is segmented, as already noted. As Halbwachs stressed, collective memory is not national memory – nations contain many collectivities. The computer literate section of a population will still be heterogeneous, but somewhat less heterogeneous than the entire population. Secondly, the computer literate section of a population probably corresponds fairly closely to the more politically active section of a population, and so is for many purposes the most important.

Google Insights reports search volume by geographical area of origin, and for practical reasons data from only a selection of Arab countries was studied. These were Saudi Arabia and Egypt (as the two most significant Arab countries), plus a selection of other GCC countries,[27] and Syria, Jordan and non-Israeli Palestine,[28] collectively described below as 'Sham'. Some of the searches measured were certainly Arab without being Islamic, especially in the case of searches originating from Egypt and Syria, which have significant Christian minorities. In all other cases, however, the vast majority of searches can be assumed to have been made by Muslims. The data can thus be considered to reflect Arab-Islamic popular historical memory.

Two varieties of search term were excluded. One was those where the motivation for the search was clearly not seeking information concerning a historical figure. Many searches for 'Ibn Khaldun', for example, are clearly directed at finding the Ibn Khaldun Center for Development Studies or the Ibn Khaldun Primary School in 'Ar'ara, in the Negev.[29] The other was terms where the names generated by students did not seem 'properly' historical. The Egyptian singer Um Kulthum and the American pop singer Britney Spears, for example, were both put in this category.

The exclusion of the first variety of terms was certainly justified. A search for the Ibn Khaldun Primary School does not reflect popular historical memory, even though the name of the school may be a channel for the distribution of memory. The exclusion of the second variety was less obviously justified, since it raises questions which this chapter cannot hope to answer, including those about the relationship between music, emotion and memory, and about that between myth, memory and popular culture more widely understood. Music,

---

[26]   This is confirmed by the extent to which the searches measured use Latin script. Arab elites tend to use English or French very readily.

[27]   UAE, Oman and Kuwait.

[28]   What Google calls the 'Palestinian Territory'.

[29]   Such motivations were identified by looking at associated search terms according to Google Insights, and also by looking at Google's suggested searches.

of course, can evoke powerful autobiographical memories, and can also colour them. Um Kulthum is strongly associated with a particular period in Arab history, and was not just a musical figure, given the often 'patriotic' content of her songs. Britney Spears also carries associations. The impact on historical myth and memory of Um Kulthum and Britney Spears, however, requires a separate study.

Major and Minor 'Icons' of Arab-Islamic Popular Historical Memory

Predictably, the top-scoring historical name for Arab internet searches was that of the Prophet Muhammad, especially during the hajj and the Prophet's Birthday.[30] The ranking of other searches is shown in Table 1.1.

A composite ranking was then derived on the basis of how frequently (i.e. in how many areas) a term was in the first 11 places, giving 11 points for first place, 10 points for second place, and so on. In the case of a tie on points, the term with most regions was placed first. The resulting composite ranking is shown in Table 1.2.

Table 1.1   Top ten Arab searches (excluding Muhammad) by area

Egypt	Sham	Saudi Arabia	Other GCC
Nasser	'Umar	Hitler	'Umar
Salah al-Din	Salah al-Din	Pharaoh	Hitler
Pharaoh	Shakespeare	'Umar	Shakespeare
Shakespeare	Hitler	Shakespeare	Nasser
'Umar	Pharaoh	Salah al-Din	Pharaoh
Hitler	Nasser	'Uthman	Lincoln
Sadat	Napoleon	Nasser	Salah al-Din
Farouk	M.L. King	Lincoln	Gandhi
Napoleon	Marx	Caesar	Napoleon
Marx	Gandhi	Abu Bakr	'Uthman

---

[30]   Actually, the 1427 hajj in 2006 and the Prophet's Birthday in 2008. It is not clear why the same pattern was not repeated from year to year.

Table 1.2   Top Arab searches

		Points	Regions	Leads
1	Muhammad	44	All	All
2	ʿUmar	34	All	Sham and GCC
3	Shakespeare	30	All	Sham and GCC
4	Hitler	31	All	Saudi Arabia
5	Pharaoh	29	All	Saudi Arabia
6	Salah al-Din	28	All	Egypt and Sham
7	Nasser	26	All	Egypt
8	Napoleon	8	All but Saudi	Sham
9	Lincoln	8	Saudi and GCC	GCC
10	ʿUthman	6	Saudi and GCC	Saudi Arabia
11	Gandhi	4	GCC and Sham	GCC
12	Sadat	4	Egypt	N/A
13	Marx	3	Sham and Egypt	Sham
14=	M.L. King	3	Sham	N/A
14=	Farouk	3	Egypt	N/A
16	Caesar	2	Saudi	N/A
17	Abu Bakr	1	Saudi	N/A

As Table 1.2 shows, the top seven terms were very popular searches in all regions, and accumulated many points (from 26 to the maximum 44). These top seven terms will be described below as 'major icons'. The remaining 10 terms accumulated significantly fewer points (from 1 to 8), and were not searched for in all regions. These 10 terms will be described below as 'minor icons', and the five of them that were popular searches in only one region will be described as 'minor regional icons'.

Two of the major icons – the Prophet and ʿUmar ibn ʿAbd al-Khattab, the second caliph – are the classic icons of the early years of Islam. The Islamic element in Arab-Islamic popular historical memory may also be considered to include Pharaoh, since searches for 'Pharaoh' were often combined with searches for the Prophet Moses,[31] and a Qurʾanic reading would suggest the defeat of the mighty enemy of God by one of God's prophets. Salah al-Din, the icon of the period of the Crusades, also belongs in the Islamic element. One minor icon and one minor regional icon (ʿUthman and Abu Bakr, the third and first caliphs respectively) also refer to the early years of Islam. The symbolic values of these 'Islamic' icons are well known, and hence will not be discussed here.

---

[31]   Google associated searches.

Two of the three remaining major icons (Shakespeare and Hitler) were from Western rather than Arab-Islamic history, as were four of the minor icons (Napoleon, Lincoln, Gandhi and Marx) and two minor regional icons (Martin Luther King and Caesar). Since Shakespeare was generally searched for using Latin rather than Arabic script, it will be assumed that searches for that term have more to do with a desire to learn English than with popular historical memory, and Shakespeare will therefore be investigated no further. The possible symbolic values of the other two major icons will be discussed below.

Modern non-Western history contributed only one major icon (Gamal Abdel Nasser) and two minor regional icons (Sadat and King Farouk). All three of these are Egyptian, and this no doubt reflects the study's starting point, which was a list of names prepared by Egyptian students. Search volumes for randomly selected modern national icons for other Arab countries[32] revealed similar national emphases, as shown in Table 1.3, which measures search volumes as multiples of searches for 'Umar ibn 'Abd al-Khattab.

Table 1.3   National searches

	Al Saud	Habib Bourguiba	Yasser Arafat	Hafiz al-Assad	Mohamed V
Saudi Arabia	123%	0%	10%	3%	9%
Tunisia	0%	194%	0%	0%	0%
Palestine	0%	0%	357%	0%	0%
Syria	27%	0%	35%	164%	0%
UAE	16%	0%	11%	5%	10%
Morocco	19%	0%	18%	0%	769%
Egypt	6%	0%	8%	0%	7%

As Table 1.3 shows, one past ruler is a major icon of popular historical memory in the country in question, but these major national icons generally register barely or not at all on the popular historical memory of any other country. Even Yasser Arafat is not, in terms of the internet search volume he generates, a major icon outside Palestine. This strongly suggests that Arab-Islamic popular historical memory of the modern period is fragmented when it comes to Arab icons, in contrast to the relative uniformity of the Islamic element in popular historical

---

32   Google Insights, 17 October 2010.

memory, and also in contrast to the greater uniformity, when it comes to global icons, of Arab-Islamic popular historical memory of the modern period.

The above data also shows that each individual national icon attracted a higher – and sometimes a very much higher – search volume than 'Umar, the most major icon of the Islamic element in popular historical memory, in the icon's country of origin. The implication is that diverse modern icons feature more prominently in Arab-Islamic popular historical memory than do universal Islamic icons. This is what calls into question the extent to which it is possible to speak of a single 'Arab-Islamic' popular historical memory in the first place. It has, of course, also been asked to what extent it is possible to speak of a single Arab public sphere.

Interpreting the Major and Minor Modern Icons of Arab-Islamic Popular Historical Memory

As has been said, the symbolic values of the major icons of the Islamic element in Arab-Islamic popular historical memory are well known, and will not be discussed here. The symbolic values of the two major icons of Arab-Islamic popular historical memory which are outside the Islamic element, Nasser and Hitler, is less well known, and requires investigation. Of the two, Hitler is more prominent: ignoring region and measuring all Arabic-language searches worldwide, there are almost one-and-a-half times as many searches for Hitler as there are for Nasser.[33]

The chief iconic value of Nasser and of Hitler in Egypt can be established on the basis of the views of students at the American University in Cairo. In-class discussions with students while teaching the formal history of the twentieth century there over many years revealed that Nasser is in many ways seen as a latter-day Salah al-Din, as the promoter of unity against the enemies of the Arabs and of Islam: the British, the Americans and the Israelis, a view which coincides with the formal history of the Egyptian state and school system. There are, of course, other readings: Nasser was blamed by some for saddling Egypt with the political system under which she struggled until 2011.[34]

The iconic value of Hitler in the Arab-Islamic world is, surprisingly for Westerners, often positive. German visitors to Cairo are often astonished when they respond to taxi drivers' enquiries about their nationality (a standard way of getting a conversation going) and are then told, 'Hitler very good'.[35] This is not a

---

[33]   Google Insights, 17 October 2010.
[34]   The relative popularity of these two opposing views is hard to assess.
[35]   Numerous German residents of Cairo have reported this exchange.

view promoted by formal history in Egypt, though it may be to some extent by family history: Hitler was at one point widely popular in the Arab world, partly because the full implications of his racial theories were not appreciated,[36] though Arab opinion was often divided.[37] Rather more is known about Hitler today, however, than was known in the 1930s.

The reasons behind Hitler's iconic value remaining positive today were suggested by a batch of essays submitted by new students at the American University in Cairo who sat an English-writing placement test in about 1990. These young and predominantly Egyptian students were asked to write about the historical figure they would most like to meet, and say why. Unsurprisingly, the Prophet was the most popular historical figure. A large number of young Egyptians also explained their desire to meet Hitler. Hitler's achievements were typically said to be that he was a strong leader who had united his people and led them in a war against England and France which was almost successful. In addition, as one student wrote: 'He was almost succeeding in evacuating most of the Israelis'.[38] Popular historical memory here indeed corresponds to 'brief and incomplete images, which are never developed in any detail', as Rappaport puts it. There are, of course, other readings of Hitler, as there are of Nasser: some Egyptians are well aware that Hitler, though undoubtedly the enemy of those seen as Egypt's enemies, also pursued policies that were entirely unacceptable. In general, though, his iconic value seems close to that of Nasser.

Although I have no similar sources for interpreting the iconic values of Nasser and Hitler in other Arab countries, there are indications that the values attributed to Hitler elsewhere are not very different from those attributed in Egypt. Disagreement about Nasser's iconic status explains the regional variation in his ranking. Given the rivalry between Egypt and Saudi Arabia during the Nasser period, it is hardly surprising that Nasser came top of the Egyptian ranking but low in the Saudi ranking, and lowest of all in the UAE, where there were actually more searches for Napoleon and for Kennedy.[39]

I have no sources for interpreting the iconic value attaching to Napoleon, Lincoln, Gandhi, Marx, Martin Luther King and Caesar. The global values of

---

[36]   Stefan Wild, 'National Socialism in the Arab Near East between 1933 and 1939', *Die Welt des Islams*, 25/1 (1985), pp. 126–73.

[37]   Peter Wien, *Iraqi Arab Nationalism: Authoritarian, Totalitarian and Pro-Fascist Inclinations, 1932–1941* (London: Routledge, 2008); Götz Nordbruch, *Nazism in Syria and Lebanon: The Ambivalence of the German Option, 1933–1945* (London: Routledge, 2008).

[38]   The quote is from memory, but the original was very memorable.

[39]   Google Insights.

some of these icons are, however, reasonably clear. Lincoln freed America's slaves, Gandhi freed India, Marx inspired Soviet attempts to free the world of British and French imperialism, and Martin Luther King freed American blacks.[40] That leaves Napoleon and Caesar, who conquered rather than liberated, and so are exceptions. Given that liberation, or perceived attempts at liberation, are among the values attaching to Nasser and Hitler, it seems that liberation may also be the common value of the modern non-Arab icons, major and minor, of Arab-Islamic popular historical memory.

Explaining Arab-Islamic Popular Historical Memory

Some of the icons prominent in Arab-Islamic popular historical memory can be easily explained in terms of the impact of the production of formal history. The presence of the Islamic icons is perhaps inevitable, given the overlap between the formal history of religion and other varieties of formal history. Since early Arab history is inextricably entwined with the early history of Islam, the relevant period is taught in Arab schools in both history and religion classes and is also referred to in Friday sermons, as well as being the subject of religious programming in the media. Similarly, the presence of one modern icon – Nasser – in Egypt can be understood in terms of the impact of formal history in that country, and also of the impact of family history: everyone alive in Egypt has family members who themselves experienced the Nasser period. The presence of major national icons such as Habib Bourguiba in the national popular historical memory of the individual countries concerned can be explained in the same terms: the local monopoly of formal history of each Arab state's school system, and the impact of family history, which generally emphasises the local.

The presence in Arab-Islamic popular historical memory of Hitler and the other minor non-Arab icons may likewise be explained in terms of the supply of global formal history. Hitler and Napoleon are prominent icons in European popular historical memory as well, as is Marx,[41] but Gandhi and Lincoln are less prominent in Europe.[42]

---

[40] This interpretation seeks to identify what the icons have in common.

[41] Hitler everywhere, and Napoleon especially in south-west Europe (parallel European study).

[42] Neither appeared in the top internet search terms.

Supply alone, however, cannot explain the emphasis given to Salah al-Din, the positive value associated with Hitler, or the emphasis given to Gandhi by Arab-Islamic popular historical memory. For this, we must look at factors determining consumption, the way in which popular historical memory is 'an image of the past which is in accord, in each epoch, with the predominant thoughts of the society', as argued by Halbwachs (quoted above). According to this model, the obvious interpretation is that the predominant thoughts of contemporary Arab-Islamic society are of liberation, to be provided by a renewal of the triumphs of Islam, to compensate for the collective trauma resulting from colonialist defeat and occupation, and later from Israeli occupation of Palestine. Care should, however, be exercised when approaching the phrase 'collective trauma', as Wulf Kansteiner has argued. Individuals may try to repress traumatic memories, but they cannot really do so, or can do so only at a price; societies, on the other hand, not only can repress or modify traumatic memories, but often do.[43] Collective memories, including popular historical memory, are highly selective. If there is a desire for liberation, then, this must be ascribed to current events, not past events.

Conclusion

As this chapter has argued, a market in myth and memory can be said to exist, where the supply is formal history and the consequence of consumption is popular historical memory. Popular historical memory has many sources, including formal history, whether of historians, states or religion. The supply of formal history, however, does not on its own determine popular historical memory. The formal history of the Egyptian state incorporated into the October War Panorama museum or postage stamps may have little impact on Egyptian popular historical memory, and Hitler occupies a prominent place in Arab-Islamic popular historical memory as a positive icon, despite the fact that no version of formal history in the Arab world presents him in positive fashion. To explain this, factors determining the consumption of myth and memory need to be included in the model. Of these, the most important are family history and the predominant thoughts of the present.

For small populations in the Sinai, or for distinct groups like the Palestinian diaspora in Cairo, standard ethnographic techniques are an excellent way of

---

43   Wulf Kansteiner, 'Finding Meaning in Memory: a Methodological Critique of Collective Memory Studies', *History and Theory*, 41 (May 2002), pp. 186.

uncovering popular historical memory. For larger populations, however, other techniques are needed: surveys like that of German schoolchildren's knowledge of the former GDR, or work on television ratings or internet search volumes. The study reported in this chapter used internet search volumes, which showed the icons occupying the most prominent places in Arab-Islamic popular historical memory, in part confirming what was already generally assumed: the importance of the early Islamic period and the period of the crusades. The study reported also revealed the extent to which Arab-Islamic popular historical memory of the modern period is segmented along national lines, however, and the important role played by one non-Arab major icon, Hitler.

One consequence of the diversity of Arab-Islamic popular historical memory of the modern period is that the only icons that attract sufficient search volume across the Arab-Islamic world to rank as minor icons common to all Arab-Islamic popular historical memory are drawn not from Arab but from global history. In contrast, the icons of European popular historical memory of all periods are exclusively Western – with Hitler, predictably, scoring top position in a comparable ranking of historical search terms emanating from Western Europe. The closest European popular historical memory gets to a non-Western icon is Buddha.[44] On the face of it, then, Arab-Islamic popular historical memory is more globalised than Western European popular historical memory. This can be understood in terms of centre and periphery. As has often been remarked, the periphery knows the centre, but the reverse is not true.

It seems, however that the periphery does not know other parts of the periphery either, despite the new Arab media. When it comes to the modern period, Arab-Islamic popular historical memory is revealed as being first national, then Islamic and then global. The only major icon in Arab-Islamic popular historical memory that is both Arab-Islamic and modern is Nasser. Otherwise, modern Arab icons are national. As a result, it is unclear whether there really is such a thing as one 'Arab-Islamic' popular historical memory.

If the modern icons of Arab-Islamic popular historical memory taken together have a common significance, that significance is an emphasis on liberation, confirmed in the case of Nasser and Hitler, and presumed in other cases. To some extent, this may be explained by the predominant thoughts of the Arab-Islamic present, though care must be taken when seeing this in terms of 'collective trauma'. It is present thoughts, not past events, that matter.

---

[44] European search volumes were measured on 5 and 8 November 2008, using methodology identical to that used for Arab searches, starting from a list produced by students at Aarhus University in Denmark.

The experiment of using internet search volumes to measure Arab-Islamic popular historical memory, then, has produced some interesting results. Other researchers are recommended also to follow the recommendations of Alon Confino, and to focus on popular historical memory as well as formal history. The use of internet search-volume data is also recommended, until, at least, further advances in communications technology make other and better techniques available. Such advances may well make possible in the future much more detailed and revealing studies of popular historical memory than the one reported in this chapter.

Chapter 2

The Ottoman Empire as Harmonious Utopia: A Historical Myth and its Function

Martin Riexinger

In early 2012, millions of Turks – both in Turkey and in Western Europe – flocked to the cinemas to watch *Fatih 1453* ('Conquest 1453'). Arguably an overlong film, with computer animations which it would be flattering to call mediocre, it would not have attracted such crowds had its subject been other than the Conquest of Constantinople.[1] The only possible exception would be the successful defence of the Dardanelles against the British in the First World War, an event associated with Mustafa Kemal and hence part and parcel of the Kemalist personality cult. The movie was financed by the metropolitan government of İstanbul led by the 'post-Islamist' Adalet ve Kalkınma Partisi ('Justice and Development Party'). This is far from surprising because the glorification of the Ottoman past has been an important issue for religious opponents of Kemalism ever since it became possible to criticize the state ideology openly.[2]

After Mustafa Kemal ('Atatürk' since 1935) had defeated the Greek and Entente troops in Anatolia in 1923, he proclaimed the foundation of the Republic of Turkey, a step followed by a number of political measures which were

---

[1]   Suna Çağapatay and Soner Çağapatay, 'Ottomania all the rage in Turkey', *Today's Zaman*, 1 April 2012, at http://www.todayszaman.com/news-275971-ottomania-all-the-rage-in-turkey.html, accessed 20 March 2013; only a very few Turkish reviews addressed the historical flaws or the chauvinist and militarist tendencies of the film, which were only slightly moderated by the Sultan's promise (which he gave in the Hagia Sophia) to treat his Christian subjects mildly. Nevertheless, it is remarkable that at least two such reviews were published in media close to Fethullah Gülen: Emine Yıldırım '"Fetih 1453" İstanbul, not Constantinople!', *Today's Zaman*, 20 February 2012; Mustafa Armağan, 'Büyük Fetih'in ışığında Fetih 1453', *Zaman*, 19 February 2012.

[2]   Etienne Copeaux, *Espaces et temps de la nation turque. Analyse d'une historiographie nationaliste 1931–1993*, (Paris, 1997), pp. 212–22.

supposed to turn Turkey into a Western country and to ensure a permanent break with the Ottoman past. The idea underlying this shift in cultural orientation was that only a nation following Western standards would be able to resist Western political dominance, something of which the decadent and reactionary (*mürteci*, today rather *gerici*) Ottoman Empire was incapable of doing.[3] However, this idea had emerged earlier: the Young Turks had already denounced the decadence of the multi-ethnic and multi-religious Ottoman Empire.[4]

The condemnation of the Ottoman Empire was not supported by the Turkish population as a whole. For all those to the 'right' of the Kemalist camp,[5] the Ottoman Empire continued to be a positive point of reference. As a result, most Turkish Islamic movements differ from those of other countries in one important respect: they refer to two 'Golden Ages', the first during the lifetime of Muhammad and the first four caliphs, commonly referred to as *asr-ı saadet* ('the age of happiness)' in Turkish-Islamic discourse, and the second during the era of the Ottoman Empire, which is seen as the establishment of God's word (*I'lâ-ı kelimetüllâh*) with a specific Turkish colouring.[6] Thus 'Ottoman nostalgia' is also one of the elements responsible for the fact that the borders between Islamic and nationalist political concepts are anything but clear-cut in Turkey.[7] Centre-right (*ortanın sağı*) politicians have also been advocating, since the 1950s, a more favourable judgement on the Ottoman Empire, in the hope of garnering support from religious circles. However, this was only an issue in the field of the 'politics

---

[3]   Şükrü Hanioğlu, *Atatürk: An Intellectual Biography* (Princeton NJ and Oxford, 2011), pp. 57–60; this interpretation of the Ottoman past is nowadays common among left-wing nationalists. See also Martin Riexinger, "'Turkey, completely independent!": Contemporary Turkish Left-wing Nationalism (*ulusal sol/ ulusalcılık*): Its Predecessors, Objectives and Enemies', *Oriente Moderno*, 90/2 (2011), pp. 358–9.

[4]   Hanioğlu, *Atatürk*, pp. 56–63.

[5]   In the Turkish context a variety of political currents, encompassing pro-business groups with very different attachment to Islam, Islamists and pan-Turkish Nationalists ('Turanists'), are commonly referred to as the 'Right' (*sağ*). The term 'Left' covers in reverse the broad spectrum from Kemalists to Marxists.

[6]   See Bukhari *Jihad* nr. 76; Sâmiha Ayverdi, *Kaybolan Anahtar* (Istanbul, 2008), pp. 22–4; Lutz Berger, 'Religionsbehörde und Millî Görüş. Zwei Varianten eines traditionalistischen Islam in der Türkei', in Rüdiger Lohlker (ed.), *Hadithstudien – Die Überlieferungen des Propheten im Gespräch. Festschrift für Prof. Dr. Tilman Nagel* (Hamburg, 2009), pp. 72–3.

[7]   Berger, 'Religionsbehörde', pp. 62–3. An exception in this regard are intellectuals without a large following who reject nationalism; see Binnaz Toprak, *Islamist Intellectuals of the 1980s in Turkey* (Istanbul, 1987), pp. 13–15. The early Republic as an ideal mythical past serves Kemalists in a similar way; see Esra Özyürek, *Nostalgia for the Modern. State Secularism and Everyday Politics in Turkey* (Durham, NC and London, 2006).

of history' until the break-up of Yugoslavia and the Soviet Bloc reopened South Eastern Europe to Turkish influence.[8] This contribution, however, is supposed to show that the purpose of a glorified and embellished vision of the Ottoman past as a period of societal harmony, yes even harmony between humans and nature, has a peculiar purpose for religious circles within Turkey. Not only does it provide a counter image to a present as distressful and illegitimate, it also contains an explanation for how the dismal present came about. An explanation which does not restrict itself to historical contingencies and political power struggles but integrates this process into the story of a larger battle between good and evil.

The Origins of the Ottoman Myth: Necip Fazıl Kısakürek and Samiha Ayverdi

The origins of the Ottoman myth can be traced back to a nostalgia that emerged first among members of the old Ottoman elite who refused to support the Republican government. Many of them came from the Balkan provinces lost in the late nineteenth and early twentieth centuries, or at least had family connections to this area. People like İsmail Fenni Ertuğrul (1855–1946), a former civil servant from Tarnovo, or Mustafa Düzgünman, a calligrapher from the conservative Asian-side borough of Üsküdar, kept alive literary and artistic traditions frowned upon by the new elite but did not challenge the political system.[9]

A gradual change towards the politicisation of this nostalgia set in during the 1940s; in 1943 Necip Fazıl Kısakürek (1905–1983), a poet and journalist from a Naqshbandi background, was allowed to publish the magazine *Büyük Doğu* ('Great East' or 'Great Orient'). In the beginning the journal desisted from open criticism of the regime; instead the authors criticised cultural aspects associated with Kemalism, like materialism and the mingling of the sexes, they denounced Communist sympathisers and tried to rehabilitate the Ottoman past. For example, many articles defended Sultan Abdülhamit II, who figures as a reactionary bogeyman in the Kemalist vision of history.[10]

---

8   Yılmaz Çolak, 'Ottomanism vs. Kemalism: Collective Memory and Cultural Pluralism in 1990s Turkey', *Middle Eastern Studies*, 42 (2006), pp. 591–3.

9   Martin Riexinger, 'Islamic Opposition to the Darwinian Theory of Evolution', in Lewis R. James and Olav Hammer (eds), *Handbook of Religion and the Authority of Science* (Leiden, 2011), pp. 487–8; Beşir Ayvazoğlu, 'Türk Muhâfazakârlığın kültürel kuruluşu', in Ahmet Çiğdem (ed.), *Muhâfazakârlık* (Istanbul, 2003), p. 510; Berger, 'Religionsbehörde', pp. 45–6.

10   M. Sami Karayel, 'Sultan Hamit müstebid midir?', *Büyük Doğu*, 31 December 1944, pp. 14–15; the author justifies the abolition of parliament with the allegation that it helped

One of the most famous conservative opponents of Kemalism, to whom *Büyük Doğu* offered an opportunity to publish her views, was the female author Sâmiha Ayverdi (1905–1993), who hailed from an elite family with a long record of government office in the Ottoman period. She had grown up steeped in the traditions of a conservative upper-class family, which implied that she received no formal education after the age of 16. In 1927 she joined the circle where the *şeyh* Kenan Rifai (Büyükaksoy) was transmitting the teachings and practices of his Sufi order, an activity which had become illegal with the 1925 Act on the Closing of Convents. The circle was, however, somewhat unconventional, since Rifai, who had also received a secular education, addressed people who, like him, had not given up their conservative, religious orientation in spite of that education. Before his death, Rifai appointed Ayverdi as his successor, whereupon she started her literary activities in the late 1930s and early 1940s with a number of novels (some of them first serialised in *Büyük Doğu*) and book-length essays. Apart from her literary activities, she supported – together with her brother Ekrem Hakkı Ayverdi, an architect who had dedicated himself to the conservation and restoration of Ottoman monuments – a number of associations intended to glorify the Ottoman past. The two thus lent support to the government formed by the *Demokrat Parti* of Adnan Menderes, which wrested power from Atatürk's state party, *Cumhuriyet Halk Partisi* ('Republican People's Party'), after the first free elections in 1950. Together with her brother, Ayverdi founded the *Kubbealtı Akademisi* in 1970, an association dedicated to conserving and promoting Ottoman arts, in particular poetry and music, and the ability to read Ottoman Turkish.[11]

Christians to gain power. Similarly, M. Sami Karayel, 'İç yüzüyle Abdülhamit: 1', *Büyük Doğu*, 27 September 1946, p. 14; 'İç yüzüyle Abdülhamit: 2', *Büyük Doğu*, 4 October 1946, p. 14; Necip Fazıl Kısakürek, 'Abdülhamîd ve Avrupalı', *Büyük Doğu*, 29 September 1965, pp. 10–11; *idem*, *Son devrin din mazlumları* (Istanbul, 1974), pp. 7–32; on Necip Fazıl Kısakürek's polemic *Ulu Hakan*, in defence of Abdülhamit, see Claudia Kleinert, *Die Revision der Historiographie des Osmanischen Reiches am Beispiel von Abdülhamid II: das späte Osmanische Reich im Urteil türkischer Autoren der Gegenwart (1930–1990)* (Berlin, 1995), pp. 15–16.

[11]   Sâmiha Ayverdi, *İstanbul Geceleri* (İstanbul, 1971), pp. 1: 'the musical order and harmony of civilization', 15; Sâmiha Ayverdi, *Mesihpaşa İmamı* (Istanbul, 1974) p. 138; the organisation's website: http://www.kubbealti.org.tr, accessed 20 March 2013; Annemarie Schimmel, 'Samiha Ayverdi – eine istanbuler Schriftstellerin', in Wilhelm Hoenerbach (ed.), *Der Orient in der Forschung. Festschrift für Otto Spies* (Wiesbaden, 1967), pp. 569–85; Nazlı Kaner, *Sâmiha Ayverdi (1905–1993) und die osmanische Gesellschaft. Zur Soziogenese eines ideologischen Begriffs: osmanlı* (Würzburg, 1998), pp. 21–43, 49–52, 112; Umut Azak, 'Sâmiha Ayverdi', in Çiğdem (ed.), *Muhafazakârlık*, pp. 248–55; Tanıl Bora and Burak

In her fictional as well as autobiographical works and in her essays, Ayverdi implicitly criticises Republican Turkey by describing Ottoman Turkey as a harmonious, spiritual society which provided to everybody a meaningful life.[12] One important aspect of this is the integrity and dignity of family life, characterised by a clear-cut division of duties and spheres between men and women and by respect for hierarchy of age. Another central aspect is the *mahalle*, the traditional city quarter, which she describes as a microcosm where people from different classes mingled and lived together harmoniously, due to the moral orientation provided by religion.[13] The *konak*, the traditional urban palace of the upper class, and its household are presented as organic models of society. Her presentation of slavery in this context is highly apologetic.[14] The villains in her vision of history are the 'rootless' (*köksüz*), 'ungrounded' (*yersiz*) and 'homeless' (*yurtsuz*) Westernising reformers, who began their attempts to undermine the Empire in the *Tanzîmât* period, and accelerated them under the Young Turks.[15] Furthermore, her writings are marked by a xenophobic,[16] anti-Semitic streak.[17]

Onaran, 'Nostalji ve Muhafazakârlık', in ibid, pp. 234–60; Beşir Ayvazoglu, 'Ekrem Hakkı Ayverdi', in ibid, pp. 238–41; Elifhan Köse, 'Muhafazakar bir kadın portresi olarak Semiha Ayverdi: Muhafazakarlık Düşüncesinde Kadınlara İlişkin Bir Hat Çizebilmek', *Fe Dergi-feminist eleştiri*, 1/1 (2009), pp. 12–14.

[12] Kaner, *Sâmiha Ayverdi*, pp. 98–102.

[13] Ayverdi, *İstanbul Geceleri*, p. 111; *eadem*, *Mesihpaşa İmamı*, p. 15; Kaner, *Sâmiha Ayverdi*, pp. 61–71; Ekrem Işın, 'Tanzimat ailesi ve modern âdâb-ı muâşeret', in Halit İnalcık and Mehmet Seyitdanlıoğlu (eds), *Tanzimat. Değişim sürecinde Osmanlı İmparatorluğu* (Istanbul, 2006), pp. 389–90.

[14] Ayverdi, *Kaybolan Anahtar*, pp. 21ff; Kaner, *Sâmiha Ayverdi*, pp. 82ff, 89–91. This apologetic attitude is common in Turkish Islamic discourse: see Berger, 'Religionsbehörde', p. 54; for a realistic assessment, see Ehud Toledano, *Slavery and its Abolition in the Ottoman Middle East* (Seattle, WA, 1998).

[15] Ayverdi, *İstanbul Geceleri*, pp. 113, 123–8; *eadem*, *Mesihpaşa İmamı*, pp. 42–4, 63ff, 68ff; *idem*, *Kaybolan Anahtar*, pp. 21–6; *yersiz* is a common term in Turkish conservative circles to denounce something as 'inauthentic'. Since it is derived from *yer* ('place') it has no precise equivalent in English; Kaner, *Sâmiha Ayverdi*, pp. 92–5. In *Büyük Doğu* the *Tanzîmât* were denounced in a similar way; see M. Sami Karayal, 'Tanzimatın içyüzü', *Büyük Doğu*, 1.7 (29 November 1943), p. 14; *idem*, 'Tanzimatın hediyesi', *Büyük Doğu*, 15 (24 December 1943), pp. 14–15; *idem*, 'Hâlis tarih ölçüsü. 2', *Büyük Doğu*, 2.44 (30 August 1946), p. 14; *idem*, 'Hâlis tarih ölçüsü. 3', *Büyük Doğu*, 2.45 (September 13 1946), p. 14; Necip Fazıl Kısakürek, 'Ve tarihçe', *Büyük Doğu*, 2.30 (24 May 1946), p. 11; 'Religious Issues in Turkish Politics', *Muslim World*, 49 (1959), p. 258.

[16] Kaner, *Sâmiha Ayverdi*, pp. 48–50.

[17] Ayverdi, *Kaybolan Anahtar*, p. 21.

Ottoman Nostalgia in the Nurcu Movement

The Nurcu Movement is one of the most influential Islamic schools of thought in Turkey. The name is derived from the *Risale-i Nur* ('Epistles of Light'), the collection of writings and sermons by the Kurdish scholar Said Nursi (1876?–1960). Born in the Eastern Provinces and educated in traditional religious schools (*medrese*), which were still common in that area, he came to the capital in 1908 to garner government support for his project for a school that was supposed to combine secular and religious learning. Abdülhamit II did not take this proposal seriously and had Said Nursi examined at an asylum. He was finally freed when the Young Turk revolution broke out. He was among those religious scholars who joined the revolutionary movement. After being taken captive by the Russian Army during the First World War, he spent two years in a prisoner-of-war camp in Russia. After his return to İstanbul he supported the National Liberation Struggle and even went to Ankara, the headquarters of Mustafa Kemal's forces. But soon it became apparent that the new government was heading in a secular direction, which was totally at odds with his own political concepts. Hence he withdrew to Eastern Anatolia, where he was arrested when religious scholars were rounded up after the Kurdish insurrection in 1925. Although he had not participated in that rebellion, he was forced to live in banishment or jail until 1951. He died in 1960, just two months before Menderes was overthrown by the first of the three military coups in Turkish history. Under the Menderes government he could again freely propagate his views and even publish the *Risale-i Nur*.[18] This collection is itself a reminder of the Ottoman past; its language is impregnated with Arabic and Persian vocabulary and grammatical constructions. Thus it is not immediately comprehensible for those Turks who grew up after the language reform that had begun after the establishment of the Republic. In the *ders*, the weekly conventions of Nurcu circles, passages from Said Nursi's works are rhythmically recited to underline their beauty and then explained in contemporary Turkish.[19] Most of the texts in the *Risale-i Nur* affirm traditional Sufi and Sunni teachings on eschatology and miracles, or the idea that Islam is compatible with science. Political issues are cautiously addressed in the guise of general moral lectures on sexuality and gender relations or economic ethics.[20]

Said Nursi regarded the Ottoman Empire as a legitimate polity, and preferable to the Republic. However, defending the Ottomans was not an issue

---

[18]   Hakan Yavuz, *Islamic Political Identity in Turkey* (Oxford, 2003), pp. 151–7.
[19]   Ibid., pp. 162–5.
[20]   Ibid., pp. 157–62.

to which he gave priority; moreover, what defence he did mount is free from any form of nostalgia. Apparently he was too well aware of the living conditions in the empire, its socio-economic deficits and the dictatorial practices of the Abdülhamit II regime.

Said Nursi's followers came from among literate people in small towns and middle-sized cities in Anatolia rather than from the disgruntled members of the old Ottoman elite. Many of them had profited from the expansion of the educational system but were wary of the secular and 'materialist' orientation of the curricula. In the first decade after Said Nursi's death, his followers concentrated on disseminating the teachings of their master, both in print and orally. Ottoman nostalgia did not become a major issue for the Nurcus before the late 1970s. In that decade some Nurcu groups began to publish newspapers, magazines and books in which they related Said Nursi's teachings to current issues.[21] With very few exceptions Nurcus kept aloof from the Islamist Milli Görüş movement and the parties which emerged from it, instead they supported centre-right parties.[22] Since the 1970s the Nurcu movement has split into various movements because of political differences, in particular regarding the coup of 12 September 1980 – which some factions welcomed, while others vehemently objected.[23] The most important group to have emerged from the Nurcu movement consists of the followers of Fethullah Gülen, who refer to themselves as the *hizmet* ('service') movement; this has built up an international network of schools and a successful media group in Turkey.[24]

---

[21] Günter Seufert, *Islam in der Türkei: Islamismus als symbolische Repräsentation einer sich modernisierenden muslimischen Gesellschaft* (Stuttgart, 1997), p. 379; Çolak, 'Ottomanism'.

[22] The founder and long-time leader of the Milli Görüş movement was the engineer Necmettin Erbakan (1926–2011) who founded his first party, the Milli Nizam Partisi ('National Order Party') in 1969 by organising (primarily) provincial businessmen with a Nakşbendi background. The party was banned after the 1971 coup but re-emerged as the Milli Selâmet Partisi ('National Salvation Party'), which joined various governments as a junior partner. The party was again forbidden after the 1980 coup, and again re-emerged, this time as the Refah Partisi ('Welfare Party'), which in 1992 became Turkey's strongest party, by appealing to residents, among others, rather than business people; it entered the government in 1996. After the 1997 'post-modern' coup the party was once again proscribed, whereas the Saadet Partisi, which Erbakan's close followers set up as its successor, never gained enough votes to enter parliament. The 'moderate' spin-off party led by Recep Tayyip Erdoğan has governed Turkey since 2002: see Yavuz, *Islamic Political Identity*, pp. 207–64, and for the local level, Cihan Tuğal, *Passive Revolution: Absorbing the Islamic Challenge to Capitalism* (Stanford, 2009).

[23] Ibid., pp. 170–77.

[24] Ibid., pp. 179–205.

In books and in articles in the newspaper *Yeni Asya* ('new Asia') and magazines like *Zafer* ('victory'), *Köprü* ('the bridge') and *Sızıntı* ('the leakage [of truth]'), Nurcus now praise the Ottoman Empire as a pious utopia unmarred by social conflicts which guaranteed that all its subjects could live a meaningful life. Under Ottoman rule there was allegedly no discrepancy between 'religion and reason',[25] and the actions of the rulers were motivated by nothing other than an honest intention to do justice.[26] Architectural remains witness that they acted exclusively for God's sake and according to the principle of *ihlas* ('faith-based honesty').[27] Yavuz Bahadıroğlu, a well-known and prolific author of historical novels, presents the *saray* as a pious household where hymns in praise of God and Muhammad (*ilahiler ve natlar*) were ceaselessly chanted.[28] According to the Nurcus the Ottomans put Islamic egalitarianism into effect.[29] Allegedly, their rulers were constantly in contact with their subjects.[30] Moreover, the system of government was supposed to be characterised by the separation of powers, as the sultan did not interfere with the proceedings of the administration or the courts;[31] the real structure of the government apparatus, the dominance of the army and the distance of the ruler from the ruled – which was to be seen in the separation between the small elite with access to the court (*enderun*) and ordinary subjects – are matters which are never dealt with.[32] Based on this ahistorical approach, Bekir Berk, a lawyer by profession and one of the most prolific Nurcu authors, describes the second Vienna Campaign (1683) as a voluntary enterprise undertaken by all Muslim ethnic groups simultaneously.[33]

According to Nurcu writers, the Ottoman subjects were able to live in harmony with all other creatures.[34] According to the reports of European

---

[25] Hekimoğlu İsmail, *100 Soruda Bediüzzaman Said Nursi, Risale-i Nur Külliyatı ve Risale-i Nur Talebeleri* (İstanbul, 1994), p. 291; and for children, *idem*, 'Osmanlı devleti neden uzun ömürlü oldu? Adalete dayanan devlet', *Yeni Nesil*, 28 October 1989.

[26] Vehbi Vakkasoğlu, *Osmanlı insanı* (Istanbul, 2004) p. 13.

[27] Ibid., p. 60;

[28] Yavuz Bahadıroğlu, *Biz Osmanlıyız* (Istanbul, 2007), pp. 66–8.

[29] Vakkasoğlu, *Osmanlı insanı*, p. 79.

[30] 'Osmanlı döneminde idareciler halkla yüz yüze görüşürdü', *Yeni Nesil*, 27 January 1985.

[31] Bahadıroğlu, *Biz Osmanlıyız*, p. 150; Fethullah Gülen, *Prizma* (İstanbul, 2003), p. 70. See, in similar vein, Mehmed Kırkıncı, *Nasıl bir maârif? nasıl bir eğitim?* (Erzurum, 2001), pp. xi–xii.

[32] V.J. Parry, 'Enderun', *Encyclopaedia of Islam*, Vol. 2, pp. 697–8.

[33] Bekir Berk, *Doğu olaylar ve tehlikenin kaynağı* (Istanbul, 1991), p. 37; 'Sultan Murad askerlere Kuran'a el bastırdı', *Yeni Nesil*, 14 February 1986.

[34] Vakkasoğlu, *Osmanlı insanı*, pp. 93–7; Yavuz Bahadıroğlu, *Biz Osmanlıyız* (Istanbul, 2007), pp. 11, 24, 149; as his main witness for the love of animals and nature he

travelers, crime was practically unknown.[35] Gülen claims that a peculiar kind of spirituality (*ruhânîlik*) had characterised the people of 'our old cities'. Theirs was a 'spick-and-span world' which enthralled everybody as soon as they approached it. Every single house resembled a mosque or a dervish convent (*zaviye*) and thus provided a connection to the 'world beyond'.[36] The glorification of the Ottoman world is hence closely connected to the critique of the condescending attitude many Kemalists display towards the traditions of the rural and the small-town population. Villages and small towns are romanticised as fragments of an idealised Ottoman world extending into the present.[37] The calm of the village is juxtaposed with the concrete architecture typical of modern Turkey and the stress and noise associated with it. This reflects a quite common dichotomy in Turkish Islamic discourse, where *huzur* ('peace of mind') is contrasted with stress.[38] Like Ayverdi, the authors highlight the importance of family values in the Ottoman Empire: mothers imbibed an awareness of the value of martyrdom,[39] and the younger generation used to honour the old.[40]

The Muslim supremacist vision of the Ottoman Empire was complemented by an irenic discourse in which the Ottoman Empire was depicted as 'another Switzerland', where different ethnic and religious groups could live together in

---

refers to the travel accounts of the French romanticist Alphonse de Lamartine; translations of such travelogues, which are often forgotten in the West, are popular reading material in Turkey. However, respect for animals is also highlighted by Ayverdi; see Kaner, *Sâmiha Ayverdi*, p. 69.

[35] Bahadıroğlu, *Biz Osmanlıyız*, pp. 14–16.

[36] Fethullah Gülen, *Zamanın Altın Dilimi* (Istanbul, 2003) pp. 43–7; see, in a similar vein, Bahadıroğlu, *Biz Osmanlıyız*, pp. 17–22.

[37] Nedim Gürbüz: 'Vah Turizm!' *Köprü*, 62 (July 1982), pp. 5–7; especially during one-party rule but also later, serious efforts were undertaken to eliminate timber houses and twisted alleys from the cityscape: see Klaus Kreiser, 'Die neue Türkei (1920–2002)', in Klaus Kreiser and Andreas Neumann (eds), *Kleine Geschichte der Türkei* (Stuttgart, 2003), p. 413.

[38] Vakkasoğlu, *İslâm*, p. 127; Gülen, *Zamanın*, pp. 40; Sema Öz, 'İslâmî geleneklerimiz yaşatılmalı', *Yeni Nesil*, 2 July 1991; Selda Gören, 'Eski Türk evleri ve özellikleri', *Yeni Nesil*, 19 July 1991; *eadem*, 'Hayatımız stres', *Yeni Nesil*, 18 January 1988; Ahmet el-Kadi, 'Bir ders daha', *Zafer 96* (December 1984), pp. 4–8; *idem*, 'Dünya İslâm'ı arıyor', *Yeni Nesil*, 7 July 1991; Muhammet Bozdağ, *İstemenin Esrarı* (Istanbul, 2007), pp. 45–9; Erika Glaßen, '"Huzur": Trägheit, Seelenruhe, soziale Harmonie. Zur osmanischen Mentalitätsgeschichte'. in Jean-Louis Bacqué-Grammont (ed.), *Türkische Miszellen. Robert Anhegger Festschrift/armağanı/mélanges* (Istanbul, 1987), pp. 163–6; Christine Jung, *Islamische Fernsehsender in der Türkei. Zur Entwicklung des türkischen Fernsehens zwischen Staat, Markt und Religion* (Berlin, 2003), pp. 161–6.

[39] 'Osmanlı annesi çocuğuna şehadet şuuru aşılardı', *Yeni Nesil*, 11 April 1986.

[40] Bahadıroğlu, *Biz Osmanlıyız*, pp. 28–31, 548.

harmony.[41] According to Bahadıroğlu the Greeks hailed the entry of Mehmet II Fatih into Byzantium;[42] although the Ottoman chronicles tell a different story.[43] Vakkasoğlu, a schoolteacher and Nurcu author, stresses that Mehmet ordered the highest-ranking Byzantine architect to construct a mosque in the city; but it is self-evidently the case that the award of contracts should be based entirely on professional considerations.[44] Furthermore, he stresses that while Bulgarians and Serbs were allowed to speak their own language the Germans forbade the Czechs to do so.[45] Hence, as is to be expected, according to Vakkasoğlu peace came to an end in the Balkans after the Ottomans had lost their territories.[46] Even the nowadays contested city of Jerusalem was a peaceful place.[47] This vision of the Ottoman past became important when the Gülen branch of the Nurcu movement began to propagate the notion of the Ottoman Empire as a role model for inter-religious harmony. This was allegedly the case because the Ottoman Empire was not simply tolerant, but *hoşgör* – a term that actually means 'tolerant', but that in the discourse of the Gülen movement is supposed to imply that the state appreciates the activities of all religious groups.[48]

In the general apologetics of the Ottoman Empire and the embellishment of its social structure promoted by the Nurcus, notable events, historical developments and ruptures are virtually absent, as is customary in romanticised visions of a historical period. The problems the empire faced from the eighteenth century

[41] Ibid., p. 9; the concept of a *pax Ottomanica* is quite common in Turkish Islamic circles: Çolak, 'Ottomanism vs. Kemalism', p. 596; Ahmet Akgündüz, 'The First Model for the EU: The Ottoman State', at http://www.islamicuniversity.nl/nl/actueel/publicaties/282-the-first-model-for-the-eu-ottoman-state.html, last accessed 9 May 2012; Berger, 'Religionsbehörde', pp. 63–6.

[42] Yavuz Bahadıroglu,'Şehre girerken Hıristiyanların da gönlünü fethetti: Fatih tekbirlerle Ayasofya'ya geldi', *Yeni Nesil*, 9 June 1987; *idem*, 'Fatih dehşet degil, şefkat yolunu seçti', *Yeni Nesil*, 13 June 1987.

[43] Berger, 'Religionsbehörde', p. 64.

[44] Vakkasoğlu, *Osmanlı insanı*, p. 36.

[45] Ibid., p. 146.

[46] *Idem*, *İslâm Dünya gündeminde* (Istanbul, 1984), 84–6.

[47] Yunus Çengel, 'Risale-i Nur ışığında terörle mücadele kitle imha silahlarından arınma', in *7. <Yedinci> Uluslararası Bediüzzaman Sempozyumu* (Istanbul, 2004), pp. 12, 9–31.

[48] For example, the conference entitled *Birlikte Yasama Sanati Hosgörü 700 Sempozyumu* ('the art of living together over 700 [years] of tolerance') in 1999; see 'Hoşgörü üç dinli bir beste', *Aksiyon* 923 (4–10 July 1999), at http://www.aksiyon.com.tr/aksiyon/haber-5395-34-hosgoru-uc-dinli-bir-beste.html, accessed 20 March 2013; Elisabeth Dörler, *Verständigung leben und lernen am Beispiel von türkischen Muslimen und Vorarlberger Christen* (Feldkirch, 2003), pp. 182–4.

onwards are simply passed over: how the emergence of nationalist tendencies in the Balkans, for instance, was motivated to a considerable degree by the fact that the educated strata were well aware of the economic and technological gap that separated the Ottoman Empire from Western Europe (or, more harshly, even from the Habsburg monarchy and Russia). And the same is true of the secularist tendencies which emerged among Muslims. A single exception is the empire's technological backwardness, with regard to which the Nurcus did not develop a common line of defence. Hekimoğlu İsmail, an author of popular books on Said Nursi and of religious novels, partially accepts the secularist narrative: in 1860 cannons had to be bought from Krupp, whereas in 1453 the Turks themselves were able to produce state-of-the-art ordnance;[49] but Gülen dismissed such manifestations of anti-Ottomanism. The slogan 'They have built mosques but not factories' is, according to him, anachronistic.[50]

When Nurcus address the last decades of the empire, they become more realist,[51] but like their Kemalist counterparts they identify the actors of the past with the political forces of the present, and thus reduce the complexity of the historical process to a simplified black and white scheme.[52] Like Ayverdi, the Nurcus decry the *Tanzîmât* as the period when the decline of the Ottoman Empire set in. According to them this period initiated the 150-year struggle of a minority of intellectuals against the nation. Pretending to renovate the Empire they wanted to erect an edifice following Western models.[53] This is a typical example of the voluntarist argumentation which dominates in the Turkish Islamic historical discourse because the questions of whether any alternatives existed, or what the consequences of alternative actions would have been, are never asked.[54] In order to bolster their critique of the *Tanzîmât* the Nurcus refer to Ayverdi's romanticising presentation. A Western witness Vakkasoğlu, to bolster his view of the Ottomans

---

[49]   Hekimoğlu İsmail, *Müslüman ve para* (Istanbul, 2004), p. 25.

[50]   Fethullah Gülen, *Asrın getirdiği tereddütler*, Vol. II (Istanbul, 2003), p. 217.

[51]   For a representative example of the Kemalist view of the Hamidian era as a period of decadence and obscurantism, see Niyazi Berkes, *The Development of Secularism in Turkey* (Montreal, 1964) pp. 256–61. The author belonged to the left-wing Kemalist circle associated with the magazine *Yön* ('direction'), cf. Gökhan Atılgan, *Yön-Devrim hareketi. Kemalizm ile Marksizm arasında geleneksel aydınlar* (Istanbul, 2002).

[52]   Yavuz, *Islamic Political Identity*, p. 153.

[53]   Safa Mürsel, 'Türkiye'de anayasa dâvâsı', *Köprü*, 54 (November 1981), pp. 6–8. By the beginning of the twentieth century this was already a commonplace in the Islamic press; see Esther Debus, *Sebilürreşad. Eine vergleichende Untersuchung zur islamischen Opposition der vor- und nachkemalistischen Ära* (Frankfurt-am-Main, 1991), pp. 207–15.

[54]   Levent Tezcan, *Religiöse Strategien der 'machbaren' Gesellschaft. Verwaltete Religion und islamistische Utopie in der Türkei* (Bielefeld, 2003), p. 135, n. 73.

and to denounce the materialist aberrations of the Young Turks, cites the French writer Pierre Loti (1850–1923), forgotten in his homeland France but still popular in Turkey because, in defiance of the *Zeitgeist*, he did not express solidarity with the Christian subjects of the Ottomans but with the Turkish Muslims.[55]

Most Nurcus accuse the Young Turks of nationalism, which reflects their rejection of any ethnic hierarchy among Muslims. With reference to Toynbee, Mehmed Kırkıncı, the leader of a Nurcu sub-group that supported the 1980 coup, denounces them as enemies of Islam and of the Arabs, having cut the bond which unified the two most important ethnic groups of the empire.[56] The Nurcus are well aware of Arab historians like Muhammad Harb who oppose the mainstream of Arab nationalist historiography and evaluate the Ottomans favourably as defenders of Islam.[57]

Although the Nurcus distanced themselves from 'anti-imperialist' slogans in the 1970s and 1980s, because they belonged to the political vocabulary of the Left, they praised the Ottoman Empire as a polity which the unfortunate Muslims of other countries could look up to. They thus follow the tradition of identifying the Ottoman Empire with the interests of the Muslims worldwide, a tradition which emerged in the nineteenth century.[58] The magazine *Sızıntı* hence reported extensively on relations between South Asian Muslims and the Ottoman Empire. They do not deny that during the First World War the vast majority of Muslims in India were loyal to the British. This is, however, explained by the assertion that according to their opinion the godless Young Turks had to be removed.[59]

---

[55]   Vehbi Vakkasoğlu, *Bozgun (bir devrin çöküşü)* (Istanbul, 1977), pp. 42–5. The importance and function of the Western Crown Witness ('Bestätiger vom Dienst') in the discourse of Islamic societies is elaborated upon in Rotraud Wielandt, *Das Bild der Europäer in der modernen arabischen Erzähl- und Theaterliteratur* (Wiesbaden, 1980), p. 57.

[56]   Mehmed Kırkıncı, *İslamda birlik* (Istanbul, 1998), pp. 47–50.

[57]   'Mısırlı Prof. Harb Yeni Nesil'de', *Yeni Nesil*, 10 June 1985; 'Mısırlı öğretim üyesi Dr. Muhammed Harb: "Avrupalılar, Araplara Türkiye'nin İslâma ihanet ettiğini yaydı"', *Yeni Nesil*, 30 June 1985; 'Türkiye ile Arap dünyası arasındaki soğukluk düzelmeli', *Yeni Nesil*, 1 July 1985. On the theses of this 'radical revisionist', see Maurus Reinkowski, *Filastin, Filistin und Eretz Israel. Die späte osmanische Herrschaft über Palästina in der arabischen, türkischen und israelischen Historiographie* (Berlin, 1995), pp. 60, 112, 128, 163ff, 166–8, 179–81, 183ff, 189, 220, 316, without, however, detailed information on his biography (p. 266).

[58]   Uriel Heyd, 'The Ottoman Ulemā and Westernization in the Time of Selim III and Mahmūd II', in Uriel Heyd (ed.), *Studies in Islamic History and Civilization* (Jerusalem, 1961), pp. 90–95.

[59]   İbrahim Refik, 'Tacın incisindeki Osmanlı'nın yetimleri', *Sızıntı*, 15 (1993), pp. 397–401, 446–50; Abdullah Çangaoğlu, 'Osmanlı devleti'nde devşirme sistemi', *Sızıntı*, 16 (1994), pp. 160–2.

Apart from ideological aberrations, the Nurcus accuse the Young Turks of incompetence. Their internal differences are supposed to have led to the defeats in the Balkan Wars and their inability to assess risks properly drew the Empire into the First World War.[60] Moreover, the Young Turks got the army involved in politics, with disastrous consequences for both politics and the military.[61] The willingness of the Ottoman sultan to cooperate with the Entente after the defeat is generally passed over.[62]

Last but not least, the Nurcus accuse the Kemalists' cultural policies of discrediting the Ottomans[63] by practising *taqlīd* ('imitation') of Westerners, for example borrowing their terminology, as in the designation of Abdülhamit II as 'Kızıl Sultan' ('the red [i.e. bloodstained] sultan').[64] In this context it is remarkable that they pass over the biography of their founding figure – remarkable but also understandable, since a presentation of his political positions before the First World War would show how strong the disaffection with the autocracy of Abülhamit II was, even among religious scholars.[65] But to rehabilitate the 'red sultan' and to defend him against attacks in the Kemalist press on the one hand, and to denounce the Young Turks on the other hand, have become two of their main concerns in the 'politics of history'. In this respect they differ from Said Nursi himself, who never denounced the Young Turks outright and was quite critical of Abdülhamit. Nursi referred to the latter's rule as *istibdat* ('despotism')[66] and claimed that only about 10 per cent of the Young Turks promoted evil designs under the influence of the Freemasons, while the rest were believing Muslims, among them scholars who had committed themselves to the nation.[67] The majority of Nurcus, however, defend the sultan against allegations by Westerners or Turkish secularists. They refer, for example, to the fact that many more newspapers – in Turkish as well as in other languages – were allowed under his allegedly infamous system of censorship than under the one-party rule of the Kemalists. They claim that the reason for this

---

[60] Mustafa Kaplan, 'Bâb-ı Âli baskını', *Yeni Nesil*, 27 November 1985.

[61] 'Siyasete giren ordu bozgunu dâvet etti', *Yeni Nesil*, 1 July 1989); 'Batı Trakya Bulgara teslim edecekti', *Yeni Nesil*, 3 July 1989.

[62] Bahadıroğlu, *Biz Osmanlıyız*, pp. 218–24.

[63] 'Tarihimiz karalanıyor', *Yeni Nesil*, 21 May 1986; Vedat Sağlam, *Köy enstitülerinden imam-hatip okullarına eğitim ve kültür* (Istanbul, 2003), p. 109.

[64] Fethullah Gülen, *Asrın getirdiği tereddütler*, Vol. II, p. 218.

[65] İsmail Kara, *İslâmcıların siyasi görüşleri*, (Istanbul, 1994), pp. 127–42; idem, 'Turban and Fez: *ulema* as Opposition', in Elisabeth Özdalga (ed.), *Late Ottoman Society: The Intellectual Legacy* (London and New York, 2005), pp. 162–200.

[66] Said Nursi, *Kastamonu Lâhıkası* (Istanbul, 2000), p. 78.

[67] Said Nursi, *Münâzarat* (Istanbul, 1958), p. 32.

denigration is Abdülhamit's relentless striving for the welfare of Muslims, both those in the Ottoman Empire and those suffering under the yoke of Western imperialism. One aspect which receives special consideration is Abdülhamit's rejection of a deal with Herzl, founder of the Zionist movement, who sought permission for Jewish settlements, for which he is allegedly well remembered in Arab countries. This is remarkable, since the Nurcus criticise Israel in a relatively moderate tone.[68] For Islamists with an explicitly anti-democratic agenda it is no problem that he dissolved parliament and ruled without parliamentary control for 33 years. For the Nurcus, with their explicitly democratic agenda, it presents a dilemma.[69] The fact that the Nurcus ignore their founder's much more nuanced view of that period shows the strong impact of the vision of history that Necip Fazıl Kısakürek propagated in *Büyük Doğu*.[70]

A minority of Nurcus dissent with regard to Sultan Abdülhamit II. Metin Karabaşoğlu, one of the most sophisticated Nurcu authors, argues that Said Nursi's ideas are basically anti-authoritarian and anti-totalitarian, and hence conflict with every top-down approach. According to Said Nursi there was no substantial difference between Abdülhamit II and the Young Turks because both subordinated the individual to the state.[71] Yamina Bouguenaya-Mermer, an Algerian physicist who after joining the Nurcu movement became one of the most important contributors on science and religion issues, and her husband Ali Mermer doubt Abdülhamit's Islamic credentials by alerting us to the fact that under his rule the secularisation of the educational system continued whereas the decline of the *medreseler* accelerated.[72]

---

[68]   'Sislerin ardında 33 yıl', *Köprü*, 95 (May 1985), pp. 24–7; Mustafa Kaplan, 'Yahudilerin emellerine sed çeken Osmanlı', *Yeni Nesil*, 31 January 1986; Sağlam, *Köy enstitüleri*, p. 32.

[69]   Kleinert, *Revision*, pp. 157–65.

[70]   A general overview can be found in Kleinert, *Revision*. Her ideological classification of many authors is to be taken with caution; when *Sebîlü'r-Reşad*, the most important Islamic magazine before the foundation of the Republic, was re-established in 1948, Abdülhamit was rehabilitated in this publication as well, in contrast to the critical attitude that had prevailed in the first series; see Debus, *Sebilürreşad*, p. 305; on another religious movement aligned with the centre-right instead of the Islamists, the *Işıkçılar*, see Esther Peskes, 'Die Wahhābīya als innerislamisches Feindbild. Zum Hintergrund anti-wahhabitischer Publikationen in der zeitgenössischen Türkei', *Welt des Islams*, 40 (2000), pp. 366–8; Islamists of the Millî Görüş movement commemorated the 100th anniversary of his toppling; see at http://www.igmg.de/nachrichten/artikel/zweite-abdulhamit-konferenz-in-hamburg.html, accessed 20 March 2013.

[71]   Metin Karabaşoğlu, 'Said Nursi', in Yasin Aktay (ed.), *İslâmcılık* (Istanbul, 2004), pp. 284–6.

[72]   Yamina Bouguenaya-Mermer and Ali Mermer, *Risale-i nur'dan toplumsal barış önerisi* (Istanbul, 1997), p. 13, n. 2.

Bahadıroğlu is the only author who presents Said Nursi's stance on the Young Turks correctly.[73] Others paint them as a negative mirror image of Abdülhamit, as a clique submitting the Muslims to foreign rulers. Gülen colours his invective with religious sub-tones: their aim was to expel the spirit of the nation, and to destroy *mihrab* and *minbar* is among the most egregious of sins.[74] The Nurcus accuse the secularists of undermining the sole legitimate sphere of action of the Ottoman woman by promoting the education of girls. The demise of the family, not unsurprisingly, led to the necessity of establishing the first old people's homes (*darülaceze*).[75] Others formulate their criticism more soberly and single out specific phenomena. But for all of them, the main culprits are the alumni of the Imperial Medical School, influenced by the materialism with which they were imbued there.[76]

From Individual Nostalgia towards a Projective Counter-image of the Present

The most striking aspect of the Ottoman myth is that it remains quite detached from everyday politics and devoid of concrete political demands. Only fringe figures call for a restoration of the Ottoman Empire. An example is the Naqshbandī Şeyh Nâzım Haqqani, a Cypriot Turk now residing in London, whose followers are now primarily converts.[77] The Ottoman nostalgia of Sâmiha Ayverdi reflects, embellished though they may be, the real experiences of a member of the privileged class in the Empire, whereas the Nurcu authors who glorify the Ottoman Empire never lived under Ottoman rule and do not usually come from the privileged classes. Their presentation of the Ottoman Empire and its 'gravediggers' reveals nothing about the Ottoman Empire but much about the discontentment of the Nurcus with the political system of the Turkish Republic. Many of the issues they address when they write on the Ottoman Empire they also raise in other contexts, without reference to a better past. They criticise modern architecture because it fails to separate the familiar and

---

[73] 'İttihadçıların bozuk kanadını reddetti', *Yeni Nesil*, 15 February 1988.

[74] Gülen, *Zamanın Altın Dilimi*, 137.

[75] 'Osmanlı annesi çocuğuna şehadet şuuru aşılardı', *Yeni Nesil*, 11 April 1986.

[76] 'Türkiye'de islâmî uyanış', *Köprü*, 103 (January 1986), pp. 26–8.

[77] http://www.osmanli.de, accessed 20 September 2013; Annabelle Böttcher: *Mit Turban und Handy: Scheich Nazim al-Qubrusi und sein transnationales Sufinetzwerk* (Würzburg, 2011), pp. 139–42; Gökhan Çetinsaya, 'Cumhuriyet Türkiyesin'de Osmancılık', in Çiğdem (ed.), *Muhâfazakârlık*, pp. 361–4.

the semi-public sphere (*Haremlik-selâmlık*),[78] and they propagate the idea of a society which is supposed to function on the basis of a harmonious social order.[79] The criticism of the army's leading role in Turkish politics is a central point in Nurcu comments on current affairs.[80] Their discourse can thus be regarded as a reconstruction of the past, in Halbwachs's sense,[81] or as an 'invention of tradition', in that of Hobsbawm and Ranger. But whereas the groundbreaking collection of essays edited by Hobsbawm and Ranger focuses on how the conscious selection of dates, dress, musical styles and so forth was used to create what was supposed to be a homogeneous nation with a homogeneous understanding of herself, with similar processes at various levels and promoted by various actors taking place in the context of many nation states, opposition groups challenge a dominant historical narrative and present their own streamlined version of the past in order to delegitimise the former. The rehabilitation of the Ottoman past by the Turkish 'Right' is a successful example. But the Ottoman Empire is only one of several counter-images for everything the Nurcus dislike about the Turkish Republic; the others are not taken from the past but from other cultural contexts. They present an idealised, or rather invented, version of church–state relations in Western countries which is used to demonstrate that the hostility of the Kemalists towards Islam has nothing to do with secularism properly understood: in Europe and the United States the state actively supports religion, or at least keeps its hands off it, and grants freedom of consciousness.[82]

———————

[78]   İbrahim Cânan, *Oturanların açışışdan Atatürk Üniversitesi lojmanları veya taklitçiliğimizin muhasebesi* (Ankara, 1979), pp. 36-7, 79-80; Cânan's dismissal of modern architecture as alien to 'the people' ties up with the critique of modern architecture initiated by *Büyük Doğu*, 42 (16 August 1946), title p., 'Yapıcılıkta şahsiyet istiyoruz' ('we want identity in constructing'), showing a picture of the Çifte-Minare Medresesi in Erzurum in front of an unfinished Western-style parcel house; *Büyük Doğu*, 70 (31 October 1947), title p., '24 yılın hikâyesi: Bu şahsiyetten bu şahsiyetsizliğe' ('a 24-year story: from identity to identitylessness'), showing an administrative building, presumably in Ankara, beneath a *muqarnas*; this view is moreover quite common in Islamic movements, and not only in Turkey; see Charles Tripp, *Islam and the Moral Economy: The Challenge of Capitalism* (Cambridge, 2006), pp. 168–80.

[79]   Fethullah Gülen, *Çağ ve Nesil* (İstanbul, 2003), pp. 117-18; 'Prof. Dr. Adnan Ziyalar: Gençlerin enerjisi cinselliğe kadırıldı!', *Yeni Nesil*, 21 December 1985.

[80]   'Demokles'in Süngüsü: Ordu ve Politka', *Köprü*, 104 (February 1986), pp. 8-15; 'Müdahalenin fatutarasını millet ödüyor', ibid, pp. 19-24; Metin Karabaşoğlu, 'Mecburî askerlik kalksın', *Köprü*, 108 (June 1986), pp. 45-7.

[81]   Maurice Halbwachs, *Les cadres sociaux de la mémoire* (Paris, 1994), pp. 27-36.

[82]   Talip Demirhan, 'Hollanda aynasında "Türk demokrasisi"', *Köprü*, 140 (November 1989), pp. 29-32; Necmeddin Oğuz, 'Dualı açılış', *Yeni Nesil*, 5 October 1987; *idem*, 'Cami inşaatına devlet desteği', *Yeni Nesil*, 14 May 1988; *idem*, '"Amsterdam" da 22

They refer to Japan for another reason: the country allegedly shows what a non-European nation is able to achieve when it is allowed to retain its culture. Thus, for example, the necessity of adopting the Latin alphabet is disputed, because Japan succeeded economically although the country stuck to its writing system, which was even more complicated than the Ottoman one.[83] This invention does also reveal more about what religious Turks dislike about the secularist state than about the enormous, sometimes disruptive, social and cultural change Japanese society has undergone since the Meiji restoration. In two respects the references to the West and Japan differ, though. They deal with other people in other places whereas the Ottoman myth ascribes the roles of the righteous and the villains to Turks in a not so distant past and at present, ergo those who use the myth and their opponents. Furthermore, the references show that tradition as such is better than imitation of the West (Japan) or that religion as such is better than irreligiosity (West). That this is the case is proven with reference to the economic and political success of the respective societies. In the Turkish case, however, it is also a question of truth and falsehood.

Another notable aspect of the Ottoman myth – as presumably other 'invented traditions' – is its flexibility, which made its adaptation to changing circumstances and predilections possible. Originally, in the case of Kısakürek and Ayverdi, tied to a religious nationalism that was no less intolerant towards the non-Turkish *cum* non-Muslim minorities, it has recently been integrated into a discourse of tolerance, based on the claim that the Ottoman Empire was a harmonious society due to its multi-cultural communitarism.

Finally, the discourse of Ottoman nostalgia is remarkable due to its projective character and worldly innocence: its focus on aesthetics and its legitimisation through aesthetics. Republican Turkey is denounced as ugly and devoid of meaning, whereas the Ottoman Empire was supposedly beautiful and meaningful. Although the exponents of the nostalgic Ottoman myth are hostile to secularism and emphasise the necessity of religion for social harmony, they appreciate cultural traditions, in particular music, which are anathema to many Islamic movements. Such an aesthetic and emotional criticism of politics and society was and is apparently not well suited to the harsh world of day-to-day

---

cami her an ibadete açık: Dinî hizmetlere devlet yardımı', *Yeni Nesil* , 16 May 1988; *idem*, '"Holanda" da ilkokul', *Yeni Nesil*, 7 April 1991; 'Laiklik ve vicdan hürriyeti', *Köprü*, 51 (August 1981), pp. 7–10. The Reagan vs Carter campaign would have been impossible in Turkey because both candidates prayed; Filiz Çırpçı, 'Amerikan usulü lâiklik', *Köprü*, 81 (February 1984), pp. 7–8.

[83] 'Latin harfleri ile medenî olunmaz', *Yeni Nesil*, 25 November 1989; more generally, Nazım Aslan, 'Kaybolan kültürümüz', *Yeni Nesil*, 18 May 1991.

politics. In their opposition to what they saw as the spiritual void of Kemalism, the Ayverdis and their circle (as well as the Nurcus) aligned themselves with the centre-right parties, which were, however, primarily interested in economic progress, were dedicated to a technocratic approach and did away with the Ottoman heritage in a quite different way. Whereas Istanbul resembled an archaeological site because intentional neglect had left many of its buildings to decay from the 1920s to the 1940s, attention was paid to monuments from the 1950s onwards; but the old structure of the cityscape was buried under multi-storey concrete buildings and freeways.[84] For center-right politicians, the Ottoman myth may have been useful in denouncing their Kemalist opponents and to mobilise certain sections in the religious camp; in order to convince a larger electorate, however, they did not rely on pictures of an embellished past but rather on symbols promising a bright future.

---

[84] Nur Altınyıldız, 'İmperatorlukle Cumhuriyet arasındaki eşikte siyaset ve mimarlık: Eskiyi muhafaza/ yeniyi inşa', in Çiğdem (ed.), *Muhafazakârlık*, pp. 179–86; Ayvazoğlu, 'Ekrem Hakkı Ayverdi', p. 239.

Chapter 3

From a Red Guard to a Jahrinya: A Chinese Author's Return to Islam

Xiaofei Tu

In this chapter I pursue a case study of the Chinese Hui (sinophone Muslim) author Zhang Chengzhi in order to shed light on how he has used religious and political symbols to imagine the past and construct the present in post-Mao China. Zhang is, without a doubt, the best-known Muslim writer in China, who has made his name with novels and essay collections such as *Xinling shi* ('history of the soul'), *Jin muchang* ('golden pasture'), *Qingjie de jingshen* ('pure spirit') and 30 other major literary works (some of which re-employ content from works with different titles). Zhang's writings are known in China both for exotic ethnic/religious stories and for their bold attacks on Western imperialism and global capitalism in the name of Islam.

Islam in China and Hui Muslims in particular are still an insufficiently studied area. Besides the pioneering work of Joseph Fletcher, Raphael Israeli's and Dru Gladney's recent works are perhaps the best English-language representations of scholarly interest on this topic.[1] However, Israeli, Gladney and other scholars of Chinese Islam have paid no attention to Zhang, since the latter is a novelist in whom literary critics rather than historians and sociologists normally show interest. On the other hand, scholars of Chinese literature – with a few exceptions – tend to show too little appreciation of the significance of Islamic symbols in Zhang's work.[2] I hope to overcome these limitations by placing Zhang within the historical context of Chinese Islam and against the backdrop

---

[1]   Joseph Fletcher, *Studies on Chinese and Islamic Inner Asia*, edited by Beatrice Forbes Manz (Aldershot, 1995); Dru C. Gladney, *Dislocating China: Muslims, Minorities, and Other Subaltern Subjects* (Chicago, IL, 2004); Raphael Israeli, *Muslims in China: Religion, Ethnicity, Culture, and Politics* (Lanham, MD, 2007).

[2]   See Jian Xu, 'Radical Ethnicity and Apocryphal History: Reading the Sublime Object of Humanism in Zhang Chengzhi's Late Fictions', *Positions*, 10/3 (2002), p. 525; Xinmin Liu, 'A Marginal Return? The Problematic in Zhang Chengzhi's Reinvention of Ethnic Identity', *Journal of Contemporary China*, 6/16 (1997), p. 567.

of the rise and fall of twentieth-century Maoist ideology. I will also make use of the concept of myth to bring out the ways in which Zhang's narrative about the Jahrinya, a Chinese Sufi brotherhood, reflect his critical views of globalisation.

This chapter first presents Zhang's life and career in an attempt to prepare the reader for later discussion of their connections to Zhang's religious and political views. It then discusses and critiques Bruce Lincoln's theory of myth and political myth-making in order to provide a theoretical framework for the analysis of Zhang's religious and political rhetoric and of his popularity in China. It then discusses his justification for 'people's violence' in contemporary politics, based on his mythical imaging of an Islamic past. With both gratitude towards and a degree of dissatisfaction with current myth theories such as Bruce Lincoln's, I argue that Zhang's political and religious views cannot be properly dealt with simply by 'revealing' their mythical nature; analysis must be complemented by anatomising the socio-political reality of China that produces these views.

The Life and Career of Zhang Chengzhi

Zhang was born in Beijing in 1948 to Hui parents with the Islamic name Said. In his later years, Zhang boasted about his family lineage that can supposedly be traced back to the Prophet Muhammad. In his childhood and youth, however, Zhang believed in the Chinese version of communism. He attended high school in the 1960s at the height of the Cultural Revolution (1966–76), in which Mao Zedong, the supreme leader of the Chinese Communist Party, managed to reshuffle his Party's power structure by eliminating internal enemies. Zhang takes pride in the fact that as a young student he was the first among his peers to call himself a 'Red Guard', meaning a foot soldier for the communist cause and the great leader Mao. Soon after, the term gained currency among idealist youth in China and millions of 'Red Guards' became the vanguards helping Mao destroy his enemies within the Party establishment. Red Guards would often bypass the government and law enforcement apparatus to denounce, detain and publicly humiliate Party cadres Mao identified as 'revisionist'. They also physically assaulted people of suspicious social status, such as former rich landowners and businessmen, former Nationalist government officials and disgruntled intellectuals. But Mao soon realised that the hot-headed young Red Guards could run out of control, and decided to send them to remote rural areas where they received their 'second education' from peasants instead of professors. Zhang was 'sent down' to Inner Mongolia in 1968, where he lived with a Mongol family for four years. Unlike many other authors who lived through the Cultural Revolution and regret the chaos it created in their lives, Zhang until this day is unrepentant about his past as a Red Guard, and nostalgic for the heightened political awareness during the Cultural Revolution, in contrast to the current consumerist Chinese society.

Zhang returned to Beijing in the 1970s, after the Cultural Revolution. He entered Peking University and the Chinese Academy of Social Sciences to study Middle Asian history. For some time he attempted to continue an academic career but was not successful. In a later novel, *Jin muchang* ('golden pasture'), he complained bitterly about his rejection in academic circles.[3]

Zhang was richly compensated, however, by his success as a writer. He began his writing career in 1978, with the publication of a poem in Mongolian entitled 'A Son of the People' and a Chinese-language short story, 'Why Does the Rider Sing Praises to His Mother?' The poem and the story are characterised by populist sentiments, melodramatic yet predictable plots and hyperbolic phrasing, which set the tone for his later writings. In the early 1980s Zhang lived in Canada and Japan for a short time, only to become disgusted by the materialism and arrogance of the industrialised world. Zhang hated the condescending writers and scholars, the mean local restaurant owner for whom he washed dishes, and practically everybody else in the two countries. He returned to China promptly and found that life at home was also unsatisfactory. But Zhang said that he preferred to be mistreated by his fellow countrymen rather than by Westerners.[4] Zhang joined the Chinese Navy in 1987 (because of its generous benefits), only to quit two years later and become a freelance writer.

In 1984 he found a meaning in his life by rediscovering his Muslim roots. According to Zhang himself, his re-embracing of Islam was a sign of providence. By accident, he ran into a folksy, uneducated fellow-Muslim from north-west China named Ma Zhiwen. Brother Ma, as Zhang would call him, led him into the tradition of the Jahrinya. Zhang had serious inner struggles at the beginning, futilely trying to run away from the divine calling he experienced. But eventually he knelt down and believed: he became a practising Muslim for the first time in his life, and a member of the Jahrinya family.[5] Later Zhang writes almost ecstatically about his encounter with the divine: 'You tore me apart, and I willingly offer my soul to you.'[6]

---

[3]   See Zhang Chengzhi, *Jin muchang* (Beijing, 2007).

[4]   Idem, *Zhonghua sanwen zhencangben: zhang chengzhi juan*, p. 130.

[5]   Ibid, pp. 90–102.

[6]   Idem, *Zhang Chengzhi wenxue zuopin xuanji: xinlingshi juan* (Haiko, 1996), p. 314.

Although he had written earlier stories about the lives of Hui people in premodern China, after his spiritual rebirth writing for Zhang turned into a mission and a religious duty. His novels and essays were more and more obsessed with the themes of religious martyrdom, resistance to materialism and urban life and fury at Western hegemony.

Bruce Lincoln's Theory of Myth: A Critical Appraisal

As this book is about myth and contemporary Islam, I would like to employ contemporary theories of myth to analyse Zhang's works, and at the same time to test the validity of such theories using his case. My starting point is that theories are indispensible tools for the analysis of social phenomena, including religion. Yet theories are always inadequate in the face of the richness of social reality, and hence have to be constantly critiqued, tested and improved.

Bruce Lincoln is a theorist in whom I have taken an interest over a lengthy period of time. His studies in religion have been motivated not only by the prospect of scholarly discoveries but also by existential and social concerns. He excels in analyses of 'the interaction of religion, politics, and culture, especially processes involving ideological persuasion, the construction of social borders, conflict over scarce resources, and the role played in history by discourses of the transcendent'.[7] Despite my admiration for Lincoln, I also have disagreements with him. Let me first begin with what I have learned from him in relation to my current topic, then spell out where I disagree with him.

Lincoln defines myth as an ideological narrative that justifies and naturalises the social order,[8] a view shared by numerous other scholars.[9] Lincoln's theory of myth, and of religion in general, has been inspired by, among others, Antonio Gramsci. Gramsci employed the term 'hegemony' to denote the consensual and ideological, as opposed to coercive, basis of a political system. As a linguist, Lincoln is particularly taken by Gramsci's insistence on the ideological nature of language and culture. Taking cues from Gramsci, Lincoln has employed ideological critique to analyse the sacrifice of the mythological 'first man' in Indo-European creation stories. In such diverse sources as the Vedas,

---

[7]   Quoted from Lincoln's personal correspondence with me in 2002.

[8]   Bruce Lincoln, *Myth, Cosmos, and Society: Indo-European Themes of Creation and Destruction* (Cambridge, MA, 1986), p. 141.

[9]   *Idem*, 'Myth and Mythology', in William A. Darity, Jr. (ed.), *International Encyclopedia of the Social Sciences*, Vol. 5 (Detroit, MI, 2008), pp. 355–8.

Old Russian folklore and Old Frisian myth, there is the common theme that creation began with the act of killing and dismembering a cosmic giant, whose body parts were transformed into myriad things and creatures in our universe. Lincoln points out that when a mythical/ideological analogy is established between human and natural worlds, a simultaneously social and cosmological order also emerges: high/low, centre/periphery, noble men/petty men, and so forth. Hence in Hinduism the socially unequal caste system is justified because, according to the Hindu myth, just as the sky is physically above earth, priests and warriors should be above commoners and servants: 'It was created this way by gods.'[10] Solidly grounded in scholarship, Lincoln's work is also deeply concerned with currently pressing social and political issues. For instance, he aptly reveals the mythical polarisation of a free, democratic 'us' and a fanatically religiously Islamic 'other' as a completely ideological construct that provides a pretext for the Bush administration's 'pre-emptive' military aggressions in the Middle East.[11]

While I admire Lincoln's erudition, penetrating insights and deep concerns for social justice, I think he overestimates the importance of myths, and consequently also the importance of his own critique of them. For Lincoln, disabusing people of religious and political myths is part of the reform of consciousness. Yet one cannot avoid the impression that by over-stressing the ideological struggle, Lincoln – a professed Marxist – is going back to the 'idealist' position that Engels repudiated in *Anti-Dühring* (1877–78); that is, he indulges in sophisticated theoretical speculations without making enough effort to address the concrete social reality that produces theory.

An additional problem with Lincoln's ideological critique is that it is geared to target traditional religious myths and right-wing, conservative political myths. It is inept in criticising such contemporary radical ideologies as Islamism, as evidenced by the fact that he has not provided any penetrating analysis of radical Islamist myths, even though he has written two books on religion and terrorism.[12] Lincoln defines the main function of myth as to preserve order: according to him, the Confucian motto 'to make social distinctions clear and to regulate men's desires according to their status' is an excellent example of

---

[10]   *Idem, Death, War, and Sacrifice: Studies in Ideology and Practice* (Chicago, IL, 1991), p. 167.

[11]   *Idem, Holy Terrors: Thinking About Religion after September 11* (Chicago, IL, 2006), p. 19.

[12]   *Idem, Holy Terrors*, and *Religion, Empire, and Torture: The Case of Achaemenian Persia, with a Postscript on Abu Ghraib* (Chicago, IL, 2007).

such social functions.[13] Even in his study of religion and conflicts, he contends that religion serves the interests of society's dominant classes by legitimising their claims and mitigating social conflicts in transcendental terms.[14] It seems to me that Lincoln has said little about myths and ideologies that purportedly dismantle order and increase conflicts, even though he does distinguish between the religion of the status quo and that of resistance/revolution,[15] and he appears unwilling to undertake the same biting dissection of the latter as he does of the former, because he wishes to be on the side of the underdog.[16] With this theoretical discussion as background, in the later parts of the chapter I will apply Lincoln's concept of myth to the work of Zhang Chengzhi, for a more complex understanding and evaluation of both.

Zhang's Imagining of History: Jahrinya as a Martyrs' Tradition

For the reader to appreciate the background and content of Zhang's writing, I will briefly present the portions of the history of Islam in China that are most relevant to our topic. Islam was first brought to China during the Tang Dynasty (618–907), when China enjoyed its heyday as a cosmopolitan culture. The first major Muslim settlements in China consisted of Arab and Persian merchants in China's capital Chang'an (today's Xi'an, in Shaanxi province) and also on the south-east coast. By the time of the Song Dynasty (960–1127), Muslims dominated China's overseas trade, and 'green-eyed Persians' became a synonym for wealth and business cunning. 'Hui', as a term for a distinct group of people, was first used at this time, for a long period as an umbrella term for Muslims in China but later referring specifically to sinophone Muslims. During the Mongol-founded Yuan Dynasty (1271–1368), hundreds of thousands of Muslim immigrants were recruited, then forcibly relocated by the Mongols to China

---

[13]   *Idem*, 'Notes toward a Theory of Religion and Revolution', in Lincoln (ed.), *Religion, Rebellion, Revolution: An Interdisciplinary and Cross-cultural Collection of Essays* (New York, 1985), p. 270.

[14]   *Idem*, 'Conflict', in Mark C. Taylor (ed.), *Critical Terms for Religious Studies* (Chicago, IL, 1998), p. 55.

[15]   Lincoln, 'Notes toward a Theory of Religion and Revolution', p. 277.

[16]   Lincoln noticed Hobsbawm's differentiation between revolution and rebellion. For Hobsbawm, rebellion 'sought to put an end to an unjust and oppressive social order, [but] they could produce little more than vague (if extreme) hopes and random outbursts of ineffective violence'. However, Lincoln did not pursue it further; see the 'Introduction' to his *Religion, Rebellion, Revolution*, p. 5.

from Western and Central Asia to help with the administration of the rapidly expanding Mongol empire. In the following Ming Dynasty (1368–1644), Muslims became more influential in China's political and cultural circles. Indeed, rumour has it that the founder of the dynasty, Zhu Yuanzhang, was himself a secret Hui Muslim, and that he concealed his religious identity out of political expedience in a Han-dominated China.[17] The Yongle Emperor ordered Zheng He, a Hui and China's foremost explorer, to lead seven expeditions to the Indian Ocean between 1405 and 1433. This adventure has inspired the speculation that the Chinese fleet, led by a Muslim, 'discovered' the Americas before Columbus.[18] Just when China was exhibiting its power on the high seas, the Muslim world lost Spain, with its open seaports, to the Christian Reconquista, and relinquished its advantage in global trade. Cut off from the *umma* of the Arab and Persian world, the Muslim immigrants in China accelerated their linguistic and cultural assimilation to their local environment.

The rise of the Qing Dynasty (1644–1911) witnessed frequent tension between the Muslims and the ruling Manchus, as well as with the majority Han Chinese population. Important to the topic of this chapter is the fact that the Hui society in northern China since the Ming Dynasty has been under the strong influence of Central Asian Sufi schools. The Jahrinya Sufi order, with which our author Zhang Chengzhi identifies, played an important role in bloody Hui rebellions in Yunnan, Shensi and Gansu provinces between 1862 and 1877. As the battles dragged on, the purpose of war for both sides turned into blind vengeance. The Manchu government and the Muslim rebels both committed mass murders, killing millions of people in their respective enemy camps.[19]

Zhang's best-known novel, *History of the Soul*, is set against this historic background. It is a loose historical account and a tribute to the Jahrinya's sacrifice and resistance. Zhang claims that his book is a spiritual adventure in search of idealism and hope – which have been abandoned by the world but been cherished by the Chinese Muslims. Zhang makes it abundantly clear that he is not writing history in the academic sense: 'chewers of the heroes' faeces'[20] is the name that Zhang gives to secular scholars of the Jahrinya who do not understand its religious, spiritual significance. Chinese critics' reception of this

---

[17]   See Fu Tongxian, *Zhongguo huijiaoshi* (Beijing, 1940).

[18]   See Gavin Menzies, *1421: The Year China Discovered the World* (New York, 2008).

[19]   For details of the Manchu persecutions of Muslims, see Hodong Kim, *Holy War in China: The Muslim Rebellion and State in Chinese Central Asia, 1864–1877* (Stanford, CA, 2004), and Jonathan N. Lipman, *Familiar Strangers: A History of Muslims in Northwest China* (Seattle, WA, 1998).

[20]   Zhang, *Zhang chengzhi wenxue zuopin xuanji*, p. 167.

book has been divided. Sympathetic commentators applaud its unapologetic, high-pitched advocacy for spiritual values in an increasingly secular age. For example, the author Zhu Sujin considers *History of the Soul* the most important book in twentieth-century Chinese literature.[21] Meanwhile, it has been warmly embraced by the Hui people in Northern China. On the other hand, detractors of the book point to its one-sidedness – a half-historical/half-fictitious narrative prejudiced towards the Jahrinya side – and its pretentious writing style.[22]

History of the Soul follows the history of the Jahrinya Muslims from the 1720s to the 1920s, and their persecution by the Qing authorities from the very beginning. The founder of Jahrinya, Ma Minxin, was an orphan, like the Prophet Muhammad. He was nevertheless able to receive a traditional religious education from childhood. In 1728 the nine-year-old Ma embarked on a pilgrimage to Mecca with his uncle. On the pilgrimage, they became separated and Ma went on alone, visiting many Sufi masters in Middle Asia. He returned to China in 1744, claiming that he carried with him secret religious messages. Soon enough, he managed to gather an increasingly large following among lower-class Muslims in north-west China with straightforward teachings and simplified rituals tailored to the needs of the poor. Ma Minxin's success attracted suspicion from the Manchu government, and in 1781 local officials arrested and eventually executed him on charges of leading an illegal religious group and disturbing peace and order. In response, his followers revolted. Since this time, intermittent rebellions against the Manchu continued for two centuries and produced ample exhibitions of heroism and martyrdom.

Zhang lavishes praises on the Jahrinya martyrs – their leaders almost without exception sacrificed their lives for the faith, and ordinary devotees followed suit. Nearly a century after the martyrdom of Ma Minxin, Ma Hualong, the leader of a Hui uprising in 1862, was slowly tortured to death, together with 300 members of his immediate and extended family, after defeat at the hands of the Manchu. He posthumously became the second most revered spiritual leader, next only to Ma Minxin. Admittedly, the glorification of tragic fallen heroes and eagerness for self-sacrifice is typical of many religions and cultures; the Roman emperor Septimus Severus wrote that the earliest Christians had sought martyrdom as eagerly as the Christians of his day a bishop's position.[23] However, the longing

---

[21] See Fu Shuhua, 'Xinlin de mikuang', *Hainan shifan xueyuan xuebao*, 5 (2005).

[22] See Zhang Yiwu, 'Cong daode xunhuan dao shenxue xunhuan – wenhua maoxian zhuyi de xingtai fenxi', *Shanghai wenhua*, 6 (1995); Xu Jilin, 'Piping de daode yu daode de piping', *Wenyililun*, 8 (1996).

[23] Quoted in Wang Weizhou, 'Meiyou hongqi lüqi yexing' I, *Duping*, 36 (2007), p. 22.

for martyrdom is so central to the Jahrinya tradition that even Zhang himself calls it masochistic. According to Zhang, Jahrinya is a faith that is not confessed but proven by deed, the foremost of which is to sacrifice one's life. The believers fought for failure rather than for victory because they were perpetual outlaws: inept at lawful resistance, martyrdom was all they were capable of:[24] 'For the Jahrinya believers, the beauty of martyrdom has already entered their blood and hearts at birth with [their fathers'] semen.'[25] The urge for self-destruction is based on a belief that is not limited to Jahrinya, but is especially pronounced within it: bloodstained clothes will be one's passport to heaven.[26] It is not surprising that for Jahrinya, *qubba*, or the leaders' and martyrs' tombs, are the centres of worship for the faithful. Indeed, Zhang's own conversion involved a visit to a holy *qubba*.[27]

This readiness for death, however, is far from fatalist passivity: rather, it is a resolution to resist injustice at all cost. According to Zhang, religious and political persecutions call for violent responses by the people. He contends that violent Muslim uprisings were carrying out punishment, inspired by a divine source, on a corrupt and oppressive regime: the demise of the Manchu dynasty, soon to come about, was evidence of divine wrath.[28]

Zhang on Contemporary Politics: Violence as Resistance to Western Dominance

The justification of resistance in the past inspires Zhang's view on the contemporary world. In his non-fictional essays, Zhang extends his defence of people's violence to a variety of actions, ranging from ancient Chinese assassins who distrusted government and took justice into their own hands to the pro-Palestine Japanese Red Army's suicide attacks in the Middle East in the 1970s.[29] According to him, the people's violence is necessary, especially at a time when global capitalism is running amok and a new, unchecked crusade against the Muslim world, led by the United States, has been unleashed. Violence is the rightful response to economic exploitation and political oppression, even though

---

24   Zhang Chengzhi, *Zhang Chengzhi wenxue zuopin xuanji*, p. 72.
25   Ibid., p. 162.
26   Ibid., p. 71.
27   *Idem, Zhonghua sanwen zhencangben*, p. 93.
28   *Idem, Zhang chengzhi wenxue zuopin xuanji*, p. 161.
29   *Idem, Zhonghua sanwen zhencangben*, p. 53.

it has been viciously labelled 'terrorism' by the new imperial propagandists. Zhang holds fashionable non-violent resistance in contempt, considering Martin Luther King, for instance, to be weak and submissive towards the powers that be. For Zhang, King is a symbol of cheap heroism and back-door servitude, because the leader of the civil rights movement and the ideals he personifies are already well accommodated by, and integrated into, the 'system'. Zhang notes that in almost every metropolis in the United States there is a street named after King, while there is no street named for Malcolm X, who made no compromises with the evil racist empire.[30]

Zhang realises that he is not alone on the anti-American, anti-capitalism bandwagon. However, he despises his Western comrades-in-arms. Even worse than Western conservatives, Western progressives and leftists are impossible to reason with: their arrogance is pathological, and they have no manners. 'The leftists unconsciously take themselves as the saviours of the poor, yet their inferior poor friends do not want their kindness. No wonder they [the leftists] are upset.'[31] The handicap of the Western liberals is not only their patronising attitude, but the way they think and act. In his response to Susan Sontag's comments on Bush's war against Islamic terrorism, Zhang chastises her for virtually participating in the collective torture of the Muslim spirit by the media and opinion makers in the West. Zhang's problem with Sontag is that she resorts to the fashionable postmodern discourse when condemning Abu Ghraib and other American cruelties committed in the name of war on terror. As such, Sontag reduces the bloody events to nothing more than wordplay. Western intellectuals condemn the war, yet they attempt unilaterally to decide for the world what kind of condemnation is acceptable. In order to protest and be heard, one has first to learn such trendy talk as 'war is a metaphor'. Thus a protesting Sontag becomes the guardian of the Western narrative hegemony.[32] Zhang is acutely aware that Western sympathisers of Islam are, after all, part of the West. Even the literary giants whom he admired as an apprentice writer, and the anti-war songwriters whom he always listened to, are not trustworthy, because at some point they are bound to reveal their brutal Westernness.[33]

Benefiting from the unjust world order it has created, the West sides with the political, economic and cultural elites in all nations. To the contrary,

---

[30] Ibid., p. 62. Zhang is in fact mistaken: there is a street in Manhattan named after Malcolm X.

[31] *Idem, Wuse de yiduan* (Hong Kong, 2007), p. 235.

[32] Ibid., p. 231.

[33] *Idem, Zhonghua sanwen zhencangben: zhang chengzhi juan*, p. 81.

Islam is the advocate for all the poor, powerless and oppressed. Zhang emphasises the fact that Islam is the only force in human history that has ever defeated the West. In medieval times, Islam protected the world from an aggressive Christendom, while the tragic defeat of Islam in Spain signalled the beginning of horrendous Western colonialism. According to Zhang, history is about to repeat itself in the twenty-first century. After the collapse of the Soviet Union, Islam has become the last hope for humanity to resist the new Western political and economical crusade.[34]

For exactly the same reason, Zhang is also a diehard fan of Mao, who was the leader of the Third World and who stood up to the West for the oppressed and exploited. Unabashed, Zhang brags: 'I admire you more than any Communist Party members, Mao!'[35] As a Chinese Muslim, Zhang considers himself doubly blessed for being able to inherit the legacies of both Islam and Mao. Yet he contends that the spirit of Mao and of true Islam has been lost in today's China. Indeed, Zhang often complains that he, as an heir to the two political and religious legacies, is misunderstood, and expresses the desire to be a proud and lonely soul: 'I do not need readers, I only need my shadow and my echo.'[36] When China is happily joining in the expansion of global capitalism, Zhang insists on identifying with his political and religious heroes – Mao and Jahrinya martyrs – precisely because he sees through the hypocrisy of wishy-washy Western liberalism and understands the inevitable clashes between Western imperialism and the oppressed peoples.[37]

Here, I believe, lies the key to understanding Zhang's religious turn in his life and literary works. While I do not intend to question the authenticity of Zhang's reconversion to Islam, one cannot escape the impression that contemporary politics – his reading of the conflicts between the West and the Islamic world, as well as the zealous Maoist years in his early life – is a decisive factor in shaping Zhang's spiritual quest.

Beyond Myth and Myth-Debunking

An interesting conclusion from Lincoln's analysis of the Hindu creation myth is that the cosmos and social orders are legitimised by an act of sacred sacrifice,

---

[34] *Idem, Xianhua de feixu* (Beijing, 2008), pp. 9, 12.
[35] *Idem, Zhang chengzhi wenxue zuopin xuanji*, p. 319.
[36] Ibid., p. 78.
[37] Ibid., p. 154.

which can and should be imitated by human beings and repeated through a similar heroic offering of one's own life. Complementary to Lincoln's theory is Dennis Klass's analysis of the sacred dead used by religions for the purpose of legitimising and maintaining political power.[38] Both theories can be fruitfully applied to Zhang Chengzhi. For him, the legitimacy of the Jahrinya hierarchy, in which the *laorenjia* or the highest leader possessed unquestionable authority, was almost completely dependent on its leaders' willing submission to, even craving for, martyrdom. With the rhetoric of selfless sacrifice, unlimited power within the order was given to the *laorenjia*, since he alone was seen as embodying the true salvation for which the martyrs had given up their lives. Romanticising the Jahrinya tradition, Zhang has turned a blind eye to the fact that some of the leaders were known for abusing the religious power bestowed on them, and unjustly punishing those who dared to challenge them.[39] Furthermore, Zhang's one-sided, simplistic emphasis on the tragic fate of Jahrinya gives him excuses to gloss over or downplay the loss of lives and properties on the part of Han people during wars.[40]

Lincoln's exposé of a modern political myth – President George W. Bush's 'war on terror' – also sheds ample light on our topic. In a similar fashion to the rhetoric of that campaign, Zhang's black and white dichotomy between the oppressor (the United States and the West) and the oppressed (Islam and the Third World) gives him reasons for blanket condemnation of an expanding global capitalism. There is no denying the existence of Western political, economic and cultural dominance in today's world, exemplified by American unilateralism, and more than a few Muslims feel frustrated and humiliated by such a reality.[41] However, Zhang's response to this does not rise above the intellectual and moral levels of his imperialist enemy. To fair-minded readers, his political analysis lacks nuances and borders on the shrill. Judging from his own accounts, he exhibits an elitist distaste for manual labour – more than capitalist exploitation, he despises the 'submissiveness and numbness' of workers who tolerate their working and

---

[38]   Dennis Klass and Robert Goss, 'The Politics of Grief and Continuing Bonds with the Dead: The Cases of Maoist China and Wahhabi Islam', *Death Studies*, 27/ 9 (2003), p. 793.

[39]   Punishments for lack of obedience to *laorenjia* include plucking out offenders' eyes and cutting off their ears. See Ma Tong, *Zhongguo yisilan jiaopai yu menhuan zhidu shilue* (Lanzhou, 1999), p. 329.

[40]   Zhang mentions the death toll of Han people in the Han–Muslim wars, but implies that the killings of civilians were committed by non-Jahrinya Muslims; see his *Zhang chengzhi wenxue zuopin xuanji*, p. 164.

[41]   Examples of such sentiments abound; see for instance, Muhammad Fathi Osman, 'Islam, Terrorism, and Western Misapprehensions', in Ibrahim M. Abu-Rabi' (ed.), *The Blackwell Companion to Contemporary Islamic Thought* (Malden, MA, 2006), p. 377.

living conditions.[42] At the top of his lungs, Zhang condemns consumerism and commodity fetishism, without seeing that often his self-righteous condemnation itself has been fetishised by politically motivated populists. Zhang extols the virtue of poor people in a way that calls to mind the old Sufi saying that 'poverty is the school of the soul'. However, one has to ask whether refinement of the soul is the answer to poverty. To the present author, religion is an insufficient substitute for the rule of law and economic empowerment for the poor in the Muslim world.[43] James Frazer put it well: all religions recommend poverty and celibacy. Yet humanity has found ways to avoid these recommendations because they have no wish to trade total extinction for the salvation of the soul.[44]

More troubling is Zhang's call for the return of the fighting spirit of Jahrinya and Mao. The fact is that the Jahrinya was a party to wars in north-west China in the 1860s and 1870s (although it should be noted that they were not solely or even mainly responsible for them) which claimed a total of 15 million lives, including 90 per cent of local Muslims.[45] If 'people's violence' caused such carnage in those times, it is terrifying to imagine such violence in the age of WMDs. Moreover, a defining characteristic of China under Mao is the destruction of lives, property, institutions and values. Richard Walker, in a study for the US Senate Judiciary Committee, estimated that the 'human cost of communism in China' after 1949 ranges from 32 million to 60 million deaths,[46] which without doubt include those of Chinese Muslims. Such killings in the names of religion or secular utopia are exactly what Lincoln calls 'holy terrors'.[47]

Having borrowed Lincoln's insights on religious and political myths – and pushed them further – to critique Zhang, I have to add one caveat. As mentioned at the beginning of this chapter, I believe Lincoln overemphasises theory and ideology at the expense of socio-economic and political history. To make it

---

[42]   Zhang, *Zhang chengzhi wenxue zuopin xuanji*, p. 130.

[43]   For instance, studies show that countries having poor records in economic and social development also have poor human rights records. Saad Eddin Ibrahim, 'The Causes of Muslim Countries' Poor Record of Human Rights', in Shireen T. Hunter with Huma Malik (eds), *Islam and Human Rights: Advancing a US–Muslim Dialogue* (Washington, DC, 2005), p. 100.

[44]   Quoted in Wang Weizhou, 'Meiyou hongqi lüqi yexing', II *Duping*, 37 (2007), p. 22.

[45]   See Cao Shuji, *Zhongguo renko shi* (Shanghai, 2001), p. 554.

[46]   Andrew J. Nathan, *China's Transition* (New York, 1997), p. 3.

[47]   *Pace* Zhang, a strong case can in fact be argued that the Islamic tradition sanctions the right to life and forbids wanton killings of innocent people. See, for instance, Shamsuddin al-Kaylani, 'Concepts of Human Rights in Islamic Doctrines (Sunnis, Shi'ites, Isma'ilis, Qarmatians, Mu'tazilis, Sufiss, Wahhabis)', in Salma K. Jayyusi (ed.), *Human Rights in Arab Thought: A Reader* (New York, 2009), p. 181.

clear what I mean here: while stressing the importance of social and political elements over theory, I have no intention of re-installing a Marxist binary system of 'economic base' and 'superstructure'. Rather, I tend to consider historical realities existing in – to use Buddhist terminology – an Indra's net, with endlessly multi-dimensional causal relationships and fundamental interdependence. Put differently, I prefer a Weberian approach that allows multiple contributing factors and non-determinist explanations (for Weber, Calvinism was only one of the causes leading to the rise of capitalism). Thus my preferred interpretation of Zhang's views can be informed by, but needs to go beyond, the Lincolnian theory about how power is mythicised by legitimising itself and marginalising the Other. Instead, I analyse Zhang's use of myth in relation to his life experiences, and the intellectual trends and political structures of the society he lives in.

For myself, the devil is in the historical details. An explanation for Zhang's popularity and a critique of his nostalgic glorification of the past, as well as for his reading of contemporary politics, has to descend from theory to concrete political and cultural situations in twentieth-century China. In what follows I shall analyse Zhang's religiosity against the background of contemporary Chinese politics and ideologies.

With regard to its treatment of Chinese Muslims, the Communist regime in China (1949–present) suffers from a schizophrenic split between a high-road Communist idealism to which lip service is paid, and the heavy-handed rule that is actually practised. Prior to the Communist rule, the Han nationalist leader Sun Yat-sen of the Republic of China (which lasted from 1911 to 1949) refused to acknowledge the Chinese Muslims as an ethnic group. Rather, they were considered to be exactly the same as the Han Chinese except for their Islamic faith. In contrast, the current Chinese constitution theoretically promises religious freedom and self-governance for the ethnic and religious minorities, in accordance with Leninist theory. On the other hand, the top-down total control that is typical of the Chinese Communist Party has been the reality for Chinese Muslims since 1949. During the Cultural Revolution, the crackdown on religion reached its peak when Muslim leaders were imprisoned and Muslim practice strictly banned. After Mao's death in 1976, the government began to loosen its policies towards Muslims, and religion in general. The Chinese people experienced simultaneous feelings of freedom and uncertainty in this early political thawing. Filling the intellectual vacuum left by a discredited Maoism, religion came back with a vengeance.[48] Starting from the 1980s, a variety of

---

[48]   There are interesting parallels between the religious revivals after the demise of political ideologies on the global scene. For instance, the Islamic activism in post-Sadat Egypt

religions and cults have come onto the centre stage. First, Christianity and Zen caught people's eye. Following Jesus and koan, exotic Tibetan lamas, Qigong masters and New Age gurus were also in fashion. Islam is also experiencing a modest revival through many channels, ranging from traditional Islamic education to online proselytisation. Islam appeals to many open-minded young Chinese as a radical alternative to Maoist 'dialectical materialism', which interprets human existence and history in terms of strictly economic determinism and of a never-ending class struggle. Christianity would fill the same bill, but for some Chinese to show interest in it would risk the impression of an opportunistic conversion – a capitulation to Western values because of the wealth and power behind them. As an advocate of Islam, Zhang's boat also rose with the tide.

Contributing to the popularity of Zhang's writings among non-Muslim Chinese intellectuals is his fervent anti-Americanism. Today, the political attitudes of Chinese people have become more and more diverse. Nevertheless, we discover certain demographic patterns. It is interesting to note that anti-Western phobia – against the United States in particular – finds a following among Chinese writers and artists as readily as it does on the 'Arab street'. The reason is that despite the rising economic and political power of non-Western countries, global standards for judging literary and artistic works remain in the hands of critics, curators and publishers located in Paris, Stockholm and New York. These standards often appear rather arbitrary and non-transparent, and fail to promise – let alone deliver – fair play. Like their political counterparts, writers, artists and musicians in the non-Western world resent the Western dominance. It is no surprise that Zhang's attack on a West that rubs its values in other people's faces resonates with Chinese intellectuals.

Moreover, Zhang's anti-Americanism is actually an example of the political cunning that has helped his success. Unlike the Tibetans and other ethnic groups that have resisted Han Chinese assimilation, the Hui Muslim community has been linguistically and culturally integrated into the mainstream way of life and has adopted a unique Hui Chinese identity. Therefore, for Zhang, as a Hui writer, the Jahrinya story has been presented in a way that glorifies Muslim sacrifice without alienating Han readers. If anyone harbours a whiff of doubt about his patriotism, Zhang effectively disperses it by warning fellow Chinese about looming foreign threats, and by promising to defend the motherland with his pen as a sword: Zhang tells his readers that after the Americans have crushed the Islamic forces

---

seems to fit this pattern, see Mahmood Monshipouri, *Muslims in Global Politics: Identities, Interests, and Human Rights* (Philadelphia, PA, 2009), p. 73.

in Iraq, 'the next target will be China'. He also condemns the Japanese ('the short-legged economic animals' and allies of the United States) for never giving up their ambition to invade China again.[49] Moving forward from *History of the Soul* to his writings on contemporary politics, Zhang has left behind the historical wars and conflicts, and found his enemies in abstract concepts of oppression and injustice that can be projected onto new targets. Hence an easy transition is made from the old grudges between Chinese Muslims and their neighbours in north-west China to a just cause: the Muslim and non-Western countries against Western imperialism. Indeed, his Muslim identity gives Zhang even more reason to take up the cudgels of righteousness. For instance, he discovers obvious Western bias in scholarly fields such as sinology and Middle Asian history. According to Zhang, most Western scholars in the fields do little to conceal their complicit role in promoting Western political and military dominance. As a Hui scholar, Zhang feels he is constantly pressured by his Western colleagues to condemn the Chinese government's policies on religious and ethnic minorities. However, he preaches that human rights are merely a disguise for Western hegemony.[50] In contrast to his grandstanding against the West, Zhang has been very careful not to offend the Chinese government. For instance, he fails to point out that Mao's time was an ordeal for the Jahrinya sect. Two of the Jahrinya leaders, Ma Teng'ai (1921–91) and Ma Zhenwu (1895–1961), were imprisoned by the Chinese Communist Party, a fact that Zhang acknowledged in his book on Islam published in Japan[51] but conveniently omitted in all his books written in Chinese.

To be fair, Zhang's political views are not entirely opportunistic, toeing the official lines of the Chinese government. Rather, his stand on political issues has shown consistency in his Maoist years and after his conversion to Islam. In my view it is important to note the analogy between Zhang's Maoism and his Islamism. First, Mao's ruthless persecution of any political dissent planted so much suspicion and hatred in the Chinese people's collective psyche that they are susceptible to the rhetoric of violence.[52] Furthermore, numerous scholars have pointed out the connection between Islamism and various Communist ideologies. Kamran Talattof maintains that Islamic fundamentalism is an emulation of 'Soviet Marxist influence in Muslim societies from the 1950s'.[53] Hendrik Hansen and

---

[49]   Zhang Chengzhi, *Zhonghua sanwen zhencangben*, pp. 65–6.
[50]   Ibid.
[51]   *Idem, Wuyuan de sixiang*, p. 198.
[52]   Tu Weiming, 'Destructive Will and Ideological Holocaust: Maoism as a Source of Social Suffering in China', *Daedalus*, 125/1 (1996), p. 177.
[53]   Kamran Talattof, 'Comrade Akbar: Islam, Marxism, and Modernity', *Comparative Studies of South Asia, Africa and the Middle East*, 25/3 (2005), p. 642.

Peter Kainz make a structural comparison of Marxism, National Socialism and radical Islamism, and find striking similarities among them.[54] It is no accident that both Maoism and Zhang's ideological presentation of Jahrinya exhibit an arrogant moralistic absolutism, a tendency to divide the world into 'good' and 'evil', and a high level of intolerance.[55] In fact, due to his lack of formal religious training, Zhang is rarely able to justify his meta-language of the 'resistance of oppressed people' on the authority of the Qur'an and other Islamic texts. Instead, he often echoes the Maoist rhetoric of 'class struggle' and 'people making history'. Yet for Maoism as well as for Zhang, the concept of people 'enters the Durkheiman realm of the sacred'[56] and ceases to be relevant to any real human beings.

Conclusion

Zhang's political and religious views thus not only share their mythical nature with ancient and contemporary ideologies, but more importantly are rooted in the political realities of 1980s and 1990s China. As already mentioned, Zhang himself emphatically and unapologetically links his version of Jahrinya spirituality to Mao's revolution against internal and foreign enemies. Perhaps Zhang has never changed, perhaps his religious conversion was simply a political confirmation. In the final analysis, his return to Islam has much less to do with a revelation coming down from seventh-century Mecca than with what has been happening in twentieth-century China. Imaginations of the past tend always to be decided by reality in the present.

Finally, I argue we should go beyond myth-debunking because it stops halfway, and risks lapsing into a self-congratulatory, elitist sense of intellectual and moral superiority. What I have attempted to do is not to discredit or condemn Zhang, but rather to understand what historical ideas, events, processes and factors have shaped Zhang's thought.[57] Generally speaking, disagreement

---

[54]   Hendrik Hansen and Peter Kainz, 'Radical Islamism and Totalitarian Ideology: A Comparison of Sayyid Qutb's Islamism with Marxism and National Socialism', *Totalitarian Movements & Political Religions*, 8/1 (2007), pp. 55–76.

[55]   Jeffrey M. Bale maintains that such traits are common to all forms of totalitarianism; as we know, Zhang's source can be none other than Maoism. See his 'Islamism and Totalitarianism', *Totalitarian Movements & Political Religions*, 10/2 (2009), p. 83.

[56]   L.C. Young and S.R. Ford, 'God is Society: the Religious Dimension of Maoism', *Sociological Inquiry*, 47/2 (1977), p. 91.

[57]   The current research can be furthered in both depth and breath. First, we can delve deeper into this individual's life and works. Gathering more details will certainly produce a

among people is a fact of life. Specifically, Zhang's views are shared by a number of people within and outside both China and other Muslim communities. The only ethical and practical way to deal with people who share his opinions is to try to understand them and to hold a dialogue with them, even if we think them mistaken. But again, we need to understand not only their views but also the realities that produced those views. Only with such understanding can there be hope of change for the better.

---

richer picture of this author, and provide a better lens for us to observe the individual and collective life of Islam in contemporary China. Second, we can expand the scope of our study by putting Zhang's views into the context of Islamic intellectuals' response to the modern West. Both Zhang and say, Sayyid Qutb, became rabidly anti-West after they travelled to Western countries. A comparative study can be a fruitful next step to this current project.

Chapter 4

Satan and the Temptation of State Power: Medieval Islamic Myth in Global Society

Ulrika Mårtensson

In the Name of God the Almighty. There is only One God, to whom we shall all return. I would like to inform all the intrepid Muslims in the world that the author of the book entitled *The Satanic Verses*, which has been compiled, printed and published in opposition to Islam, the Prophet and the Quran, as well as those publishers who were aware of its contents, have been sentenced to death. I call on zealous Muslims to execute them quickly, wherever they find them, so that no one will dare to insult the Islamic sanctions. Whoever is killed on this path will be regarded as martyr, God willing. In addition, anyone who has access to the author of the book, but does not possess the power to execute him, should refer him to the people so that he may be punished for his actions. May God's blessing be on you all. *The Observer*, 19 February 1989

This notorious 'death sentence' or, as it has come down in global public memory, *fatwa* against the British novelist Salman Rushdie was issued by the Islamic Republic of Iran's Supreme Leader, Ayatollah Khomeini, on 13 February 1989, and broadcast by Tehran Radio the following day – Valentine's Day. The reason was Rushdie's novel *The Satanic Verses*, published in September 1988, which contained passages about how the novel's main character, Mahound, had received revelations from Satan. Since Mahound was described in almost identical terms to those in which the Prophet Muhammad is described in the historical Islamic sources, Rushdie was seen as implying that the Prophet himself was guided by Satan.

According to Fred Halliday, the violent reactions to Rushdie's book have spawned the public myth that the novel really was blasphemous and offensive to Muslims, which is why Ayatollah Khomeini issued his *fatwa*. For Halliday, a myth signifies something 'not factually true', and he corrects the public myth on several accounts. First, Rushdie did not invent a blasphemous story but was commenting on a well-known report about the Prophet's satanic temptation contained in, among other sources, al-Tabari's (d. AD 923) *The History of the Messengers and the Kings*. Secondly, 'blasphemy' in Christian terminology means offensive speech against God, which Rushdie did not engage in. Thirdly, Khomeini did not issue a *fatwa* ('binding legal pronouncement') but a *hukm* ('non-binding judgment') that Rushdie was an unbeliever (*kafir*). Fourthly, many intellectuals and authors in Muslim-majority countries defended the principle of freedom of expression, and thus Rushdie's right to publish, so Khomeini's judgment cannot be seen to express the feelings of all Muslims.[1]

So where do we find this public myth? Wikipedia, the most conveniently accessible encyclopaedia of a truly global outreach, is one important disseminator of it. Its account of 'The Satanic Verses' contains the same elements which Halliday sought to debunk:

> The novel caused great *controversy* in the *Muslim* community for what some Muslims believed were *blasphemous* references. Rushdie was accused of misusing freedom of speech. As the controversy spread, the import of the book was banned in *India* and burned in demonstrations in the United Kingdom. In mid-February 1989, following a violent riot against the book in *Pakistan*, the *Ayatollah Ruhollah Khomeini, Supreme Leader of Iran* and a *Shi'a* Muslim scholar, issued a *fatwa* calling on all good Muslims to kill Rushdie and his publishers, or to point him out to those who can kill him if they cannot themselves. Although the British Conservative government under *Margaret Thatcher* gave Rushdie round-the-clock police protection, many politicians on both sides were hostile to the author. British Labour MP *Keith Vaz* led a march through Leicester shortly after he was elected in 1989 calling for the book to be banned, while Conservative MP *Norman Tebbit*, the party's former chairman, called Rushdie an 'outstanding villain' whose 'public life has been a record of despicable acts of betrayal of his upbringing, religion, adopted home and nationality'. Meanwhile the *Commission for Racial Equality* and a liberal think tank, The Policy Studies Institute held seminars on the Rushdie affair. They did not invite the author *Fay Weldon*, who spoke out against burning books, but did invite Shabbir Akhtar, a Cambridge philosophy graduate who called for 'a negotiated compromise' which 'would protect Muslim sensibilities against gratuitous provocation'. The journalist and author Andy McSmith wrote at the time 'We are witnessing, I fear, the birth of a new and dangerously illiberal "liberal" orthodoxy designed to accommodate Dr Akhtar and his fundamentalist friends.'

> Following the *fatwa*, Rushdie was put under police protection by the *British government*. Despite a conciliatory statement by *Iran* in 1998, and Rushdie's

---

[1]   Fred Halliday, *100 Myths about the Middle East* (London: Saqi Books, 2005), pp. 182–5.

declaration that he would stop living in hiding, the Iranian state news agency reported in 2006 that the fatwa would remain in place permanently since fatwas can only be rescinded by the person who first issued them, and Khomeini had since died.

Rushdie has never been physically harmed for the book, but others associated with it have suffered violent attacks. *Hitoshi Igarashi*, its *Japanese* translator, was stabbed to death on 11 July 1991; Ettore Capriolo, the *Italian* translator, was seriously injured in a stabbing the same month; *William Nygaard*, the publisher in *Norway*, survived an attempted *assassination* in *Oslo* in October 1993, and *Aziz Nesin*, the *Turkish* translator, was the intended target in the events that led to the *Sivas massacre* on 2 July 1993 in *Sivas*, Turkey, which resulted in the deaths of 37 people. Individual purchasers of the book have not been harmed. The only nation with a predominantly Muslim population where the novel remains legal is Turkey.[2]

While the Wikipedia entry does not frame the controversy over the book in terms of state interests, it mentions the reactions by heads of state at the time: the Supreme Leader Khomeini in Iran and the British Prime Minister, Margaret Thatcher. Other accounts of *The Satanic Verses*, such as Malise Ruthven's early academic study and Kenan Malik's recent analysis, ascribe more significance than the public Wiki-myth does to the different and conflicting interests of India, Pakistan, Saudi Arabia, Iran and the UK.[3] Ruthven believes that the leftist-liberal Rushdie, seeking to provoke fundamentalist Muslims and seeing religion as no more than a social construct to bolster worldly power, underestimated both the strength and fury of Islam as lived religion and of states' interests: Rushdie was misguided to ignore the fact that reality obliges us to step down from idealistic heights of freedom of expression and artistic liberty.[4] Malik, on the other hand, supports artistic liberty and finds the state-level involvements in the controversy highly problematic. He would find Ruthven's realism characteristic of the nominally 'liberal' myth that diversity requires some sacrifice of freedom, a myth that has contributed to the current 'culture of grievance in which being offended has become a badge of identity, cleared a space for radical Islamists to

---

[2]   At http://en.wikipedia.org/wiki/The_Satanic_Verses, under the heading 'Controversy'. Accessed 21 August 2012.

[3]   Malise Ruthven, *A Satanic Affair: Salman Rushdie and the Rage of Islam* (London: Chatto & Windus, 1990); Kenan Malik, *From Fatwa to Jihad: The Rushdie Affair and Its Legacy* (London: Atlantic Books, 2009).

[4]   Ruthven, *A Satanic Affair*, pp. 158–63.

flourish, and made secular and progressive arguments less sayable, particularly within Muslim communities'.[5]

A third approach is Pnina Werbner's argument, that Rushdie's novel is neither an attack on Islam nor rested on the assumption, as Ruthven put it, that religion is nothing but a social construction. In Werbner's view it is 'a serious modernist vision of Islam as a universal, liberal and tolerant tradition', which draws on Islamic traditions that are highly reminiscent of the Enlightenment in their probing of reason and faith, doubt and certainty, and individual freedom and traditional authority.[6] The controversy resulted from the failure of non-Muslim and Muslim intellectuals to identify both at a more profound historical level and in the context of the controversy the affinities between Western and Islamic thought.[7]

In this chapter 'myth', 'state power' and 'freedom of expression' are the main topics. The contribution must be defined primarily in relation to Werbner and her sources.[8] Where these studies describe the Qur'anic and Islamic concepts which Rushdie draws on as deliberations about certainty and doubt, and reason and dogma, here the same concepts are referred more narrowly to problems of state power and legal authority. By using Roland Barthes' concept of myth, these concepts are here historicised in such a way that their relevance for Rushdie's context can be even further explored. This context is one of global legal debates about religion and freedom of expression, and where the Islamic myths are employed as criticism of state power, although on conflicting ideological grounds and with different intended outcomes. With reference to Malik's argument that the *Satanic Verses* controversy signifies limitations in freedom of expression, it is argued here that at the global legal level freedom of expression has triumphed over blasphemy.

Myth

In *Mythologies* (1957), Roland Barthes has defined myth not as an idea but as a *form*: a linguistic sign. All linguistic concepts communicate meaning by

---

    5   Malik, *From Fatwa to Jihad*, p. 210.

    6   Pnina Werbner, 'Allegories of Sacred Imperfection: Magic, Hermeneutics and Passion in *The Satanic Verses*', *Current Anthropology*, 37, Supplement, February 1996, pp. S55–S86; cit. p. S55.

    7   Werbner, 'Allegories', pp. S56–S58.

    8   Especially Michael M.J. Fischer and Mehdi Abedi, 'Bombay Talkies, the Word and the World: Salman Rushdie's Satanic Verses', *Cultural Anthropology*, 5:2 (1990), pp. 107–59.

combining signifier, signified and sign. What is special about myth is that it reproduces this combination in relation to an already existing concept, in order to change its meaning.[9] It does so by invoking memories and investing them with emotional responses. For example, Barthes refers to an image on the front cover of *Paris Match* from the early 1950s, where a French soldier of African origin looks up to and salutes the French flag. The context is the wars of liberation in the French colonies. In itself, the image is only an African soldier saluting the French flag. However, since the flag is a symbol of the French Republic and the context is colonialism, the emotions invoked by the image turn the concept of 'The French Republic' into a myth which says: 'Oh, look, Africans like the French Republic; it *is* good, after all! It's only difficult Africans who don't want to see that!'[10]

Barthes' concept of myth comes with a method of de-mythicisation. While myth presents itself as a factual system, it is 'but a semiological system'[11] which 'hides nothing and flaunts nothing: it distorts'.[12] The *Paris Match* image distorts the reality that the French Republic was experienced as oppressive by those who were fighting for independence. The interpreter's task is to identify the distortion, by way of the myth's emotional invocation.

Global Society

The broadest context used here to frame the *Satanic Verses* controversy is what Peter Beyer calls 'global society'. Inspired by Niklas Luhmann's sociology, Beyer defines society as a system of communication. Consequently, a society reaches as far as communication reaches. Today, international organisations, law, economy, education systems and mass media, together with the internet, provide communicative codes that are worldwide, and thus, for Beyer, constitute a global society.[13]

The basic societal system of global society is the nation state and its set of common function systems (i.e. government, law, economy, education, science and religion) and social systems (i.e. organisations and social movements). The highest-level international organisations are constituted by nation

---

[9]   Roland Barthes, *Mythologies* (London: Vintage, 1993), pp. 109–27.
[10] Barthes, ibid., p. 116.
[11] Barthes, ibid., p. 131.
[12] Barthes, ibid., p. 129.
[13] Peter Beyer, *Religions in Global Society* (London: Routledge, 2006), pp. 10, 34–41.

states – the UN, OIC, EU, NATO, and so forth. Nonetheless, global society is more than the sum of its nation states: it is the many different communications that occur *within* the nation states at the same time as they *transcend and challenge* national boundaries.[14]

The fact that communication is global does not mean there is global agreement; on the contrary, debate becomes more intensive the more we know what others think. The most significant debates concern what Beyer defines as 'key values', which historically are connected with nation-state-oriented modernity and are communicated through systems of global society, i.e. enlightenment, progress, equality, freedom and solidarity. While these values are global, their implications are contested, and through contestation they are perpetuated. Identity – whether related to class, gender, ethnicity or religion – plays a significant part in that contestation.[15] But political ideologies also matter. While liberals are concerned primarily with the individual's enlightenment, progress, equality, freedom and solidarity, for some religious and conservative thinkers it is primarily the community (variously defined) that is at stake.

This perspective on global communication might explain how there can be simultaneously value agreement and intense debate and even conflict, i.e. the failure of translation between 'Islamic' and 'Western' intellectual legacies involved in the *Satanic Verses* controversy that Werbner describes. It also means that the internal Islamic debate is both about doctrinal issues *and* about these global ideological divides. Rushdie can thus be seen as representing a liberal approach while his targets, the 'Islamic fundamentalists', represent a community-oriented approach. Take, for example, two organisations: The Society of the Muslim Brotherhood and Jama'at-i Islami. They were founded in the first half of the 1900s in the context of Egyptian and Indian struggles for national independence from British colonial rule. Their main objectives are to foster Islamic solidarity, unity and progress, and to protect Muslims' freedom and dignity, in the face of Western colonialism and cultural imperialism, through reform – i.e. by returning to the Qur'an and the Prophet's *sunna* and embodying the principles of Sharia, the Muslim community will be enlightened, and Muslim individuals and nations will prosper and progress and become free to rule their own destinies.[16]

---

[14]   Ibid, pp. 41–53.

[15]   Ibid, pp. 53–4.

[16]   See for example, Muhammad 'Abd Allah al-Samman, 'al-Ma'ani al-hayya fi'l-islam', *Rasa'il al-fikra al-islamiyya*, 3 (Cairo, 1953), pp. 14–15: 'Of Islam's live meanings, three stand out as exceptionally important: the liberation of the intellect; the liberation of the selves; and the awakening of humanity. These three meanings were established at the very moment when the sun of Islam began to rise, and so they are enclosed in the first revelation to Muhammad,

These 'fundamentalist' theologies of reform are critical of established governments and religious institutions. For the Muslim Brotherhood, successful reform will manifest itself in government based on the Islamic principles of solidarity and equality contained in the Qur'an and the *sunna*.[17] The Brotherhood's communitarianism is expressed, for example, in the founder Hasan al-Banna's description of Islamic government as involving surveillance of government functionaries to ensure their adherence to Islamic values, in public *and private* domains.[18] Individual freedoms are thus made subject to Islamic government. In the current platform of the Muslim Brotherhood's Freedom and Justice Party in Egypt, it is declared: 'Concerning the minority who are not suited by this program, they will be counteracted through legislation, surveillance technology and punitive measures; "indeed God restrains through the ruler what He does not restrain through the Qur'ân" (*inna Allaha layazaʿu bi'l-sultân mâ lâ yazaʿu bi'l-qurʾân*)'.[19] The statement appears in a context where it is claimed that Islamic values are necessary to combat corruption.

At the level of international organisations, the Organisation for Islamic Cooperation (OIC) was founded in 1969 with the objective of fostering solidarity among Muslim-majority countries on the basis of Islam, and defending the dignity and freedom of Muslims the world over. Among OIC's 57 member states, Iran, Sudan and Pakistan represent at state level a reform theology similar to that of the Muslim Brotherhood and Jamaʿat-i Islami.

---

peace be upon him: (1) "Read by the Name of your Lord who created", (2) "Created man from a clot of blood", (3) "Read, for your Lord the Most Bounteous who taught by the pen, He taught man what he did not know" (Q. 96: 1–5). In the first verse the intellects are turned towards servitude to God alone; in the second verse the selves are turned towards the fact that they are of one kind, made for equality and freedom from servitude of other men; and in the remaining verse attention is turned to the importance of knowledge (*ʿilm*) to support the unrestricted awakening of mankind'.

[17] Regarding al-Banna and the Muslim Brotherhood's ability to 'link issues which were usually associated with reactionism and backwardness, such as Islamic laws and strict public morality, to the national issues of independence and development', see Brynjar Lia, *The Society of the Muslim Brothers in Egypt: The Rise of an Islamic Mass-movement, 1928–1942* (Reading, PA: Ithaca Press, 1998), citation, p. 213; on the Muslim Brotherhood in Egypt, Syria and Europe, see Alison Pargeter, *The Muslim Brotherhood: The Burden of Tradition* (London: Saqi, 2010).

[18] Hasan al-Banna, 'Nahwa'l-nûr', published in *Al-Rasâʾil al-thalâtha* (Cairo: Dar al-Tibaʿa wa'l-nashr al-Islamiyya, 1977), pp. 109–10.

[19] Platform: Freedom and Justice Party (in Arabic), downloaded from the Carnegie Endowment for International Peace website, at http://www.carnegieendowment.org/2011/06/01/egypt-s-freedom-justice-party-to-be-or-not-to-be-independent/hy, accessed 12 August 2011.

Thus, while the OIC communicates at state level, the communications include the reformist perspective.

OIC concerns itself also with Muslims as minorities in the USA and Europe, where the transnational Muslim Brotherhood and Jama'at-i Islami are also established. Some Western Muslims are inspired by their reform programmes, but the majority are not.[20] While increasing numbers of Western Muslims perceive the global key values of enlightenment, progress, equality, freedom and solidarity in a liberal way, the Islamic reformists' view of these values as instrumental to their vision of the community's development sometimes generates tensions between the reformists and proponents of more liberal individual-oriented understandings of the same values.[21] Yet many Western Muslims are united in concern over negative stereotypes and public resentment against Islam and Muslims which since the 1990s have become expressed with increasing frequency in European media and radical right-wing politics.[22] Reflecting this development, OIC has become concerned with protecting the rights of Muslim minorities in Western countries. A key role here is played by freedom of expression.[23]

If we add Barthes' concept of myth to this perspective of global communication and ideology, the question of what common grounds are lost in translation, in Werbner's terms, can also be seen as a question of what is distorted. The public myth of the *Satanic Verses* controversy which claims that freedom of expression regarding Islam and the Prophet is offensive to and enrages Muslims, distorts the reality of common values/grounds between the Islamic sources on which Rushdie drew, Rushdie himself and the parties in the ensuing controversy.

The Satanic Verses

One of the most well-known and, in both Islamic and Western academic milieus, widely read sources for Rushdie's concept 'the satanic verses' is al-Tabari's *History of the Messengers and the Kings* (*Ta'rikh al-rusul wa'l-muluk*). Hailing from Tabaristan on the southern shore of the Caspian Sea, Abu Ja'far Muhammad

---

[20]   Pargeter, *Burden*, pp. 135–76.

[21]   Ibid., pp. 173–4, 202–6.

[22]   *Muslims in the European Union: Discrimination and Islamophobia*, European Monitoring Centre on Racism and Xenophobia (2006), at http://fra.europa.eu/fraWebsite/attachments/Manifestations_EN.pdf, accessed 21 August 2012.

[23]   Ekmeleddin Ihsanoglu, *The Islamic World In the New Century: The Organisation of the Islamic Conference, 1969–2009* (London: Hurst, 2010), pp. 143–71.

b. Jarir al-Tabari (d. AD 923) was a resident of Baghdad and a historian, Qur'an commentator, *hadith* expert, jurist and theologian of lasting fame.[24] He represented the Shafi'ite 'semi-rationalist' methodology in *fiqh*[25] and a 'proto-Ash'arite' rationalist position in *kalam*; he is reported to have said that the man or woman who has reached puberty but does not employ reason to explore God, together with His names and attributes, is an infidel (*kafir*) whose life and property are forfeit.[26] It appears that Tabari's definition of unbelief was directed partly against the Hanbalites, who opposed the idea that human reason could be employed to deduce knowledge about God, since the only valid source of knowledge about God was His self-revelation to the Prophet (the Qur'an) and the Prophet's direct knowledge of God expressed in his *sunna*. Tabari faced occasionally strong opposition from the Hanbalites of Baghdad, among other things because of a debate about whether the Prophet would, as stated in a *hadith* commenting on Q.17:79, sit beside God on the Throne on Judgement Day. The Hanbalites claimed he would because the Prophet had said so, while Tabari held that their quoted *hadith* was inauthentic, and that no created being can sit next to God in the physical sense – to seat the Prophet next to God would imply giving him a share in the divine, which is *shirk* ('giving humans a share in the divine nature').[27] The Prophet's special status consisted in his capacity to intercede on behalf of the believers on Judgement Day.[28] Tabari thus insisted on God's absolute difference from *all* humans, including the Prophet. This has implications also for knowledge: only God is infallible, while all humans are fallible.

Related to the problem of fallibility is the myth of how the Prophet recited to his Companions and his tribe Quraysh a sign which unlike his other signs was from Satan, not from God. The report was contained in both historical sources and Qur'an commentaries, and expressed the generally held view that prophets were subject to temptation and fallacy, the only difference between them and

---

[24] For biographical information about al-Tabari, see Franz Rosenthal, *The History of al-Tabari*: Vol. 1, *General Introduction and From the Creation to the Flood* (New York: State University of New York Press, 1989), pp. 10–78.

[25] Christopher Melchert, *The Formation of the Sunnī Schools of Law, 9th–10th Centuries CE* (Leiden: Brill, 1997), pp. 75, 182, 191–7.

[26] Claude Gilliot, *Exégèse, langue et théologie en Islam. L'Exégèse coranique de Tabari (m. 311/923)* (Paris: Libraire Philosophique J. Vrin, 1990), ref. to Ibn Hazm, *al-Fisal fī al-Milal wa'l-Ahwâ wa'l-Nihal* (Beirut: Dar al-Ma'rifa, 1975), Vol. I, p. 35, Vol. IV, p. 67.

[27] Tabari, *Ta'wil*, Vol. 9, pp. 179–85; Rosenthal, *Introduction*, pp. 70–78; Mustafa Shah, 'Al-Tabari and the Dynamics of *tafsir*: Theological Dimensions of a Legacy', *Journal of Qur'anic Studies*, 15:2 (2013), pp. 83–139, esp. pp. 108–10.

[28] Tabari, *Ta'wil*, Vol. 9, p. 179.

others being that prophets were corrected by God while ordinary humans could persist in error.[29] Shiite scholars, however, never accepted the report, due to their doctrine about the infallibility of the Prophet's successors: the imams. Sunni scholars associated with the movement for making the Prophetic *sunna* (embodied in the *hadith*) the principal source of law from the ninth century AD tended to emphasise the infallibility of the Prophet, and consequently to deny the historicity of the report about 'the satanic verses' because it was seen as damaging to his image as a law-giver. By the fourteenth and fifteenth centuries this stance was dominant among Sunni scholars. In the twentieth century especially, reformers like Muhammad 'Abduh, Sayyid Qutb and Abu A'la al-Mawdudi have reaffirmed the non-historicity of the report and the infallibility of the Prophet. The fact that Western Orientalists were now also studying the report was a significant factor in their need to readdress the issue.[30] Perceiving the Prophet's *sunna* as the source of a reformed, powerful Muslim community that could withstand the West, the Prophet's infallibility became a non-negotiable issue for them.

Following Barthes, a myth invests an existing concept with new significance. Since Tabari's reports often refer implicitly or explicitly to the Qur'an, it is relevant to search for the 'original' concept for his report about the satanic verses there. In Q.20:120 we find a definition of what exactly satanic temptation consists in:

> But Satan whispered to [Adam], saying: 'Adam, shall I show you the Tree of Immortality and a kingdom which will never perish?'

In Tabari's Qur'an commentary, *Jami' al-bayan fi ta'wil 'ay al-Qur'an*, he explained this verse as follows:

> From Musa – 'Amr – Asbat – al-Suddi: 'Adam, shall I show you the Tree of Immortality and a kingdom which will never perish?' means 'if you eat from it you will be a king in the manner of God ... and you will never die'.[31]

The interpretation stays with the Qur'anic text's reference to eternal life and eternal kingship, but adds that eternal kingship belongs to God alone, meaning that the

---

[29]   Mohammed Shahab Ahmed, *The Satanic Verses Incident In the Memory of the Early Muslim Community: An Analysis of the Early Riwâyas and their Isnâds*. Unpublished PhD dissertation, Department of Middle East Studies, Princeton University (1999).

[30]   Ahmed, *Satanic Verses*, pp. 3–5.

[31]   Tabari, *Ta'wil*, Vol. 9, p. 277.

original satanic temptation is about comparing oneself with God, particularly with reference to kingship. The implication is that satanic temptation was seen to be primarily an issue for rulers, or those aspiring to rule, a meaning consistent with the Qur'an's historical origins in the Prophet's state-building effort.

In Tabari's History, satanic temptation is already mentioned in the introduction, where Tabari defined his aim as to explore which kings and caliphs follow Satan and which follow God.[32] The subsequent contents of the history show that the matter concerns the 'rule of law': rulers who follow Satan put themselves *above* the law and pursue narrow self-interest at the expense of the common good, while those who follow God rule by the law and for the common good.[33] As for the actual report about the Prophet's satanic temptation, Tabari transmitted it from the Prophet's biographer Muhammad b. Ishaq (d. AD 767). The Prophet was tempted as he struggled to convert Quraysh from worshipping three female deities (al-Lat, al-'Uzza and Manat) to worship of One God, and to recognising the Prophet as the Messenger of God and political leader of the Arabs. Quraysh refused, and threatened to cast out the Prophet unless he ceased attacking their deities. The Prophet was in deep agony, wanting to please his people as much as he wanted to be true to the divine message:

> From Muhammad b. Ishaq: Satan cast on [the Prophet's] tongue, because of his inner debates and what he desired to bring to his people, the words: 'These are the high-flying cranes; verily their intercession is accepted with approval.' When Quraysh heard this, they rejoiced and were happy and delighted at the way in which he spoke of their gods, and they listened to him, while the Muslims, having complete trust in their Prophet in respect to the messages which he brought from God, did not suspect him of error, illusion, or mistake. When he came to the prostration, having completed the *sura*, he prostrated himself and the Muslims did likewise, following their Prophet, trusting in the message which he had brought and following his example.[34]

The Prophet was tempted at the moment when he was preparing to sacrifice the truth to accommodate Quraysh, and thus secure a *political* victory.

---

[32] See Rosenthal, *Introduction*, pp. 166–9, 249–57; Ulrika Mårtensson, 'Discourse and Historical Analysis: The Case of al-Tabari's History of the Messengers and the Kings', *Journal of Islamic Studies* (2005), Vol. 16, No. 3, pp. 287–331.

[33] Mårtensson, *Tabari*, in Farhan A. Nizami (ed.) *Makers of Islamic Civilization* (Oxford: Oxford University Press, 2009), esp. p. 79.

[34] W. Montgomery Watt and M.V. McDonald, *The History of al-Tabari. Volume VI: Muhammad at Mecca* (New York: SUNY Press, 1988), p. 108.

But God intervened and revealed to the Prophet – through Gabriel – that he had been tempted by Satan and that God forgave him, for 'there had never been a prophet or messenger before him who desired as he desired and wished as he wished but that Satan had cast words into his reading (*qur'an*), as he had cast words on Muhammad's tongue'.[35] God then withdrew the 'satanic' sign (*'aya*) from the revelation.

Tabari's report historicises the concept of satanic temptation in Q.20:120 by providing it with a concrete memory of the Prophet's desire to unite and lead the Arab nation; of his fallibility; and of God's mercy. The emotions described in the report are anxiety, relief and doubt: anxiety over not knowing what to do; the false relief of 'the fall'; and the true relief of God's mercy. But even the final relief cannot dispel the lingering feeling of doubt: neither the Prophet nor the Muslims knew *who the revelation came from*. Doubt is at the heart of this report, and Tabari's History continues to provide one example after another of how hard, even impossible, it is for those in authority to know whether they are really following God, even when their intentions are the best possible.

It appears that Tabari's report emphasised doubt to dissuade Muslims from thinking that by emulating the Prophet they could become immune to error: 'You see,' Tabari implied, 'the Companions followed the Prophet without questioning, even when his revelation came from Satan.' Even though the myth is reported by Ibn Ishaq, and as such is independent of Tabari, it is tempting to interpret its significance in the context of Tabari's history from the viewpoint of his conflict with the Hanbalites, who saw the Prophet's revelations and the eyewitness Companions as the only valid sources of law, and refused to concede to human reason the capacity to deduce law beyond the revealed writings.[36] The myth shows the Companions failing to exercise critical reasoning and to speak out against the Prophet when he did something evidently wrong. Viewed in this way Tabari's report about the satanic verses signifies the value of freedom of expression, in the sense of criticising the powerful, including the Prophet himself, when they use revelation to legitimise illegitimate grabs for political power.

Compared with the Qur'anic concept of satanic temptation as essentially concerned with state power, Tabari's myth has invested it with the feeling of doubt over the source of revelation and authority; arguably, this feeling reflects also the context that Tabari's generation of scholars found themselves in, debating the sources of legal authority.

---

[35]   Ibid., p. 109; I have changed Watt and McDonald's 'recitation' (*qur'an*) to 'reading'.

[36]   David Vishanoff, *The Formation of Islamic Hermeneutics: How Sunni Legal Theorists Imagined a Revealed Law* (New Haven, CT: American Oriental Society, 2011), p. 232.

The Satanic Verses

Salman Rushdie was born in Mumbai on 19 June 1947 to a Muslim family with roots in Kashmir. He grew up in an intellectual atmosphere, and pursued university studies (including Islamic studies) at Cambridge University in Britain, where he settled and became a famous novelist. The problems of power and religion are recurrent themes in Rushdie's novels. *Shame* (1983) is a reflection over Pakistan under General Zia ul-Haq's 'Islamisation' of the country through *sharia* laws, supported by Jama'at-i Islami, a reformist organisation which strongly rejected the historicity of Tabari's report on the satanic verses.

The Satanic Verses was published in India in September 1988. Critics warned even before publication that many would find it offensive, but it took until winter 1989 for violent protests to break out in India and Pakistan, and among Indian and Pakistani communities in the UK.[37] In an interview just after publication Rushdie described his personal relation to the novel's theme:

> The point is that I am not a religious person any more, formally; but I have remained all my life very attached to and interested in the subject of Islam. I studied it at university – indeed the place where I first heard about the satanic verses (of which a fictionalized version is in this book) is when I was studying Islam. So it's an image which has remained with me for 20 years ... I don't believe Mohammad had a revelation but I don't doubt his sincerity either.[38]

In another interview he stated that he intentionally criticised rulers who used Islam for purposes of authoritarian state power, referring to General Zia ul-Haq.[39] And 'Even *Shame* was attacked by fundamentalist Muslims. I cannot censor. I write whatever there is to write.'[40] Explaining his interest in the satanic verses myth, Rushdie said: '[T]he image out of which the book grew was of the prophet going to the mountain and *not being able to tell the difference* between the angel and the devil.'[41] As in Tabari's report, Rushdie related the problem

---

[37] For surveys of the controversy surrounding *The Satanic Verses*, see Lisa Appignanesi and Sara Maitland (eds), *The Rushdie File* (London: Fourth Estate, 1989); Ruthven, *A Satanic Affair*; Malik, *From Fatwa to Jihad*.

[38] Salman Rushdie, interview, *Sunday*, India, 18–24 September, 1988; published in Appignanesi and Maitland, *Rushdie File*, pp. 40–1.

[39] Rushdie, interview, *India Today*, 15 September 1988; published in Appignanesi and Maitland, *Rushdie File*, pp. 38–40.

[40] Rushdie, interview, *India Today*.

[41] Ibid. (italics added).

of distinguishing between the angel and the devil to power; in an interview in early 1989: 'When you're weak, do you compromise? When you're strong, are you tolerant?'[42] He elaborated, referring to the satanic verses myth:

> When weak, there seems to have been a brief flirtation with a possible compromise – about monotheism – which was very rapidly rejected. Now I don't think this diminishes Mohammed. All prophets face temptation. When Gibreel ... comes to Mohammed and tells him that the verses are satanic verses and should be removed – and here are the real verses – he forgave him. He said, 'Never mind, it's understandable, things like this have happened before.' I mean, it seems that Gibreel is more tolerant than some of these people attacking the book.[43]

Even though Rushdie compared his work with the Islamic historical sources, his novel is not about the Prophet Muhammad but about Mahound. Mahound, Rushdie explains in the novel, is not the historical Prophet Muhammad but a figment of the imagination of Islam's medieval enemies, the Christian crusaders. Like prejudicial epithets and nicknames in general, this image is in the eye of the beholder, not in the object beholden:

> His name: A dream-name, changed by the vision. Pronounced correctly [as 'Muhammad'], it means he-for-whom-thanks-should-be-given, but he won't answer to that here; nor, though he's well aware of what they call him, to his nickname in Jahilia down below – *he-who-goes-up-and-down-old-Coney*. Here he is neither Mahomet nor MoeHammered; has adopted, instead, the demon-tag the farangis [Crusaders] hung around his neck. To turn insults into strengths, whigs, tories, Blacks all chose to wear with pride the names they were given in scorn; likewise, our mountain-climbing, prophet-motivated solitary is to be the medieval baby-frightener, the Devil's synonym: Mahound.[44]

Mahound is historically the name that Crusader polemists gave to the Prophet Muhammad, and by which they meant a 'false prophet' whose sole concern was worldly power and sexual lust for subordinate women.[45] What Rushdie says in the passage cited above is that *people live up to the prejudices held against them*,

---

[42] Rushdie, interview, *Bandung File*, 27 January 1989, broadcast on BBC Channel 4, 14 February 1989; published in Appignanesi and Maitland, *Rushdie File*, pp. 27–31.

[43] Rushdie, interview, *Bandung File*.

[44] Salman Rushdie, *The Satanic Verses* (London: Viking Penguin, 1988), p. 93.

[45] Ruthven, *Satanic Affair*, pp. 35–6.

and this character lives up to the Crusader image Mahound (just as another character in the novel, Saladin Chamcha, is physically transformed into the goat-hoofed Devil when he is bestially abused by English policemen).[46] But most importantly of all, Mahound is an image of the Quranic concept of satanic temptation: his sole concern is worldly power.

Rushdie's narrative about Mahound mirrors the historical accounts of the Prophet's life found in Muhammad Ibn Ishaq's biography and Tabari's history, including the report about the Prophet's satanic temptation:

> Mahound's anguish is awful. He *asks*: is it possible that they *are* angels? Lat, Manat, Uzza ... can I call them angelic? Gibreel, have you got sisters? Are these the daughters of God? And he castigates himself, O my vanity, I am an arrogant man, is this weakness, is it just a dream of power? Must I betray myself for a seat on the council? Is this sensible and wise or is it hollow and self-loving? ... But I, too, have much to gain. The souls of the city, of the world, surely they are worth three angels? Is Allah so unbending that he will not embrace three more to save the human race? – I don't know anything.[47]

Eventually Mahound falls for the temptation – the 'dream of power', in Rushdie's words – and pronounces that the 'three angels' could be worshipped. But, in contrast to Tabari's report where the Companions simply followed the Prophet, Mahound's followers are devastated by his betrayal of the message, and questioned him. When the revelation is withdrawn, Rushdie added a new twist to Tabari's report:

> 'It was the Devil,' [Mahound] says aloud to the empty air, making it true by giving it voice. 'The last time, it was Shaitan' ... Gibreel, hovering-watching from his highest camera angle, knows one small detail, just one tiny thing that's a bit of a problem here, namely that *it was me both times, baba, me first and second also me.*[48]

In contrast to Tabari's report, there is no God and no divine forgiveness in Rushdie's myth. Gibreel is not the mediator of God's words but the voice of Mahound's own desires, and Mahound falls not for an external but an internal

---

[46]   Fischer and Abedi, 'Bombay', p. 131. For the view that 'Mahound' is intended to represent Muhammad, see, e.g., Shabbir Akhtar, 'Art or literary terrorism?', in Dan Cohn-Sherbok (ed.) *The Salman Rushdie Controversy in Interreligious Perspective* (Lampeter: Mellen, 1990), pp. 1–23; ref. to pp. 12–14.

[47]   Rushdie, *Satanic Verses*, p. 111.

[48]   Ibid., p. 123.

temptation; both the 'satanic' and the 'divine' revelations came from within himself. However, Mahound's withdrawal of the revelation signifies a dramatic shift: he ceases to doubt his own motives and starts persecuting his opponents, destroying the cult of the three female deities, and controlling his women. This is also different from Tabari's report where doubt remains. By removing doubt from Mahound, Rushdie distorted the historical portrait of the Prophet, changing its semiotics from the doubt of true faith to the certainty of authoritarianism.

In Rushdie's novel, Mahound has a follower: the Imam from Desh, easily recognisable as Ayatollah Khomeini (d. 1989), founder of the 'reformed' Islamic Republic of Iran in 1980. In the following passage the Imam destroys the goddess Al-Lat:

> '[The people] love me,' the Imam's voice says, 'because I am water. I am fertility and she [Al-Lat] is decay. They love me for my habit of smashing clocks. Human beings who turn away from God lose love, and certainty, and also the sense of His boundless time, that has no need to move. We long for the eternal, and I am eternity. She is nothing: a tick, or tock. She looks in her mirror every day and is terrorized by the idea of age, of time passing ... After the revolution there will be no clocks; we'll smash the lot. The word *clock* will be expunged from our dictionaries. After the revolution there will be no birthdays. We shall all be born again, all of us the same unchanging age in the eye of Almighty God' ... Down she tumbles, Al-Lat queen of the night; crashes upside-down to earth, crushing her head to bits; and lies, a headless black angel, with her wings ripped off, by a little wicket gate in the palace garden, all in a crumpled heap. – And Gibreel, looking away from her in horror, sees the Imam grow monstrous, lying in the palace forecourt with his mouth yawning open at the gates; as the people march through the gates he swallows them whole. The body of Al-Lat has shrivelled on the grass, leaving behind only a dark stain; and now every clock in the capital city of Desh begins to chime, and goes on unceasingly, beyond twelve, beyond twenty-four, beyond one thousand and one, announcing the end of Time, the hour that is beyond measuring, the hour of the exile's return, of the victory of water over wine, of the commencement of the Untime of the Imam.[49]

The Qur'anic concept of satanic temptation is echoed in the Imam's utterance 'I am eternity', while the image of him swallowing up the people alludes to the war between Iran and Iraq, which killed hundreds of thousands of Iranians, to whom Khomeini promised eternal salvation in return for their lives.

---

[49]   Ibid., pp. 214–15.

Following the book's logic, the Imam is following Mahound, the Crusader image of a false prophet who never had any divine revelations, only dreams of power and oppression of women. The last twist in this logic is Rushdie's remark: 'To turn insults into strengths, whigs, tories, Blacks all chose to wear with pride the names they were given in scorn; likewise, our mountain-climbing, prophet-motivated solitary is to be the medieval baby-frightener, the Devil's synonym: Mahound'[50] – the implication being that if Mahound is a Western prejudice against Islam, and the Imam is associated with Khomeini, then the latter is also seen as living up to Western prejudice rather than following the *sunna* of the Prophet Muhammad. And according to this double mythicising manoeuvre, Khomeini also lives up to the Qur'anic concept of satanic temptation, seeking God's eternal kingdom. In reality Khomeini was a follower of the Iranian mystical tradition of *'irfan*, 'immediate knowledge of God'.[51] While *'irfan* traditionally served the religious scholars in their quest for justice, Khomeini wedded it to state power and claimed that he himself shared the Hidden Imam's infallibility.

According to Ruthven, Khomeini took action against Rushdie in response to a situation where the Jama'at-i Islami, backed by Saudi Arabia, was posing internationally as defenders of Islam against Salman Rushdie's and the West's infamous attacks. Responding to this demonstration of Sunni power, Khomeini sought to bolster Shi'ite Iran's Islamic credentials.[52] According to Halliday, Khomeini's 'death sentence' was not an official, binding and irreversible *fatwa* but an unofficial, unbinding and reversible *hukm* ('judgment'). Mehdi Mozaffari has pointed out that the corresponding Farsi term is *firman*, a 'decree' by the head of state.[53] While no one is forced to act on such a decree, it is certainly intended to be acted upon.[54]

---

[50]   Ibid., p. 93.

[51]   Alexander Knysh, '"Irfan" Revisited: Khomeini and the Legacy of Islamic Mystical Philosophy', *Middle East Journal*, 46: 4 (Autumn 1992), pp. 631–53.

[52]   Ruthven, *Satanic Affair*, pp. 151–3.

[53]   Mehdi Mozaffari, *Fatwa: Violence and Discourtesy* (Aarhus: Aarhus University Press, 1998), p. 54. Historically, the Shah's *firman* was sometimes issued as an order to persecute the state's enemies, e.g. the Jews or the Nestorian Christians; see John Stewart, *Nestorian Missionary Enterprise: The Story of a Church on Fire* (Piscataway, NJ: Gorgias Press, 1928/2007), p. 18.

[54]   Hashemi Rafsanjani, speaker of Parliament, claimed: '[T]he importance of the issue merits our great leader – who usually does not involve himself in personal issues – involving himself in force to express his anger. It is always incumbent on us to obey his orders. We always know that he raises issues related to Islam in a timely manner and that he makes a confrontation in due time'; in Appignanesi and Maitland, *Rushdie File*, p. 86, from Tehran

When Khomeini pronounced his decree, Iran had emerged battered but unvanquished from the First Gulf War (1980–88), and had spawned a Lebanese satellite organisation, Hezbollah, which had eventually forced the Islamic Republic's arch-enemy Israel to evacuate south Lebanon. Iran was self-confident and eager to assume global Islamic leadership, and its Supreme Leader Khomeini would not tolerate insults to his person by a snooty British ex-Muslim author. While the decree says that death is the punishment for insulting Islam and the Prophet, it was the Supreme Leader himself who was insulted – Rushdie's caricature of the Imam/Ayatollah Khomeini implies that he is an unbeliever because he follows Mahound, not the Prophet.[55] The decree proved Rushdie's point: as Mahound killed those who ridiculed him, Ayatollah Khomeini sought to have Rushdie killed, and thus he 'adopted, instead, the demon-tag the farangis ['foreigners'] hung around his neck'. In Rushdie's own words: 'The zealot protests serve to confirm, in the Western mind, all the worst stereotypes of the Muslim world.'[56]

Freedom of Expression

Khomeini's decree can also be seen as related to Iranian activities in the OIC. In 1984, Iran's UN ambassador Said Rajaie-Khorassani declared that the human being is a divine creation, and since the UN Human Rights Charter ignores this fact it requires emendation. According to the Iranian Constitution, *sharia* is sovereign in relation to international law and UN Human Rights, and Article 24 of the Iranian Constitution limits freedom of expression by *sharia*.[57] Inside Iran, freedom of expression had been curtailed on 'Islamic' grounds since 1980.

Home Service, 10.30 am GMT, 15 February 1989, reported by BBC *Summary of World Broadcasts*, 17 February 1989.

[55] According to Malik, Ghayasuddin Siddiqui, founder of the then Iran-sympathising British Sunni organisation, The Muslim Institute, 'was frequently in Tehran and in the autumn of 1988 had plenty of discussions about *The Satanic Verses*, in street cafés and government ministries. "There was little hostility to the novel," [Siddiqui] recalls. "It was widely discussed. There were even some good reviews in the press"'; Malik, *From Fatwa to Jihad*, p. 7.

[56] Rushdie, Interview, *Sunday Times*, 19 February 1989, published in Appignanesi and Maitland, *Rushdie File*, p. 4.

[57] Anicée van Engeland, 'Le droit international des droits de l'homme et la République Islamique d'Iran: respect des obligations internationales par un gouvernement islamique', *European University Institute Working Papers*, Max Weber Program 2008, No. 8, pp. 3, 5.

In August 1990, the OIC produced the Cairo Declaration of Human Rights in Islam after a committee of legal experts had assembled in Tehran in December 1989, some 10 months after Khomeini's decree against Rushdie and in the midst of the subsequent international turmoil.[58] The Cairo Declaration did not replace the UN Human Rights Charter, as most OIC member states had ratified the latter. Rather, the OIC issued the Declaration to 'serve as a general guidance for Member States in the Field of human rights'.[59] According to the preamble the Declaration was issued 'in contribution to the efforts of mankind to assert human rights, to protect man from exploitation and persecution, and to affirm his freedom and right to a *dignified* life in accordance with the Islamic Sharia'.[60] In accordance with the connection between dignity and *sharia* that is established in this first paragraph, the Cairo Declaration consistently limits rights and freedoms by reference to *sharia*. Article 22, which concerns 'freedom of expression', states:

> (c) Information is a vital necessity to society. It may not be exploited or misused in such a way as may violate sanctities and *the dignity of Prophets*, undermine moral and ethical values or disintegrate, corrupt or harm society or weaken its faith.

> (d) It is not permitted to arouse nationalistic or doctrinal hatred or to do anything that may be an incitement to any form of racial discrimination.

Paragraph 22(c) limits freedom of expression by protecting the dignity of Prophets and a number of other abstractions: sanctities, values, harm to society and the weakening of faith. This allows states great freedom to limit information and expression. Given that the final meeting of the legal experts who drafted the Cairo Declaration took place in Tehran 10 months after Khomeini's decree, paragraph 22(c) might have been a response to *The Satanic Verses*. While the OIC called for Rushdie's novel to be withdrawn, the organisation never condoned Khomeini's decree against his person.[61]

In 1999, Pakistan, as representative of the OIC, presented to the UN Commission on Human Rights a draft resolution banning defamation of Islam,

---

[58] The Cairo Declaration (1990), in the University of Minnesota Human Rights Library, at http://www1.umn.edu/humanrts/instree/cairodeclaration.html, accessed 5 January 2010.

[59] The Cairo Declaration.

[60] Ibid.

[61] 'Islamic States Refuse to Back Rushdie Death Sentence', *The Guardian*, 17 March 1989, published in Appignanesi and Maitland, *Rushdie File*, p. 145.

to be included under the UN Human Rights paragraph against racism, not under the freedom of expression article, in order to commit the Commission to combat discrimination against Muslims. In the UN context the issue was expanded to defamation against religion in general. Since 1999, the issue of anti-defamation of religion has been raised annually in the Commission on Human Rights (from 2006 the Human Rights Council), and since 2005 also in the UN General Assembly.[62]

Since the 9/11 attacks in 2001 the campaign has become more focused on Muslim minorities in the West. In Europe, 9/11 triggered an intensification of anti-Muslim feelings in the public sphere, partly seen in conflicts surrounding 'artistic' productions such as Ayaan Hirsi Ali's and Theo van Gogh's film, and van Gogh's subsequent murder by a Muslim fundamentalist activist; the Danish cartoons of the Prophet Muhammad, and the violent surge of reactions in Islamic countries and the death threats against the cartoonists; and the Dutch film *Fitna*. The insulting images of the Prophet and Islam that were constructed in these works can be seen as replicas of Rushdie's Mahound myth: they are *farangi*-produced demon tags, which Muslim individuals and states lived up to by their violent reactions. These events and the perceived vulnerability of Muslim minorities in the West are reflected in OIC's latest Charter, amended in March 2008, which places certain obligations on its member states:

> 12. To protect and defend the true image of Islam, to combat defamation of Islam and encourage dialogue among civilizations and religions;

> 16. To safeguard the rights, dignity and religious and cultural identity of Muslim communities and minorities in non-Member States;[63]

On 12 November 2009 the UN General Assembly adopted a draft resolution which to some extent endorsed OIC's campaign, due to concerns over an increasingly vociferous international campaign of defamation of religion and incitement to religious hatred, combined with new security measures after 9/11 and the economic and social exclusion of Muslim minorities in the West. The Assembly concluded that freedom of expression 'carried with it special duties

---

[62]   Becket Fund for Religious Liberty Brief, 2 June 2008, 'Combating Defamation of Religions', 2 June 2008, at http://www.becketfund.org/files/a9e5b.pdf, p. 2, last accessed 5 January 2010.

[63]   OIC Charter (2008), at http://www.oic-oci.org/is11/english/Charter-en.pdf, p. 4, accessed 25 August 2009.

and responsibilities, and might therefore be subject to limitations as provided by law, and which were necessary for respect of the rights or reputations of others, protection of national security or of public order, public health or morals.'[64] In favour of the resolution were all 57 OIC member states, plus Russia, Venezuela and North Korea, while the USA, the EU, South Korea and most East European countries voted against; non-Muslim African, Caribbean, Latin American and south Asian countries, including India, abstained.

The abstainers worried that anti-defamation of religion would have detrimental effects for freedom of expression. There are several historical cases which show that this has indeed been the case. After OIC adopted the Cairo Declaration in 1990, with its commitment to defend the dignity of sanctities and prophets, attacks against 'defamers of Islam' have taken place across the globe. Rushdie's Japanese publisher was murdered in 1991; his Italian and Norwegian publishers were attacked and wounded in 1991 and 1993 respectively.[65] In Egypt, where the Muslim Brotherhood and the militant Gama'a Islamiyya were strong, Muslim writers and public intellectuals received the same kind of death threats as Rushdie: Farag Foda, a secularist writer, was declared an apostate by the Brotherhood-affiliated judge Muhammad al-Ghazali and murdered by Gama'a Islamiyya activists in 1992;[66] in 1994 Nobel laureate Naguib Mahfouz was severely injured in a murder assault by Gama'a Islamiyya activists for having defended Rushdie's right to freedom of expression, even though he strongly criticised his novel; and in 1995 Nasr Hamid Abu Zayd, professor of literature, was declared apostate for applying literary-critical methods to the Qur'an; he left the country as a precautionary measure. Sayed al-Qimni, sociologist at Cairo University, has written about the historical rise of Islam in political and economic terms. By 2005, al-Qimni had received so many death threats that he stopped writing. In July 2009 the Minister of Culture, Farouk Hosny, gave him the State Award of Merit in Social Sciences. Muslim Brotherhood MPs and lawyers tried to get the award rescinded, charging al-Qimni with 'defamation of Islam', and Gama'a Islamiyya hinted that he appeared to be an apostate.[67]

---

[64] UN General Assembly GA/SHC/3966, 12 November 2009, at http://www.un.org/News/Press/docs/2009/gashc3966.doc.htm, accessed 5 January 2010.

[65] Malik, *From Fatwa to Jihad*.

[66] Regarding Muhammad al-Ghazali and Faraj Foda, see Pargeter, *Burden*, p. 207.

[67] 'Egypt and Global Islam: The Battle for a Religion's Heart', *The Economist*, August 8–14 2009, pp. 48–9; 'Author asserts He Is Muslim, Refutes Apostasy Accusations: Egyptians Protest Award to Controversial Writer', *Al-Arabiyya*, 13 July 2009, at http://www.alarabiya.net/articles/2009/07/13/78580.html, accessed 26 August 2009.

Even though the Egyptian state apprehended some attackers, it never challenged the climate of religious censorship fuelled by the Islamic reformers. Rather, since the state was authoritarian, it saw any form of censorship as beneficial, and the state's religious bulwark, al-Azhar University mosque, has been complicit in condoning persecution of secular intellectuals. This was plainly manifest in the Egyptian state's orchestration of an international campaign against Denmark on account of the Danish cartoons of the Prophet Muhammad, published in a Danish newspaper in September 2005. As Jytte Klausen has shown, the Egyptian government used the cartoons and the OIC's campaign against defamation of religion to thwart US and EU pressure for democratisation. Denmark – through the Danish Egyptian Dialogue Institute – had allied itself with the US push for democracy and freedom of expression.[68] As Egypt was unable to punish the superpower USA itself, Denmark presented itself as the perfect scapegoat, having violated the dignity of the Prophet. Ibrahim al-Hudaybi, grandson of the Muslim Brotherhood's second General Guide, independently confirmed Klausen's finding that the Egyptian government's anti-Danish campaign was an attempt to discourage US pressure for democratic reform.[69]

The year 2011 marked not only popular uprisings against authoritarian regimes in Arab countries but also a significant change in OIC's campaign against the defamation of religion. In March 2011 the OIC altered, dropping the campaign, and decided to back a new strategy proposed by the UN Human Rights Council to promote anti-discrimination against minorities and freedom of religion.[70] OIC's readiness to abandon its campaign in exchange for acknowledgement of discrimination against Muslims shows that the vulnerability of Muslim minorities in Europe had become the principal motivation behind the campaign to regulate freedom of expression regarding religion.[71] However, demands on non-Muslim majorities to protect Muslims' civil and human rights have produced a situation where Muslims must reciprocate by committing to human rights. OIC thus now defines the Danish cartoons as incitement to hatred against Muslims, rather than as defamation of Islam.[72]

---

[68]   Jytte Klausen, *The Cartoons that Shook the World* (New Haven, CT: Yale University Press, 2009), pp. 165–84.

[69]   Klausen, *Cartoons*, pp. 173–6.

[70]   'Islamic Bloc Drops 12-Year U.N. Drive to Ban Defamation of Religion', Reuters, 24 March 2011, at http://blogs.reuters.com/faithworld/2011/03/24/islamic-bloc-drops-12-year-u-n-drive-to-ban-defamation-of-religion/, accessed 8 May 2011.

[71]   Ihsanoglu, *Islamic World*, pp. 149–71.

[72]   Ibid.

By March 2011 the regimes of Ben Ali in Tunisia and Mubarak in Egypt had fallen, and that of Gaddafi in Libya was on the ropes. While it cannot be proven that the OIC's change was related to these political developments, the switch from anti-defamation to anti-discrimination represents a change from state-centred interests to minorities' rights. In the same countries popular support for democratic government is strong. Yet the Muslim majority countries rank considerably lower when it comes to liberal democratic values or the 'self-expression values', including freedom of expression.[73] While weak support for self-expression might be expressed as defence of religion, it is not causally related to religion. Data from the World Values Surveys show that high rates of 'self-expression values' correlate positively with high economic well-being on both *country* and *individual* bases.[74] Consequently, Western Muslims' values are closer to the Western national averages than the averages in their countries of origins.[75] OIC's desire to represent Western Muslims, combined with the popular demand for democracy in the Middle East, might have motivated the OIC to move towards an anti-discrimination approach to freedom of expression. Such a development is in line with the global systemic values of solidarity, equality, progress and freedom, as well as with the true Islamic faith, as gleaned from the Qur'an, Tabari's History and Rushdie's *The Satanic Verses*.

De-mythologising the Public Myth of the Satanic Verses Controversy

It has been argued here that Salman Rushdie's novel *The Satanic Verses* is a myth about the Crusader image Mahound which caused controversy because it rammed straight into a global contestation over freedom of expression between those who associate Islam with absolute state power and certainty and those who associate it with faith and doubt. This contestation is still going on, at the global level of the UN and the OIC, and domestically through different kinds of assault tactics. Assaults range from government abuse of human rights and civil liberties, to Islamic reformist activists' threats against secular intellectuals and artists, to Western intellectuals' and artists' assaults on Muslim minorities

---

[73]   Ronald Inglehart, 'How Solid is Mass Support for Democracy – and How Can We Measure It?', *Political Science and Politics*, 36 (2003), pp. 51–7.

[74]   Ibid., pp. 56–7.

[75]   Ronald Inglehart and Pippa Norris, 'Muslim Integration into Western Cultures: Between Origins and Destinations', unpublished draft, 28 February 2009, at http://www.hks.harvard.edu/fs/pnorris/Acrobat/Muslim%20Integration%20Into%20Western%20Societies.pdf, accessed 4 April 2010.

by offending their feelings about the Prophet. While Rushdie was targeted by Islamic reformers in the same way as some of the Danish cartoonists have been, his assault is substantially different. He did not question Muslims' reverence for the Prophet, nor their feelings of humiliation at the hands of Western powers. His point in *The Satanic Verses* was that centuries-old European prejudice against Islam and the Prophet had come to life in the authoritarianism and inter-communal violence perpetrated by Islamic reformers in their quests for empowerment. The reformers' criticism of the authoritarianism of, for example, Mubarak's Egyptian state and its abuse of institutionalised Islam to legitimise its own indeterminate power has striking similarities with Rushdie's critique. Yet the ideological breaking-point between them is, as yet, insurmountable: Rushdie stands for individual rights to freedom of expression while the reformers put the collective aim of the Islamic state above freedom of expression. Thus, according to Rushdie's message, they have fallen for the satanic temptation that they seek to obliterate.

The public myth about the satanic verses controversy has been de-mythologised here through three moves. First, a Qur'anic concept of satanic temptation as boundless state power was identified. Secondly, Tabari's myth about the Prophet's satanic verses was both referred back to the original Qur'anic concept of satanic temptation and to the context where Tabari and his fellow scholars were deliberating prophetic authority and law. This move showed that Tabari's report mythologised the original Qur'anic concept by introducing the feeling of doubt that must accompany true faith. Thirdly, Rushdie's *The Satanic Verses* was referred back to Tabari's myth and found to replace the doubt that lingered with the Prophet with Mahound's absolute certainty, addressing a historical context of modern Islamic reformism and global debates about Islamic law, human rights and freedom of expression. This final move also brings out some striking similarities between Tabari's and Rushdie's myths: true faith is characterised by doubt, which in turn needs to find public expression.

Finally, then, how do Tabari's and Rushdie's myths relate to the Wikipedia public myth? Both Tabari and Rushdie use the myth of the satanic verses to draw attention to what they perceived to be the greatest issue at stake: the faithful person's right to express doubt. While Tabari wrote in a time where there were no global legal bodies or systems of communication, he inevitably communicated this issue in exclusive Islamic terms, even though the fact that he lodges satanic temptation in Creation and the first human being implies that he saw it as a universal challenge to authorities. Rushdie writes in the global idiom of English, and he creates characters from different cultures (the UK, India, 'Desh' and 'Jahiliyya') who illustrate the universality of the core issue. Tabari's and Rushdie's universalism contrasts with the public myth of the controversy, which casts the issue in terms of a conflict between liberal Western and traditional or 'fundamentalist' Muslim values. Thus the public myth diverts attention from Islam's original critique of boundless state power and from its intellectual heritage where the right to express doubt was considered the prerequisite of true faith.

PART II
Sacred Places and Persons

Chapter 5

The Glocalization of al-Haram al-Sharif: Designing Memory, Mystifying Place

Nimrod Luz

The Haram al-Sharif is considered the third most important sacred Islamic site (*thalith al-Haramayn*) but it is surely "the first political qibla" (*ula al-qiblatayn*).[1] The sacred, through its physical manifestations (sacred sites), plays an essential role in contemporary political debates of a multi-scalar nature. In this chapter I seek to develop a deeper understanding of the spatial, political, and social aspects of Islamic resurgence, both at large and—in particular—in Israel. I ask how the most holy Islamic place there, the Haram al-Sharif, is being perceived, produced, and promoted as a nexus for Palestinian communities, as both a religious symbol and a national icon. I explore how its unique status as the third most important Islamic site, and its role as a sacred religious icon among contesting parties, transform it into one of the most intriguing localities, where images, meaning, and actual control are constantly being contested and fought over. The local Islamic movement is certainly the most tenacious and active force behind the mystification of the place, not only as a global Islamic monument but also a local national icon. Concomitantly with global processes of Islamic resurgence, the place has become a spatial metaphor for the status and state of the Israeli-Palestinian minority, on both the local-national and the global scale. This is achieved through various processes: contestation and over-surplus of meaning, inclusion (mystification), and exclusion of other (demystification).

It is the premise of this chapter that through ideas of sanctity and myth, and through the agency of the sacred, we may understand better aspects of Islamic resurgence, in the context of the secularization debate and of the nation state in

---

[1] Yitzhak Reiter, "Third in Holiness, First in Politics: Al-Haram al-Sharif in Muslim Eyes," in Yitzhak Reiter (ed.), *Sovereignty of God and Man: Sanctity and Political Centrality on the Temple Mount* (Jerusalem, 2001), pp. 155–80; *idem, Jerusalem and Its Role in Islamic Solidarity* (New York, 2008), pp. 11–35.

the age of globalization.[2] My exploration of the Haram al-Sharif and the role of the Israeli-Palestinian Islamic movement therein are based on contextualization of place as an open-ended, ever-changing locality. The theoretical foundation of this work rests on three concepts to be found in recent developments of cultural, political, and economic geography: place, scale, and glocalization. I promote an understanding of place as the outcome and the process of production, as open to multiple possibilities.[3] The sacred in this respect is but one example (intriguing as it may be) of "place." "Scale" refers to the ways places are perceived, understood, and promoted on different levels and between different levels from the personal (body scale) to the global. Understanding places within a multi-scalar configuration allows a better understanding of the forces that shape them and of the reasons leading to these configurations.[4] The neologisms "glocal" and "glocalization" stem from the theoretical understanding that the global and global flows and phenomena are local at any given time. Through this contextualization of the Haram I analyze the ways in which the Israeli-Palestinian Islamic movement is producing, promoting, and actively changing the ways the Haram is being perceived within varying scale levels.

The Contested Nature of the Sacred: Sacred Sites as the Nexus of Conflicts

Rodney Needham postulates that the sacred is indeed a contested category.[5] Far from being locations where faith is quietly practiced, God peacefully worshipped, and brotherly love rejoiced, sacred places are often to be found at the center of conflict. They often serve as a stage where violence and bloodshed take place. Sacred places become contested first and foremost because they are places—that is, they are spatial. This last observation justifies further elaboration

---

[2]   I think one cannot discuss Islamic resurgence in disconnection to current anthropological and sociological debates on religion, modernism, and nationalism. Indeed, I follow here the contextualization put forward in Talal Asad, *Formation of the Secular: Christianity, Islam, Modernity* (Stanford, CA, 2003), esp. pp. 181–201.

[3]   Henri Lefebvre, *The Production of Space*, trans. D. Nicholson-Smith (Oxford, 1991); Doreen Massey, "Places and their Past," *History Workshop Journal*, 39 (1995), pp. 182–92.

[4]   Eric Swyngedouw, "The Mammon Quest: 'Glocalization,' Interspatial Competition and the Monetary Order: The Construction of New Scales," in Mick Dunford and Grigoris Kafkalas (eds), *Cities and Regions in the New Europe* (London, 1992), pp. 39–67; *idem*, "Territorial Organization and the Space/Technology Nexus," *Transactions of the Institute of British Geographers*, 17 (1992), pp. 417–33.

[5]   Rodney Needham, cited in David Chidester and Edward T. Linenthal (eds), *American Sacred Space* (Bloomington, IN, 1995), p. 5.

and inquiry into the inherent political and contested nature of places. In what follows I discuss, rather succinctly, the way places have been theorized and contextualized by contemporary political and cultural geographers.

In recent years the question of place has been raised among scholars from an array of disciplines. In his invariably persuasive manner, Foucault observed that place is fundamental to any exercise of power.[6] Put differently, places are by their very nature political entities, or at least politicized through various human agencies. A useful definition in understanding place as a socially constructed entity is: "Place is space to which meaning has been ascribed."[7] If this is the case, then place is the outcome of a process of construction, which implies that it is invested with meaning, ideology, and (surely) politics. By its very nature, place is full of power and symbolism. It is a complex web of relations, of domination and subordination, of solidarities and cooperation.[8] At the same time, place is inexorably linked with controversies, conflicts, struggles over control, and debates (as well as more physical contestations) over meaning and symbolism. Being a "web of signification" inevitably transforms place into a site where that significance and its "true" nature is up for grabs by those already in, or in search of, power.[9] Places are spatial metaphors through which people and peoples can represent themselves and thus concretize their culture; that is, through places, cultural ideas and abstracts become concrete. Therefore, the struggle over the ownership and control of places needs to be seen also as a cultural struggle for autonomy and self-determination.[10] Place provides both the real, concrete settings from which culture[11] emanates, to enmesh people in webs of activities and meanings and in the physical expression of those cultures in the form of landscapes.[12]

---

[6] Michel Foucault, *Power/Knowledge: Selected Interviews and Other Writings, 1972–1977*, trans. Catherine Gordon (New York, 1980), p. 63.

[7] Erica Carter, James Donald, and Judith Squires (eds), *Space and Place: Theories of Identity and Location* (London, 1993), p. xii.

[8] Doreen Massey, "Power-Geometry and a Progressive Sense of Place," in Jon Bird, Barry Curtis, Tim Putman, George Robertson, and Lisa Tickner (eds), *Mapping the Futures: Local Cultures, Global Changes* (London, 1993), p. 144.

[9] David Ley and Kris Olds, "Landscape as Spectacle: World's Fairs and the Culture of Heroic Consumption," *Environment and Planning D: Society and Space*, 6 (1988), p. 195.

[10] Arturo Escobar, "Culture Sits in Places: Reflections on Globalism and Subaltern Strategies of Localization," *Political Geography*, 20/2 (2001), p. 162.

[11] As place, culture is always in the process of becoming, and must not be reified or understood as a rigid and specific setting of human ideals, norms, etc.

[12] James A. Agnew and James S. Duncan (eds), *The Power of Place: Bringing Together Geographical and Sociological Imaginations* (Boston, MA, 1989), preface.

Thus far I have established that places are always in the "way of becoming," that is, they are always in the process (or open to the possibility) of change, and that conflict and competition are inherent in spatiality, along with collaboration in the negotiation, and indeed production, of understanding and meaning.[13] Sacred places make for an intriguing example of the socio-political and constructed nature of place. The specificities of the politics of sacred places will be discussed in what follows.

Eade and Sallnow focus our attention to the highly contested nature of the sacred: "The power of a shrine, therefore, derives in large part from its character almost as a religious void, a ritual space capable of accommodating diverse meanings and practices."[14] In this they break free of former paradigms and the contextualization of pilgrimage sites to establish a dynamic and a highly political understanding of the role of sacred sites for communities and sub-groups, while competing and performing their religious practices therein.[15] Geographers dealing with religion have pointed also to the presence of conflict and contestation involved in the production of sacred sites.[16] Indeed, the very word "production," when applied to the allegedly transcendent outward quality[17] of a sacred site's spatiality, immediately grounds the place and locates it within the realm of everyday life. Chidester and Linenthal present us with an understanding of the multivalence of sacred sites and their inherent contested

---

[13]   Allen Pred, "Place as Historically Contingent Process: Structuration and the Time-Geography of Becoming Places," *Annals of the Association of American Geographers*, 74/2 (1984), pp. 279–97.

[14]   John Eade and Michael J. Sallnow (eds), *Contesting the Sacred: The Anthropology of Christian Pilgrimage* (London and New York, 1991), p. 15.

[15]   Emile Durkheim, *The Elementary Forms of Religious Life* (New York, 1912/1995); Victor Turner, "Pilgrimages as Social Processes," in *idem, Drama, Fields, and Metaphors: Symbolic Action in Human Society* (Ithaca, NY, 1974), pp. 166–230.

[16]   Christine Chivallon, "Religion as Space for the Expression of Caribbean Identity in the United Kingdom," *Environment & Planning D: Society & Space*, 19/4 (2001), pp. 461–84; Lily Kong, "Negotiating Conceptions of Sacred Space: A Case Study of Religious Buildings in Singapore," *Transactions of the Institute of British Geographers*, 18/3 (1993), pp. 342–58; *idem*, "Ideological Hegemony and the Political Symbolism of Religious Buildings in Singapore," *Environment and Planning D: Society and Space*, 11 (1993), pp. 11–23; *idem*, "Mapping 'New' Geographies of Religion: Politics and Poetics in Modernity," *Progress in Human Geography*, 25/2 (2001), pp. 211–33; Simon Naylor and James R. Ryan, "The Mosque in the Suburbs: Negotiating Religion and Ethnicity in South London," *Social & Cultural Geography*, 3/1 (2002), pp. 39–59.

[17]   This intangible quality is what Otto defined as "numinous." See Rudolph Otto, *The Idea of the Holy: An Inquiry into the Non-rational Factor in the Idea of the Divine and its Relation to the Natural*, trans. James. W. Harvey (Harmondsworth, 1959).

nature. They claim that "a sacred place is not merely discovered, or founded, or constructed; it is claimed, owned, and operated by people advancing specific interest."[18] Therefore, becoming a sacred place involves a process of production, but is also inescapably linked to cultural-political contests over the multiple meanings assigned to the place. The conflict is not just over the production, Chidester and Linenthal continue to argue, but also over the "symbolic surpluses that are abundantly available for appropriation."[19] Sacred sites are arenas where resources are transformed into a surplus of meaning; they are heavily invested with symbolism, emotions, and indeed mystification. This also explains why sacred sites are locations for competing discourses. Too much is at stake and there is too much to lose for contesting groups or influential actors. Taking over and controlling the sacred involves various forms of politics;[20] thus the sacred is always to be found intertwined with political power, agency, and rather profane[21] social forces. As argued by Lefebvre, the production of places is inexorably linked to politics.[22] The very concept of the production of space necessitates a human agency and activity, and therefore implies politics in various manifestations. This is all the more apparent in the case in point, the Haram al-Sharif. Indeed, the process of sanctifying the site in Islamic understanding was heavily engaged with politics and the invention of traditions. But the contesting and competing narratives about the place are not confined solely to the past, but also involve "tinkering with the past" by various contemporary competing groups.

Scale, Glocalization, Resistance

The geopolitical changes that followed the 1967 war—and Israel's consequent taking-over of direct control in the area concerned—were responsible for the increase of tension and friction over the Haram al-Sharif. The place became one of the most controversial issues between Israel and the Muslims around the world and, the focal point of regional Israeli-Arab conflict, and a major site of contestation between Israel, as a self-proclaimed Jewish state, and Palestinians

---

[18]   Chidester and Linenthal, *American Sacred Space*, p. 17.

[19]   Ibid., p. 18.

[20]   Gerardus van der Leeuw, *Religion in Essence and Manifestation*, trans. J.E. Turner (New York, 1933/1986).

[21]   Indeed, the use of the term "profane" here needs to be understood as turning Eliade's concept of the nature of the sacred on its head.

[22]   Lefebvre, "Production of Place."

on both sides of the Green Line.[23] Israel, like any other modern nation state, sees itself as the only legitimate authority authorized to execute power and exercise violence against whoever challenges its authority within its political boundaries.[24] Thus, since 1967 Israel has opposed most endeavors challenging its control of the Haram al-Sharif and its environs, and stubbornly seeks to dictate the socio-spatial interaction there. The way to overcome these restrictions is to scale up the level of resistance to the state, whether personal, local, national, or global. In what follows I contextualize the issues of scale, scalar politics, and resistance in order to understand better the nature of the activities of Palestinian citizens in Israel with respect to the Haram. Further, I address the term "glocalization" and show its relevance to the case in point.

The inflammatory visit on 28 September 2000 of a former Knesset member (MK), Ariel Sharon, later Israeli Prime Minister, to the holy Islamic compound[25] in Jerusalem may be seen as the ultimate trigger, the spark that ignited the second Palestinian civilians' uprising, commonly known as the al-Aqsa (or Second) Intifada. Sharon's visit was a highly calculated political response to the political stalemate that followed the failure of the second Camp David summit. In the days after the visit the Second Intifada got under way, and civilian acts of resistance and defiance of Israeli state authority spread among Palestinian communities within and outside the Green Line. When interviewed about the riots (also known as the "October 2000 Events") and the reactions among Israeli-Palestinians, 'Abd al-Malik Dhamsha, an MK and head of the Islamic party in the Knesset at the time, supplied the following rejoinder:

> It is a war that every Muslim should be part of. There is no Green Line when al-Aqsa is concerned and this [the reactions] will continue throughout Israel ...
> I cannot see this murderer transgress the most holy place in this land and idly observe from the sideline. Am I not a human being? Am I devoid of emotions, am I not a Muslim? He entered the most holy mosque of the Muslims in order to defile it as a murderer, as a powerful man, a Zionist. Do you honestly believe that

---

[23]   Roger Friedland and Richard D. Hecht, *To Rule Jerusalem* (Cambridge, 1996).

[24]   James C. Scott, *Seeing Like a State: How Certain Schemes to Improve the Human Condition Have Failed* (New Haven CT, 1998).

[25]   The term "Haram al-Sharif" is coterminous with the al-Aqsa Mosque in everyday parlance. Throughout this paper I use them both interchangeably, with reference to the compound in Jerusalem constructed by King Herod to serve as the platform for the second Jewish Temple, and was later the construction site for various Islamic structures, including the Dome of the Rock and the Al-Aqsa Mosque.

we will not face up to it? This act is addressed against our very existence, but we do exist. Our sole culpability is that we are humans and that we have a life and that we have a mosque and a land.[26]

Above and beyond this highly emotional response, Dhamsha is also engaged in intriguing spatial language, weaving a complex multi-scalar configuration. While talking about the Haram and trying to explain the magnitude of Sharon's provocation he moves at random between different scalar settings. He begins with the global scale by asserting that the defence of al-Aqsa against the transgression of profanity is the task of all Muslims. He then moves to a supranational scale and addresses the role of Palestinians on both sides of the Green Line. Subsequently he touches on the national scale by focusing on the Israeli-Palestinians. This is followed by a personal scale as he alludes to his own rage and the humiliation he experienced as a human being and a Muslim. He concludes by jumping again to the community scale, in speaking on behalf of Israeli-Palestinians at large.

The concept of geographical scale has become a buzzword of sorts in recent debates among political, economic, and urban geographers.[27] I exploit it here as I think it can be conducive to any critical discussion of the spatialities (and other aspects) of Islamic resurgence. Spatial scale needs to be understood as something that is produced. It is a process that involves politics and therefore is constantly being fought over by contesting forces. Scale is the spatial configuration where socio-political relations are contested.[28] Scalar configurations are not pre-given platforms upon which social life simply takes place, but are constantly being remade through socio-political struggle.

Scale and its production ("scaling") are indeed political and social projects. Scale is socially constructed, which implies that at each and every level of analysis—that is, from the personal to the global—our understanding of scale is the outcome of social processes and political struggle. The question of scale and how it is set is a matter of political struggle, involving power relations and the changes in or contestation of existing power geometries.[29] Scale and scaling

---

[26]   *Haaretz*, 3 October 2000, p. 3.

[27]   Neil Brenner, "The Limits to Scale? Methodological Reflections on Scalar Structuration," *Progress in Human Geography*, 25/4 (2001), pp. 591–614.

[28]   Eric Swyngedouw, "Neither Global nor Local: 'Glocalization' and the Politics of Scale," in Kevin R. Cox (ed.), *Spaces of Globalization: Reasserting the Power of the Local* (New York and London, 1997), pp. 137–66.

[29]   Neil Smith, "Homeless/Global: Scaling Places," in Bird et al. (eds), *Mapping the Future*, pp. 81–119.

are not politically neutral; they are both the outcome of struggles for power and control. Scale is a constitutive dimension of socio-political processes. It demarcates the site of social or political contest. It is also about setting a context for the struggle. Scale is an active progenitor of specific social processes; it sets the boundaries for struggles over identity, and for control over places. In the face of a scale superimposed by a hegemonic power, subaltern groups may opt actively to thwart this power by jumping scales. Against the backdrop of Israeli control over the Haram, Dhamsha moves between scales as a way of subverting and resisting a pre-given geographical production of scale in that specific place. Jumping scales allows the subordinate or the controlled to dissolve spatial boundaries largely imposed from above, and that contain rather than facilitate their production and reproduction of everyday life. By discussing challenges to and political contestations over specific scales I hope to indicate and make clear ways in which Islamic resurgence "takes place," and uses scale within the boundaries of nation states. This approach is defined here as the glocalization of the place.

Glocalization refers, first, to the contested restructuring of the institutional level from the national scale, both upwards to supranational or global scales and downwards to the scale of the individual person or of local, urban, or regional configurations; and second, to the strategies of global localization of key forms of industrial, service, and financial capital.[30] Glocalization is also concerned with processes of de- and re-territorialization. This is achieved again through reconfiguration and the contestation over spatial scale. Since all social life is inevitably situated in a local context, Swyngedouw suggests that we need to rethink the global phenomenon. The global and the local are deeply intertwined, and mutually constituted. The overarching and dramatic processes that currently shape the world under the canopy of the concept of globalization are of course always local.[31] The global always takes place at the local, and the latter is constantly being shaped and altered by the former. But in coining the term "glocalization," Swyngedouw focuses our attention on the fact that, regardless of the importance and magnitude of world globalization, we need to pay special attention to the localities in which these changes are taking place. Glocalization refers, then, to the changes to and struggles over scalar configurations. Scale relates to existing social power-relationships as dictated by authority. Scale reconfiguration, in turn, challenges existing power

---

[30] Swyngedouw, "The Mammon Quest"; *idem*, "Territorial Organization".

[31] Bruno Latour, *We Have Never Been Modern*, trans. Catherine Porter (Cambridge, MA, 1993).

relations and questions existing power geometries.[32] Jumping scales—as in the case in point, approaching other than the national scale—is therefore central to any emancipatory project. Glocalization, which refers to addressing the global within a local context (but also promoting a local/national understanding of the global) should be understood as such a project. In what follows I describe this process of scalar reconfiguration as a strategy of resisting state control. Part and parcel of these endeavors are the mystification of the place and the exploitation of the past—put differently, a specific reading of the past—to reconfigure the scale at which the struggle is being fought. By focusing on the process of scaling I aim to explore the continuous reorganization, through political struggle, of the hierarchical interrelationships between scales.[33]

The Construction of a Sacred Palestinian National Site: The Islamic Movement as an Agent of Change

Shortly after the failure of the second Camp David summit, the mayors of Israeli-Palestinian municipalities were convened for an "emergency meeting." The reason behind this meeting was a news item in an article published in *Sawt al-haqq wa-l-huriyya*, the weekly publication of the Islamic Movement's more extreme wing,[34] relating to an alleged government plan for constructing a synagogue inside "Solomon's Stables."[35] During the meeting Dr Hanna Swaid, the mayor of Eilabun, supported Shaykh Ra'id Salah's[36] response, in which he had stated that this construction, should it materialize, would equal the destruction of al-Aqsa. Swaid is a Christian-Arab, now serving as an MK for Hadash, the Democratic Front for Peace and Equality (currently the only joint Arab-Jewish party in the Israeli parliament). Nonetheless, his ideological, ethnic, and religious background does not seem to deter him from encouraging

---

[32]   Eric Swyngedouw, "Globalisation or 'Glocalisation'? Networks, Territories and Rescaling," *Cambridge Review of International Affairs*, 17/1 (2003), pp. 25–48.

[33]   Brenner, "The Limits to Scale".

[34]   In 1996 the Islamic Movement in Israel was divided into two main wings. The more extreme is also called "The Northern Islamic Movement" (as opposed to the "Southern") and professes a more subversive approach toward the state.

[35]   *Sawt al-Haqq w-al-Huriyya*, 11 August 2002, p. 10. The term "Solomon's Stables" derives from the Crusader period in Jerusalem, when the al-Aqsa mosque was erroneously understood to be none other than Solomon's Temple. The commonly accepted dating of these underground halls is c. 20 BC.

[36]   Ra'id Salah is head of the Northern wing.

Israeli-Palestinians to join in a special annual rally of the Islamic Movement conducted under the slogan: "Al-Aqsa is in Danger."[37] His devotion to al-Aqsa surely cannot rest on religious grounds; for him publicly to demonstrate such a commitment to the site can only imply that al-Aqsa is perceived as much more than just a religious symbol, indeed as a national one. It seems that this transformation started with the charismatic mufti Hajj Amin al-Husayni during the Mandate period.[38] The project of transforming the site into a religio-national symbol has been carried further in recent years by the Islamic Movement in Israel. I would like to concentrate on three aspects of those activities. First, I explore the physical changes initiated at the Haram by the Islamic Movement; second, I address the latter's social activities, throughout the country, regarding the status of al-Aqsa; and third, I look at the Movement's use of public media (mostly its own journals) as a way of elevating the status of the Haram.

The Physical Construction of the Site

In the 1980s there was an increase in the presence and influence of Israeli-Palestinian Muslim citizens in the al-Haram al-Sharif compound. The driving forces behind these activities were by and large the two wings of the Islamic Movement in Israel. This is especially true regarding the "Northern" section of the Movement, headed by Shaykh Ra'id Salah. The Islamic Movement's most prominent contribution is to be found at the southern tip of the platform below the al-Aqsa Mosque, commonly known as "Solomon's Stables." In recent years, save for an occasional visit by archeologists, the place has mostly remained closed to the public. It was known also as al-Aqsa al-qadima (ancient al-Aqsa), but was not part of the pilgrimage routine at the Haram. Since 1967 the management of the Haram, like that of other Islamic religious buildings in East Jerusalem, has been in the hands of the Jordanian Ministry of Endowments.[39] This arrangement was agreed upon, shortly after 1967, almost by accident, and as unobtrusively as possible, by the Israeli government. Thus the actual daily routine of the Haram was managed by an administration that was financed by, and followed instructions coming from, Amman. The creation of the Palestinian Authority

---

37   *Sawt al-Haqq wa-l-Huriyya*, 10 September 2000, p. 5

38   Yoram Porath, *The Emergence of the Palestinian-Arab National Movement 1918–1929* (London, 1974), pp. 194–200; Taysir Jbara, *Palestinian Leader: Hajj Amin al-Husayni, Mufti of Jerusalem* (Princeton, NJ, 1985).

39   Reiter, "Third in Holiness," p. 160.

(PA) following the Oslo Accords in 1993 heavily distorted this arrangement, as the Palestinians under Arafat were constantly striving to better their position and to undermine both Israeli and Jordanian control of the Haram.[40]

In 1996 the Israeli-Palestinian Islamic Movement was about to prove that it also was a significant player, in addition to the unholy triad of Israel, Jordan, and the PA. In the summer of that year the Endowment Authority (by now under the PA) received the approval of the Israeli government to perform some necessary maintenance work on the underground halls. The idea as explained to the Israeli authorities was that this was a much-needed step to enable prayers to be held on rainy days, expected during that year's Ramadan. It would seem that Ra'id Salah was simply waiting for this challenge: a few months earlier he had been a prominent player in a rupture within the Israeli-Palestinian Islamic Movement. The official ideological reason behind the split was the issue of whether the Movement should establish itself also as a political movement and run in the general elections for the Israeli parliament. Under his leadership, the Northern faction was responsible for the mobilization of thousands of volunteers, and the collection of money and materials, all indispensable to the building project. The Movement was responsible for the execution of a large-scale renovation project that ultimately transformed the halls into one of the largest mosques in the Middle East.[41] The project was carried through to the accompaniment of fierce and constant encounters with the Israeli authorities—both in the courts, and on the ground with Israeli police. It was a great success for the Movement, and for Salah personally. The fact that he had confronted the Israeli authorities directly and prevailed not only won him the title of "shaykh of al-Aqsa" but also positioned him as the most influential Islamic leader among Israeli-Palestinian Muslims. It was a live demonstration that the power of the place, combined with the organization skills of the Movement, could lead to massive public support among Israeli-Palestinian citizens. One of the outcomes of the 1996 al-Aqsa campaign was an annual rally conducted under the slogan "al-Aqsa is in danger," initially organized as a fund-raiser for the 1996 renovation campaign, but such an astounding success that it then became the Northern faction's biggest and most meaningful event of the year. This surely attests to the importance assigned to the Haram by Israeli-Palestinians, but it is also a sign of the Movement's role and its significance in contemporary politics.

---

[40]   Shmuel Berkovits, *The Battle for the Holy Places: The Struggle over Jerusalem and the Holy Sites in Israel, Judea, Samaria and the Gaza Districts* (Or Yehuda, 2000), p. 133.

[41]   Abd al-Malik Dahamsha, interview with author, September 2002.

Social Activities among Israeli-Palestinian Muslims

In addition to grand-scale, flamboyant operations such as the creation of al-Musalla al-Marwani,[42] as the underground place of prayer is called, the Islamic Movements are engaged year round with various social activities targeted at bringing the Haram closer to the people's hearts. Thus throughout the year the two factions maintain a subsidized bus service around Israel to bring devotees to the site. This is far from being a sporadic or a concentrated effort, but rather a continuous and tenacious project.[43] In such a manner the Movement is reaching more and more people, including those who are not exposed to written or electronic media on a regular basis. My observations in Sakhnin, a town of 25,000 people in the Galilee, revealed that no less than 12 buses (roughly 600 people) depart regularly to Jerusalem at weekends. This means that, routinely rather than only on special occasions, thousands of visitors (pilgrims as the case may be) are transported to the Haram from across the country.

A unique association that goes by the name "The al-Aqsa Association for the Upkeep of Islamic Endowments and Sacred Places," headed by Shaykh Kamal Rayan, is working year round to initiate numerous projects to maintain public connections with the site. The association was established in 1990, its explicit *raison d'être* being to preserve and defend *awqaf* and Islamic sacred sites throughout Israel.[44] But the al-Aqsa Association is also actively concerned to keep alive the memory of specifically Palestinian iconic sites. In recent years a special project was carried out by various research teams to complete a map of historical Palestine: "Let every Palestinian know whether he is from here or is an immigrant, where his mosque is and where his ancestors' graves are."[45] Special attention is paid to projects that concern the sacred center of Jerusalem, two of which are addressed directly at commemorating the Haram and connecting to it as large an audience as possible. The first is called *Shadd al-rihal* ("fastening the saddles"), a name derived from a well-known hadith, transmitted by Ibn Shihab al-Zuhri, according to which the prophet Muhammad acknowledged that beasts may be saddled for holy pilgrimage to only three mosques (those

---

[42]   The name is supposed to mean the praying area of al-Marwani, after the family of Abd al-Malik, the caliph responsible for the building of al-Aqsa and the Dome of the Rock. However, it is totally fictitious in the sense that there is no valid source, nor even an indication, pointing to the use of this name in any previous historical period, and connecting it to Abd al-Malik's project.

[43]   *Al-Shuruq*, 4 February 2002, p. 6.

[44]   Kamal Rayan, interview with author, October 2002.

[45]   Ibid.

of Mecca, Medina, and Jerusalem).[46] The importance of this hadith is primarily the fact that it establishes Jerusalem's status as equal to the two most important sanctuaries already existing in Islamic piety. According to Rayan, the project's objective is to establish a direct and unobstructed connection between Israeli-Palestinian Muslims and the al-Aqsa mosque, especially now during these "dire days that are upon us."[47] Literally this means contributing to increase the number of visits to the Haram and raising the number and value of donations to it. The second project involves tree-planting at the site and its environs, with a commitment to tend the trees on a regular basis. These two projects are constructed in a fashion that will ensure the linkage and commitment of Israeli-Palestinian Muslim devotees to the Haram on a practical, daily level. Indeed, in recent years there is a growing tendency among Israeli-Palestinian Muslims to decorate new houses, mostly above the main entrance, with signs and pictures of the Dome of the Rock. The casual and mundane manner in which this has become a convention indicates clearly that the Islamic Movements are making headway with their objectives with respect to the Haram.

Use of Public Media

The media are one of the main arenas used to advance and promote the status of the Haram and its importance among Israeli-Palestinians. It should come as no surprise that both factions' magazines are strongly engaged with the site, often publishing articles concerning its role in history as well as news on contemporary politics. The Northern faction's magazine, *Sawt al-haqq wa-l-huriyya*, explores in a very detailed and elaborate manner the religious status of the Haram, historical anecdotes that emphasize its Islamic nature, and, since 2000, the political implications of future peace negotiations.

As of 2000, and particularly after the October 2000 "Events,"[48] the printed and electronic Arab media in Israel pay a great deal of attention to the Haram, which is all the more apparent when exploring the "Islamic" media. The writing style is highly religious and saturated with quotations from the Qur'an, *tafsir* (exegesis), and the hadith literature. A special supplement entitled "al-Aqsa in

---

[46]   Meir J. Kister, "You Shall Only Set Out for Three Mosques: A Study of an Early Tradition," *Le Museon*, 82 (1969), pp. 173–96.

[47]   Kamal Rayan, interview with author, October 2002.

[48]   As explained above, this is the common Israeli term for the riots among Israeli-Arab citizens in October 2000.

Danger" is dedicated to the history and religious importance of the site, and concerned with contemporary challenges (mostly violations of its sanctity) by Israeli authorities.[49] A prominent picture of the Dome of the Rock fills the front page; following this is a series of articles and news items all revolving around the Haram, both in history and the present. The first article is a survey of various attempts by Israeli authorities to tighten their control in the compound since 1967. Particular attention is given to recurring events in which Jewish groups try to gain access to the site in order to conduct prayers there; among the violations considered are the archeological excavations along the Haram walls from 1967 to the present. In an article headed "Al-Aqsa is above and beyond any would-be negotiator," Tawfiq Muhammad 'Ari'ar presents us with an uncompromising view of the Haram's Islamic character.[50] The conflict is essentially a religious one, claims 'Ari'ar, and since it is one of the three most important Islamic shrines it cannot be subject to negotiation or compromise. The author exploits all the standard religious justifications in order to warn PA officials against making concessions when negotiating with Israel. He is particularly averse to the idea that Jews will be allowed to continue to pray at the Western Wall. Interestingly enough, 'Ari'ar does not substantiate this position (which is commonly found among members of the Northern wing) with any religious precedent nor with any *shari'a* ruling. Intriguingly enough, this was already agreed upon by the two sides in the July 2000 talks, as referred to in the Clinton minutes.[51] An even more confrontational and adamant approach is advanced in an article by Ra'id Salah, who vows to defend the Haram with his life and warns against even the smallest concession of any part of it:

> This is the destination of the nocturnal journey of the Prophet (*isra'*) and from here he ascended to heaven (*mi'raj*). This place witnessed the conquest of Jerusalem by Umar ibn al-Khattab and the liberation of Jerusalem from the hands of the Crusaders by Salah al-Din ... and because it is so important it is beyond negotiation and no voice will rise higher than the voice of al-Aqsa. And those of feeble character that say that America is stronger than them, the blessed al-Aqsa answers and says God is stronger. And the Western Wall from within and from without is part of al-Aqsa, and so are the other buildings and mosques within it, including al-Musalla al-Marwani. This being the true nature of al-Aqsa, we will renew our covenant with God and our covenant with al-Aqsa and we will pin our

[49]   *Sawt al-Haqq wa-l-Huriyya*, special supplement, 15 September 2002.
[50]   Ibid., p. 3.
[51]   *Haaretz*, 23 December 2000, p. 1.

hopes on our Islamic *umma* and our Arab world and our Palestinian people and reiterate: we shall redeem you in spirit and blood.[52]

Rhetoric of this nature positions the Israeli-Palestinian Islamic movement as the most hawkish with respect to any concession over the Haram. Salah's attitude, which is backed by daily and visible action, not only produces a public image of a zealot of al-Aqsa but also reflects badly on anyone willing to consider a less obstinate approach. Against the backdrop of the continuous work to elevate the public status of al-Aqsa, any alternative and more lenient understanding amounts to being disloyal to the fundamentals of Islam, and even sinful. Salah also makes a connection between the local, the regional, and the global as part of his strategy to thwart any Israeli efforts to exert control over the site. This will be addressed further; for the moment I will confine myself to the construction and production of the place by the Islamic Movement.

The Islamic Movement's two wings in Israel are both in play where al-Aqsa is concerned. Both, in their own style and with their own emphases, are working towards the elevation of the place's status, certainly in Israeli politics, but also on a larger scale. Whether through renovation projects, fund-raiser events or the use of the mass media, al-Aqsa is constantly being produced, promoted, and reminded. The audience varies greatly and a multi-scalar politics is at work. But before I address the issue of scaling and rescaling directly I turn now to an exploration of the way the place is being mystified, mythologized, and construed.

Mystification and Demystification of the Sacred: Tinkering with the Past

Myth, argues Lincoln, has the task of giving an historical intention a natural justification.[53] The strength of the myth is discovered when contingency and the temporary appear eternal—or in a different take, as if it has always been like that. Thus the act of mystification is exposed and projected as a highly politicized act which aims to answer a group's contemporary needs. This realization is never truer than in the case of al-Aqsa. The idea that the past, often presented as history, is instrumental for the needs of contemporary groups is far from being earth-shattering news. This understanding was painfully addressed by scholars of different persuasions, whether environmental historians, students of religion,

---

[52]   *Sawt al-Haqq wa-l-Huriyya*, special supplement, 15 September 2002, p. 5.

[53]   Bruce Lincoln, *Discourse and the Construction of Society: Comparative Studies of Myth, Ritual, and Classification* (Oxford, 1989), p. 5.

political theorists, or anthropologists.[54] My only contribution here is to suggest that while exploring the very act of mystification the role of places should be taken into consideration. The past of a place, argues Massey, is as open to multiplicity of means as is its present.[55] Claims and counter-claims about the present character of a site depend in almost all cases on particular, rival interpretations of the past. The past is up for grabs, as it were, and it is in the present that we may produce a certain understanding of it, one that promotes our most urgent needs and political necessities. In the case in point, the Islamic Movement is moving in two opposite directions, albeit with complementary measures. On the one hand its representatives continually try to promote the Haram's status and religious importance among Muslims in a multi-scalar configuration. On the other hand these representatives advance a specific reading of the site's past which basically refutes any Jewish connection or relations with it, or indeed any Jewish history. The following excerpt from an essay of Ra'id Salah fleshes out these two aspects of the site's current mystification:

> The Mosque of al-Aqsa is an Islamic, Arab, and Palestinian property and no one save them, regardless of their identity and who they are, and particularly the Jews, have any rights over there until the end of days. Whoever accepts their right on even a stone or anything else there is a traitor! It is our duty to confront this person and inform him he is indeed a traitor. It is a treacherous act against God, Muhammad, the believers, the Islamic nation, the Arab world and the Palestinian people. It is an act of betrayal in the first of the *qiblas*, in the second mosque, and the Prophet's ascension to heaven and it is a betrayal of the mosque in Mecca and the mosque of Medina. It is a betrayal of the infant martyrs, of Muhammad Durra[56] and others. We say to whoever tries to undermine these standpoints: you will not succeed, the mosque of al-Aqsa is ours and no one of the Jewish public has any part in it. We firmly believe that no Muslim, Arab, or Palestinian with

---

54   David Lowenthal, *The Past is a Foreign Country* (Cambridge, 1985); Bruce Lincoln, *Discourse and the Construction of Society*; Benedict Anderson, *Imagined Communities: Reflections on the Origin and Spread of Nationalism* (London and New York, 1983); Eric Hobsbawm and Terrence Ranger (eds), *The Invention of Tradition* (Cambridge, 1983); Nadia El-Haj, *Facts on the Ground: Archaeological Practice and Territorial Self-fashioning in Israeli Society* (Chicago, IL, 2001).

55   Massey, "Places and their Past."

56   Muhammad al-Durra was killed during an IDF operation in Gaza in September 2000. The dispute over the cause and instigation of his death made him a symbol of the Second Intifada; hence he became an iconic martyr in the Arab world and a symbol of Palestinian grievances against Israel.

a shred of pride in his heart will forsake any part, stone, wall, path, monument, dome, or structure in the blessed al-Aqsa within and without, above ground or underground.[57]

In order to establish the myth that supports his political aims (and surely religious beliefs) Salah is promoting a twofold understanding of the site. First, its religious and political significance for Palestinians and Muslims worldwide; second, total denial of any Jewish heritage in the site, despite early Islamic traditions openly acknowledging its Jewish history.[58] That the very name Bayt al-Maqdis (Temple Mount) was a common name for Jerusalem during the early Islamic period surely attests to this. In the face of these rarely disputed facts about the city's history, how can we understand Salah's uncompromising position and his decisive denial of any Jewish heritage? It should be clear that he is not the only one voicing such opinions. MK 'Abd al-Malik Dhamsha denies all historical evidence attesting to the existence of a Jewish temple in the compound: "There are neither archeological findings nor historical evidence that can imply that a Jewish temple actually existed on site."[59] A complete denial of the Jewish-Israeli narrative is not, however, endemic to leaders of the Islamic movement. Shawqi Khatib is a well-known political figure among Israeli-Palestinians. He served as chair of the Arab Follow-Up Committee[60] as well as several terms as mayor of Yafia, a town in central Galilee. He is a member of Hadash, a political party that states in its manifesto that in any would-be peace agreement Jerusalem will be divided among the two nations. In addition, special arrangements will be made in order to facilitate the continuation of Jewish worship at the Western Wall. However, when asked directly he made it clear that for him the Jewish linkage to Jerusalem is indeed a myth based on lies and historical distortion: "I did not conduct serious research but I heard people saying that you [the Jews] have based your research on Jerusalem on lies."[61]

---

[57] *Sawt al-Haqq wa-l-Huriyya*, 25 January 2002, p. 5

[58] In the earliest traditions concerning Jerusalem (literature in praise of the city) the temple of Solomon or the Jewish history of the city is often referred to. See Ofer Livne-Kafri (ed.), *Abu al-Ma'ali al-Musharraf b. al-Murajja b. Ibrahim al-Maqdisi, Kitab fada'il bayt al-maqdis wa-al-khalil wa-fada'il al-sham* (Shfaram, 1995); Amikam Elad, *Medieval Jerusalem and Islamic Worship: Holy Places, Ceremonies, Pilgrimage* (Leiden, Köln, and New York, 1995).

[59] Interview with the author, September 2002.

[60] This is the leading politically independent body of Israeli-Palestinians. Its members, including leading intellectuals and public figures, come from all (or no) political parties.

[61] Interview with the author, August 2002.

How are we to understand the complete denial of Jewish heritage? And along the same lines how can Islamic leaders promote al-Aqsa as the very kernel of Palestinian nationalism as well as a highly significant Islamic site? It would seem that we cannot sever the contemporary political situation of Israeli-Palestinians from the way the Haram's past is being mythologized, both as an Islamic national symbol and as an all-encompassing Islamic sacred site. The past of the place is highly instrumental for the political aims of Israeli-Palestinians—although it is a very specific past, in much the same sense as Nora distinguished between memory and history. While history is the representation of the past, memory is life, borne by living societies.[62] Put differently, memory is the vehicle through which myths are being carried on, but at the same time it is also the medium through which agents can alter and change the way their respective communities uphold those myths. The current understanding of al-Aqsa cannot be disconnected or understood in isolation from the Arab-Israeli conflict and the current situation of Israeli-Palestinians. The process of nation-building is advanced through the construction of a common past, shared symbols, and accepted mythologies. The creation of an imagined community necessitates anchors of identity which are commonly accepted and shared by all. In the Palestinian case the Haram in Jerusalem is put forward as such a shared symbol. Indeed, the very fact that Christians, at least when confronting Israeli authorities and the Jewish majority, share this understanding clearly attests to the place's status as a national symbol. The invention of traditions is part and parcel of the social construction of the nation; thus, as part of the nation-building project, histories, memories, myths are blended together and invested in specific sites. These are the places where the cultural attributes of a group/nation are becoming accessible and concrete. The collective amnesia demonstrated by Salah and other Palestinian public figures needs to be understood above all as a much-needed component of the construction of a Palestinian national narrative. The existence of a competing and successful other (Israel as a Jewish state), especially where the Haram is concerned, is paving the way for the circulation of specific traditions of the past that serve the contemporary needs of the Palestinians.

As a marginalized minority within Israel, and for Palestinians outside the Green Line an often suspect group, Israeli-Palestinians have been moving in recent years more and more toward the Islamic and Palestinian vertices of

---

[62] Pierre Nora, "Between Memory and History: Les Lieux de Mémoire," *Representations*, 26 (1989), pp. 7–24.

their identity.[63] The promotion of the Haram as a national icon is conducive to such inclinations and to contemporary political needs. The role of the Islamic movement is crucial in this process. Not only is it an agent in the transformation of al-Aqsa and the way it is perceived among local devotees, but it also has a vital role in promoting this understanding far beyond the local/national scale. The mystification of al-Aqsa along with the demystification of the relevant Jewish past is under way through a constant and massive socio-political endeavor. The process of Islamic resurgence is indeed local tinkering with the past, but it reaches far beyond the local political scene. I would like to address now the very process of glocalization as performed mostly by the Islamic movement in Israel.

Jumping Scales: Nationalizing, Globalizing and Glocalizing al-Aqsa—Concluding Remarks

Recently, Rekhess has promoted the idea that ever since the Oslo Accords Israeli-Palestinians have been localizing their national struggle.[64] By this he refers to a variety of actions in which their Palestinian-Arab heritage is fused locally with their Israeli daily lives and identity. Thus the memory of the Nakba, for example, is publicly discussed and commemorated as part of what he calls the opening of the "48 files." By internalizing their cultural/national heritage, Israeli-Palestinians are empowering themselves against the hegemony of the state and the Jewish majority. This "jumping of scales," as defined by Smith, is part of their project of emancipation from the hurdles and control imposed on them by the Israeli state through its various agencies.[65] This tactic (or strategy, as the case may be) is quite common to subaltern groups and should be understood as a form of resistance. Moving between scales and publicly displaying their Palestinian identity empowers Israeli-Palestinians and enables them to oppose state regulatory force. It seems that this is exactly what Jonas was referring to when theorizing scale and the politics of spatiality:

> This is a process driven by class, ethnic, gender and cultural struggles. On the
> one hand, domineering organizations attempt to control the dominated by

---

[63] The use of vertices is consistent with the metaphor of analyzing Israeli-Palestinians' identity as a triangle of three vertices: Islamization, Palestinization, and Israelization. Sammy Smooha, *Index of Arab-Jewish Relations in Israel* (Haifa, 2005).

[64] Eli Rekhess, "The Arabs of Israel after Oslo: Localization of the National Struggle," *Israel Studies*; 7/3 (2002), pp. 1–44.

[65] Smith, "Homeless/Global: Scaling Places."

confining the latter and their organizations to a manageable scale. On the other hand, subordinated groups attempt to liberate themselves from these imposed scale constraints by harnessing power and instrumentalities at other scales. In the process, scale is actively produced.[66]

The nation state is one of the most effective domineering organizations where scaling our lives is concerned. Jumping scale from the national, either upward or downward, allows the subordinate national minority at least a partial liberation and some control over its life. Following this understanding I argue that the Islamic movement (indeed resurgence) in Israel is promoting new understandings regarding the Haram as a way actively to produce scale, within a multi-scalar configuration.

Promoting the Haram as a national Palestinian symbol is effectively challenging prevalent notions about the place within the Jewish majority in Israel, but at the same time it enables the Palestinian minority to play a more active and meaningful role among their compatriots. This explains perfectly the active role the Israeli-Palestinian Islamic Movement is taking up in opposing various state initiatives regarding the site. A case in point is the abovementioned demonstrations against the intentions of the police to allow Jewish groups to pray at the Haram during the Passover of 2009. But it does not stop there. The Israeli-Palestinian Islamic movement, and Ra'id Salah in particular, vehemently opposes any PA concessions to Israel regarding right of access to the site. The Israeli Islamic Movement proves to be more hard line than some of the spokespeople of the PA. By advancing the place as a Palestinian national icon and actively defending it as such, the Movement is bettering its position on both the local and the national Palestinian scale. At the same time it is also actively approaching the regional (Arab) and the global (Islamic).

I would like now to address directly what I initially termed the "glocalization" of the Haram. By this I refer to the emancipatory project of rescaling the local and of promoting it to the supranational and the global, while simultaneously introducing a global understanding of the site within the local. The Islamic Movement in Israel is actively engaged in a process of multi-scalar configuration of the site, as a way on the one hand of transcending the control of the national state (de-territorialization) and on the other hand of bringing about a new understanding of the site into the national and local scale (re-territorialization). The interaction between the local and the global is mediated by signs and symbols,

---

[66] Andrew Jonas, "The Scale Politics of Spatiality," *Environment and Planning D: Society and Space*, 12/3 (1994), p. 258.

images and narratives, and by circulating meanings.[67] Swyngedouw suggests that the glocalization of the world's political-economic geography addresses the ways in which the former hegemony of the national scale is weakening and the local (sub-national) and global (supranational) scales are gaining more importance.[68] Following this, I argue that through the process of glocalizing the Haram the Islamic Movement is indeed trying to work for a weakening of the national and the strengthening of the local and the global. Through the active engagement in the mystification of the place and circulating specific meanings of the Haram, the Islamic movement is globally promoting a certain symbolic meaning of the site, but at the same time promoting this understanding locally in what I address here as the constant glocalization of the place. Needless to say, this process also introduces the Movement as an active player and a glocal agent of the place, thus gaining respectability and agency not only locally and nationally within Israel but also reaching for the global.

---

[67] Adrian Ivakhiv, "Toward a Geography of 'Religion': Mapping the Distribution of an Unstable Signifier," *Annals of the Association of American Geographers*, 96/1 (2006), pp. 169–75.

[68] See, for example, Eric Swyngedouw, "Neither Global nor Local: 'Glocalization' and the Politics of Scale," in Kevin Cox (ed.), *Spaces of Globalisation: Reasserting the Power of the Local* (New York and London, 1997), pp. 137–66.

Chapter 6

The Myth of Perpetual Departure: Sufis in a New (Age) Global (Dis)Order

Itzchak Weismann

The Haqqaniyya is one of the most visible Sufi brotherhoods on the global scene. An heir to the activist Naqshbandi mystical tradition, it has adapted more than most other contemporary Sufi branches to the new realities of globalisation. Shaykh Nazim 'Adil al-Haqqani, its founder and head, travels constantly among his diverse communities of followers around the world. His son-in-law and deputy in the United States, Shaykh Hisham Kabbani, maintains for the brotherhood a strong presence on the internet. The Haqqani teachings combine the rejection of Western civilisation, nostalgia for the lost Ottoman Caliphate and unbridled animosity to the Islamist trends with the cultivation of Western discipleship, interest in New Age culture and a belief in the imminent appearance of the awaited one – the Mahdi.

There are different ways to evaluate the messianic vision of Shaykh Nazim, which employs Christian and universal symbols along with traditional Muslim ideas and is constantly updated to take account of current events in the international arena. Nazim's view of the end of days may be seen as part of the general upsurge of apocalyptic literature in the troubled Muslim world, which largely coincides with the contemporary resurgence and radicalisation of Islam.[1] It may also reflect the efforts of a devout Muslim to exploit the new opportunities offered by the current technological revolution in communications to spread the Islamic call to the West.[2] But above all, as I claim in this chapter, the evolving Haqqani apocalypse is a mythic articulation of the anxiety felt by an adept of an orthodox Sufi brotherhood in a cosmic struggle against the rising tide of global militant Islamism.

---

[1] For contemporary radical Muslim apocalyptic and messianic writing, see David Cook, *Contemporary Muslim Apocalyptic Literature* (Syracuse, NY: Syracuse University Press, 2005); Timothy R. Furnish, *Holiest Wars: Islamic Mahdis, Their Jihads, and Osama bin Laden* (Westport, CN: Praeger Publishers, 2005).

[2] For an overview, see Jamal Malik and John Hinnels (eds), *Sufism in the West* (London and New York: Routledge, 2006).

This chapter begins with a theoretical consideration of the tensions inherent in the adaptation of Sufism, and religion at large, to contemporary realities. For this purpose the ongoing scholarly discussion on the spatial and temporal dimensions of globalisation are confronted with premodern and modern conceptualisations which Mircea Eliade has defined as the myth of eternal return. In the following two sections I introduce Shaykh Nazim al-Haqqani and analyse the workings of his brotherhood at the local and global levels. My main concern here is to demonstrate how Nazim's hagiography, the main source of information on his life, and his communities, on which we have several anthropological studies, are constructed in the light of his overall project of globalising Sufism. The final section deals with Shaykh Nazim's apocalyptic-messianic vision. I present his writings and utterances on the subject as a transformed myth of perpetual departure that reflects the transnational characteristics of the Haqqani brotherhood and its quest for religious authority and spiritual realisation in the face of the general and Islamist global (dis)order.

Globalisation and the Myth of Eternal Return

Globalisation refers to the transnational cultural economy of the late twentieth and early twenty-first centuries. It involves easy and swift flows of goods, capital, people, information and risk across the globe, combined with the emergence of social networks and political organisations which constrain the nation-state.[3] These rely on the technological revolution in communications, which progressively eliminates limitations of time and space. Globalisation has dialectical relations with its modern past and its local present. Temporally, as late modernity, it marks the continuation of the nation-state system, the acceleration of capitalist production, and scientific and technological progress. As a new historical era, which is associated with postmodernity, it denotes the proliferation of transnational organisations, consumerism, the flourishing of diaspora and hybrid identities, and the heterogenisation and relativisation of Western values. Spatially, as glocalisation, which is a composite of the global and the local, it denotes 'the intensification of worldwide social relations in such a way that local happenings are shaped by events occurring many miles away and vice versa'.[4]

---

[3]   Kate Nash, *Contemporary Political Sociology: Globalization, Politics, and Power* (Oxford: Blackwell, 2000), p. 47.

[4]   Anthony Giddens, *The Consequences of Modernity* (Cambridge: Polity, 1990), p. 64.

The technological annulment of temporal/spatial distances across the globe accentuates the modern experience of the world and of oneself as 'in perpetual disintegration and renewal, trouble and anguish, ambiguity and contradiction'.[5] It also reproduces as well as transforms the class polarisation of the modern era. For some, globalisation augurs an unprecedented freedom from physical obstacles and unheard-of ability to move and act from a distance, while for others it portends the impossibility of appropriating and domesticating the locality from which they have little chance of cutting themselves free.[6] While the global wayfarer engages in networking on a worldwide scale, the local resident seeks an anchor in the power of identity.[7]

The temporal and spatial realities of globalisation seem to be incompatible with traditional religious worldviews, which are habitually associated with specific times and places. According to Mircea Eliade, the renowned scholar of comparative religion, premodern religious man marked a fundamental difference between his territory, the cosmos he inhabited, and the unknown surrounding space, the chaos from which he stayed away. He similarly distinguished between intervals of festivity, which form a meaningful circular and recoverable present, and the ordinary temporal duration, which has no real meaning.[8] Sacred time and space are sustained by the myth of the eternal return. Eliade defines myth as a sacred history that relates what the Gods or culture heroes did at 'the beginning of time'.[9] Eternal return refers to the periodic reactualisation of these mythic events through rituals, gestures and pilgrimages to 'the centre' (temple or city), which provide the paradigmatic model for all human activities.[10] The myth of the eternal return thus helped the premodern religious person to understand the world and to organise life in an orderly repetitive manner. Myths of the end (and renewal) of the world normally appear when this ordered cosmos seemed to be breaking down.

---

[5]   Marshal Berman, *All That Is Solid Melts into Air* (New York: Simon and Schuster, 1982), p. 345.

[6]   Zygmunt Bauman, *Globalization: The Human Consequences* (Cambridge: Polity, 1999), p. 18.

[7]   The concepts feature in the titles of the first two books of the trilogy by Manuel Castells, *The Information Age: Economy, Society and Culture, Vol. 1: The Rise of the Network Society* (Oxford: Blackwell, 1996), *Vol. II: The Power of Identity* (Oxford: Blackwell, 1997).

[8]   Mircea Eliade, *The Sacred and The Profane: The Nature of Religion* (San Diego, CA: Harcourt Brace, 1959), chs 1 and 2.

[9]   Ibid., pp. 95–9.

[10]   Mircea Eliade, *The Myth of Eternal Return: Or, Cosmos and History* (Princeton, NJ: Princeton University Press, 1954), ch. 1.

Archetypal and repetitive myths have persisted into modern societies, despite the cultivation of historical consciousness and the belief in personal freedom and progress. They have been particularly conspicuous in the formation and maintenance of the nationalist imagery. The major components of national/ethnic myths evoke and also historicise the premodern conceptions of sacred time and space. Anthony Smith includes among them stories about the temporal origins of the community, the territory to which it once migrated and where it is now located, its common ancestry, the heroic age of its establishment and the course of its decline and regeneration. These modern myths have created national group identity (an aspect that Eliade's phenomenological approach tended to overlook), encapsulated its meanings and visions, and guided its collective action.[11]

With the advent of globalisation 'the myth of eternal return' has been called into serious question. Globalisation has greatly intensified the modern processes of the 'emptying of time and space' or, in other words, their homogenisation through the uniformity of the clock and the universal map, and the disembedding of social systems, the 'lifting out' of social relations from local contexts of interaction and their restructuring across indefinite spans of 'time-space'.[12] Supra-national networks, immigration, mass consumption and New Age spirituality have weakened the power of myths embedded in time and place and made their periodic reactualisation seem superfluous. For traditional men of religion the present time has therefore been a time of crisis, demanding a radical reformulation of their myths. For the more globally conscious among them such reformulation could take an apocalyptic turn. In the Islamic case, this is the story of the Wahhabi–Salafis' trans-historisation of the *jahiliyya* (pre-Islamic barbarity) and of the Crusades in the worldwide fight against unbelief, and this is also the counter-story of Shaykh Nazim al-Haqqani's reactualisation of the coming of the Mahdi.

The Construction of a Global Wayfarer

The remarkable spreading of the Haqqaniyya brotherhood in the West, along with the idiosyncrasies of its leader's conduct and teachings, has attracted the attention of the scholarly community. Still, our knowledge of Shaykh Nazim's life, especially of the early stages relating to his upbringing and initiation, depends

---

[11]   Anthony Smith, *Myths and Memories of the Nation* (Oxford: Oxford University Press, 1999), pp. 57–96.

[12]   Giddens, *Consequences*, pp. 17–29.

heavily on the brotherhood's official version of events. This hagiography has been expounded, undoubtedly under the Shaykh's authorisation, in both English and Arabic respectively by his foremost deputies, Hisham and 'Adnan Kabbani.[13] I use here the English version, which naturally is attuned to Western consumption.[14]

Muhammad Nazim 'Adil al-Haqqani was born in 1922 in Larnaca, Turkish Cyprus, into the family of a junior Egyptian administrator in the British colony. He claims descent on his father's side from 'Abd al-Qadir al-Jilani, the eponymous founder of the worldwide Qadiri brotherhood, and on his mother's side from the noted mystical poet Jalal al-Din Rumi, founder of the mostly Turkish Mevlevi brotherhood. Nazim also claims, as Sufi shaykhs often do, to belong to the family of the Prophet (p. 376).

Like many contemporary Islamic activists, Shaykh Nazim's upbringing combined religious studies, in his case the Sufi path and the sciences of jurisprudence and *hadith* (traditions on the sayings and deeds of the Prophet), with official education including modern sciences. He completed high school in Larnaca in 1940 and then enrolled in the University of Istanbul from which he received a degree in chemical engineering. At that time he continued to pursue spiritual education and was introduced to the Naqshbandi brotherhood (pp. 377–8).

The Naqshbandiyya[15] originated in fourteenth-century Bukhara, from where it spread far and wide. Its foremost offshoot in modern times has been the Khalidiyya, which played a conspicuous role in the modernisation of the Ottoman Empire,[16] as well as in leading the resistance to the Russian conquest of the Caucasus.[17] The Naqshbandiyya regards itself as the most orthodox and

---

[13] Muhammad Hisham Kabbani, *The Naqshbandi Sufi Way: History and Guidebook of the Saints of the Golden Chain* (Chicago, IL: Islamic Supreme Council of America, 1995), pp. 375–408; 'Adnan Muhammad al-Qabbani, *al-Futuhat al-haqqaniyya fi manaqib ajilla' al-silsila al-dhahabiyya li'l-tariqa al-Naqshbandiyya al-'aliyya* (n.p, n.d.), pp. 326–47. See also the brotherhood's website at: http://www.naqshbandi.org.

[14] The page numbers in the text that follows refer to Kabbani's work.

[15] For the history of the brotherhood, see Itzchak Weismann, *The Naqshbandiyya: Orthodoxy and Activism in a Worldwide Sufi Tradition* (London and New York: Routledge, 2007). See also Hamid Algar, 'A Brief History of the Naqshbandi Order', in Marc Gaborieau, Alexandre Popovic and Thierry Zarcone (eds), *Naqshbandis: cheminements et situation actuelle d'un ordre mystique musulman* (Istanbul and Paris: ISIS, 1990), pp. 3–44.

[16] Butrus Abu-Manneh, *Studies on Islam and the Ottoman Empire in the 19th Century (1826–1876)* (Istanbul: ISIS, 2001).

[17] Moshe Gammer, *Muslim Resistance to the Tsar: Shamil and the Conquest of Chechnia and Daghestan* (London: Frank Cass, 1994); Anna Zelkina, *In Quest for God and Freedom: The Sufi Response to the Russian Advance in the North Caucasus* (London: Hurst, 2000).

activist of the Sufi brotherhoods. Its distinctive features include subordination of the *tariqa* (the mystical path) to the *shari'a* (divine Law); a silent form of *dhikr* (recollecting God's name, the mystical rite), which shuns unlawful dance and music; a *silsila* (spiritual lineage) that returns to Abu Bakr, the first Caliph and immediate successor of the Prophet; and the principle of *khalvat dar anjuman* (solitude in the crowd), which encourages active involvement in the affairs of society and state.[18]

Nazim's principal master in the Naqshbandi–Khalidi brotherhood was Shaykh Abdallah Faiz al-Daghestani (1891–1973). Abdallah left the Caucasus as a boy with his family and when he grew up was initiated into the Naqshbandi path in Turkey. After his master's death in 1936 he moved to Damascus, where he spent the rest of his life.[19] Nazim relates a vision he had after graduation from the university which directed him to this specific spiritual master. A prolonged journey in wartime Syria took him in 1945 to Shaykh Abdallah, who initiated him in one night and sent him back to spread the path in his homeland Cyprus (pp. 379–81). Seven years later, in 1952, Nazim returned to live beside his master in Damascus, from where he was regularly sent to establish communities of followers throughout Syria and Lebanon (p. 385).

Shaykh Nazim began to extend his activities to the West with a visit to London in 1974, a year after Abdallah al-Daghestani's death. He was warmly welcomed by the English mystic John Bennett, who had visited Abdallah in Damascus in 1955 and heard from him that a great messenger of God would soon come to the West.[20] Nazim made it his habit to spend Ramadan in the British capital, and then return across Europe to guide disciples and give lectures at various spiritual centres. From 1978 he added a three- to four-month stay in Turkey to his annual travels, where he became involved in local affairs and claimed to be the Sufi shaykh of the late President Turgut Özal. In 1986 he undertook an extensive journey to South and Southeast Asia, from Pakistan and India to Malaysia and Brunei, and from 1991 he began to regularly visit the United States, leaving behind Hisham Kabbani to manage his affairs. Of particular symbolic value were Nazim's visits in 1993 to Bukhara, the birthplace of the Naqshbandiyya, shortly after Uzbekistan's independence (pp. 387, 396), and in 1997 to Daghestan, the original homeland of his master.

---

[18]   Weismann, *Naqshbandiyya*, pp. 9–13.
[19]   On Abdallah al-Daghestani, see Kabbani, pp. 347–73.
[20]   Available at: http://www.duversity.org/institute_2.htm (accessed 25 July 2010). See also, Andrew Rawlinson, 'A History of Western Sufism', *Diskus* 1 (1993): p. 63.

Despite his advanced age, Shaykh Nazim is constantly on the move. According to his hagiographer:

> His life is always intensely active. He is a traveler in God's way, never staying home, always moving from one place to another. One day he is in the East and the next he is in the West. One day he is in the North and the next he is in the South. You do not know where he will be from one day to the next. (p. 408)

Sufis have often migrated from one place to another, either in search of spiritual knowledge or out of necessity. Shaykh Abdallah, as we have seen, was no exception. He was forced to leave his country twice, once in 1890, when his family escaped Russian rule in Daghestan, and then in 1938, when he emigrated from Turkey after it had adopted secularisation and outlawed the Sufi brotherhoods. Nazim's movement is different. He has no need for a territorial base, as the whole world is open to him. His house in Cyprus is merely a place of rest between his constant travels, far less important for his global mission than London, Istanbul or Washington. Shaykh Nazim is a global wayfarer on perpetual departure.

Networking into a Virtual Community

The growing attention to the Haqqaniyya since the 1980s has produced a number of studies on local communities of the brotherhood. The earliest fieldwork was carried out in Lebanon, whereas most subsequent studies have focused on the Western settings of Britain and the United States. Taken together, they allow us to examine the specific operation of each local community, the evolution of the *tariqa* as a whole and, most importantly from our point of view, the overall structure of its global networking.

The Tripoli branch of the Haqqaniyya began to form in 1975, when Shaykh Nazim's visits to the city were regularised. Daphne Habibis, who studied this community five years later,[21] maintained that it actually existed only when the Shaykh was present: in the periods of his absence many failed to attend even the weekly *dhikr*. Nazim's following in Tripoli consisted of two main groups – the marginalised lower classes, which exhibited the conventional attitude of humility and reverence to the master, and a segment of the old notability,

---

[21]   Daphne Habibis, 'Change and Continuity: A Sufi Order in Contemporary Lebanon', *Social Analysis* 31 (1992): pp. 44–78.

which though partly westernised sought the spiritual blessing of a holy man. All disciples were male. The principal means of recruitment to the brotherhood was Nazim's charismatic attraction. It was enacted through his piety and exemplary behaviour, and augmented by his apocalyptic prophecies. When in Tripoli he spent the bulk of his time with his disciples, normally through the Naqshbandi practice of *sohbet* – informal discussion with the shaykh. The Naqshbandi tradition of independence from formal centres and rituals helped the Tripoli community to continue its gatherings when the Muslim Brothers' revolt in Syria brought the wrath of the government upon all Sunni groups.

Habibis explains the highly flexible and fluid structure of the Haqqaniyya in Tripoli as characteristic of many traditional Sufi brotherhoods, which operate as loose networks and associations rather than formal groups. Still, in a clear departure from old practices, at his master's instigation Shaykh Nazim constantly travelled around in search of new disciples instead of waiting for them to come to his centre (*tekke*).[22] Habibis is more to the point when she describes the brotherhood as a transitional stage in the transformation of Sufism from an organic part of traditional society to a private inner theosophy which provides a sense of location in the cosmos. The Haqqaniyya was not only a new religious movement offering a solution to the existential wilderness of modern society, however; for its upper-class followers it was also the means to connect to a fledging transnational religious network.

The hub of this transnational network is London. Tayfun Atay, who studied the Haqqani community in the city in the early 1990s,[23] noted that it consists of two diasporas: one is Turks, Shaykh Nazim's first followers in Britain, and South Asians, who comprise the majority of his following; the other is Western converts, who are mostly British but also include other European nationals and Americans. These groups are separated and the differences between them are epitomised in the ways they perform the *dhikr*. The Turkish disciples (*murids*) gather for a sober ritual in the brotherhood's centre in the north of the city and the South Asians hold more enthusiastic meetings at their private homes, while the Westerners conduct open ceremonies that present Sufism to the British public and promote interfaith dialogue. In the latter, women are allowed to

---

[22]   'Abdallah's inspiration for this departure from traditional ways of acquiring disciples may have come from Abu al-Nasr Khalaf, the Naqshbandi master of Homs, who is responsible for the wide spread of the brotherhood throughout northern Syria. See Itzchak Weismann, 'The Politics of Popular Islam: Sufis, Salafis, and Muslim Brothers in Twentieth Century Hamah', *International Journal of Middle East Studies* 37 (2005): pp. 39–58.

[23]   See Tayfun Atay, *Naqshbandi Sufis in a Western Setting* (DPhil thesis, University of London [SOAS], 1995).

participate together with men. Nazim's discourse likewise varies according to which group he attends: to the Turks he talks about the glorious history and current politics of the Ottoman Empire and Turkey, with the South Asians he dwells on the spiritual powers of the saints, and to the Westerners he lectures about the deficiencies of modern life and the need for spirituality.[24]

The class structure of the Haqqani community in London reproduces the duality we observed in Lebanon since the Turks and South Asians normally belong to the working and lower middle classes, while Westerners are typically well educated and some even have an aristocratic background.[25] Just as in Tripoli, though on a larger scale, the brotherhood may be said to exist only when Shaykh Nazim is present. When he arrives at Ramadan the local groups come together, followers from all over the world flock to the city to be with him, and the more educated and affluent Turkish and South Asian disciples also become active. At this time the transnational character of the brotherhood is most visible. Far more than in Tripoli, the Shaykh's appeal to Westerners relies on his charming personality as well as an attitude of tolerance and flexibility toward other religions and creeds. Endorsing the liberal doctrine of free choice, he asserts that every person must take the decision to accept Islam by himself.

Shaykh Nazim's critique of modernity notwithstanding, he professes to have adapted to the Western setting and allows the use of technology, including video and tape recordings of his own speeches. Concomitantly, he has drawn closer to the New Age culture of spirituality and self-fulfilment. Following a visit in 1999 to Glastonbury, the centre of alternative spirituality in Britain, Nazim established there a Sufi community and charity shop which holds weekly *dhikr*s and uses the vocabulary of 'energies' and 'light' rather than Islamic language.[26] On the other hand, the Shaykh constantly refers to the danger of 'Wahhbism', by which he means all forms of worldwide Islamism. He describes it as the archenemy of Sufism, a disgrace to the Muslims and the cause of the militant image that is now associated with Islam in the West. These are all accompanied by the further elaboration of his apocalyptic vision.

---

[24]   For similar divisions in Birmingham and Sheffield, see Jørgen S. Nielsen, Mustafa Draper and Galina Yemelianova, 'Transnational Sufism: The Haqqaniyya', in Malik and Hinnels, pp. 105–6.

[25]   For a study of a British group of Shaykh Nazim's disciples who belong to the lower classes, see Ali Köse, *Conversion to Islam: A Study of Native British Converts* (London and New York: Kegan Paul International, 1996), pp. 157–75.

[26]   Ian K.B. Draper, 'From Celts to Kaaba: Sufism in Glastonbury', in David Westerlund (ed.), *Sufism in Europe and North America* (London and New York: Routledge, 2004), pp. 144–56.

The global potential of the Haqqaniyya came to fruition after the brotherhood was transplanted to the United States. Annabelle Böttcher, author of a preliminary study on the American community in 2000,[27] claims that Hisham Kabbani, Nazim's 'deputy in the western hemisphere', deviated from the characteristically discreet approach of his master by adopting modern capitalistic marketing strategies and by making ample use of the media. Kabbani, who like Shaykh Nazim combined Islamic studies with modern sciences, was able to establish in a short time 23 Sufi centres throughout North America, with a convention centre on farmland in Fenton, Michigan, and a lobbying office in Washington, DC. The various websites of the brotherhood are dedicated to the diffusion of Islamic and Sufi teachings among Muslims and non-Muslims, the promotion of peace and tolerance, and the selling of books, videos, rosaries and perfumes. The Haqqaniyya became known to the general public in the USA after Kabbani appeared before the State Department to testify against 'Wahhabi' preaching in American mosques.

A subsequent study by David Damrel[28] sought to interpret the shape and trajectory of the Haqqaniyya in North America in the context of the interface between the dynamics of its multiple Muslim communities and the general interest in New Age spirituality. The Haqqani sources themselves explain the introduction of the brotherhood into America as part of Shaykh Nazim's 'foreseeing of the great spiritual hunger of people in the Western Hemisphere'. Subsequently Kabbani strove to establish his flagship organisation, The Islamic Supreme Council of America, as the representative voice of American Muslim sentiment. The two key points of its agenda have been to impart religious education to Muslims who are ignorant of their faith and to present Islam as a peaceful and tolerant religion to non-Muslims who hold a bad opinion of it. The Haqqani endeavour to educate American Muslims was seriously undermined after Kabbani declared in his testimony to the State Department that 80 per cent of them are affected by 'Wahhabi' extremism. As a result, the brotherhood was boycotted and slandered by most other Muslim organisations in the USA. The Haqqaniyya was much more successful in its appeal to the non-Muslim spiritually oriented segments of the American society, and most of its following today are converts.

Damrel is right to attribute the success of the Haqqaniyya in North America to its extensive use of the internet. Like his master, Kabbani travels almost

---

[27]   Annabelle Böttcher, 'The Naqshbandiyya in the United States', http://www. naqshbandi.net.

[28]   David Damrel, 'Aspects of the Naqshbandi-Haqqani Order in North America', in Malik and Hinnels, pp. 115–26.

constantly to the centres of the brotherhood throughout the United States and abroad. Reaching further, however, are the 'live' prayers and sermons streamed from its sites during Ramadan and on the Prophet's birthday, and the information they provide on Nazim's and Kabbani's whereabouts, which allows all who are interested to take part in this virtual religious community and to be with their virtual shaykh whenever they like. Nazim's critiques of consumerism and environmental degradation, his ecumenical approach to other religious traditions, the relatively high public status he now offers to women and, last but not least, his apocalyptic prophecies find resonance among broader sections of the New Age culture. Yet these are by no means confined to the American arena. Through the internet, Shaykh Nazim's charisma, messages and rituals are also being carried to his followers and the New Age community at large in Western Europe, the Middle East, South and Southeast Asia, and all corners of the globe.

Reflecting on the transnational character of the Haqqani Sufi community, Nielsen et al. conclude that it is surprisingly traditional and only marginally constructed around migration. Like *tariqa*s of old, the Haqqaniyya is an aggregate of a variety of local groups held together by certain shared teachings and rituals and by adherence to a commonly acknowledged Shaykh. Unlike other contemporary transnational communities, it generates little movement, normally to Shaykh Nazim's base in Cyprus or in Europe and the USA.[29] But this is only one side of the coin. The Haqqani network has shown a remarkable flexibility in its adaptation to the transnational spiritual market along with stern objection to the equally transnational Islamist trend. It has also reproduced within its ranks the glocalised class polarisation between Western spiritual seekers, who normally are physically and virtually free to move around the globe, and indigenous and migrant Muslims, who typically remain fettered to their place. The Haqqani brotherhood has thus become part of the global New Age movement.

Geospirituality and the End of Days

Muslim apocalyptic expectations have witnessed a new efflorescence in the past few decades as part of the contemporary resurgence of Islam. Reacting to the defeat in the Six Day War in 1967 and subsequent disastrous events, the new apocalyptic writers have relied on the classical descriptions of the

---

[29]   Nielsen et al., 'Transnational Sufism', p. 113.

end of days,[30] but have departed from the ulama's traditional conventions by relating their scenarios to current political events and natural calamities, assimilating anti-Semitic conspiracy theories and using evangelical exegeses of the Bible.[31] This ferment materialised on the first day of the Muslim fifteenth century (November 1979) when a group of Saudi dissidents, who claimed to have the Mahdi among them, stormed the Grand Mosque in Mecca.[32] Nazim al-Haqqani's messianic vision is part of this literature. However, he is unique among the Mahdists, who are usually sympathetic to the Islamic fundamentalist agenda and oppose the mystical aspect of Islam.

Belief in the imminent appearance of the Mahdi and the last days has been a constant feature in Nazim's preaching. Like everything else, he attributes his eschatological prophecies to his shaykh, Abdallah al-Daghestani, who is also supposed to appear at the appointed time beside the Mahdi; in fact, the Mahdi himself and his entire entourage will belong to the Naqshbandi brotherhood.[33] The available sources allow us to follow the development of Nazim's apocalyptic teaching from 1975, shortly after his global mission was established. In addition to the aforementioned fieldwork in Lebanon in 1980 and 1981, they include a collection of the Shaykh's talks on the subject in Switzerland and England in 1985–1986, various reports on his prophecies around the Christian millennium and a work published by Hisham Kabbani in 2002 concerning Armageddon.

The basic components of Nazim al-Haqqani's apocalyptic mythology were already in place when Habibis studied his community in Tripoli.[34] Shaykh Nazim claimed to be in spiritual contact with the Mahdi, who was living in solitude in a cave in the Rub' al-Khali desert in Arabia, and predicted that he would appear 'this year' or 'next year' to fulfil the prophecies contained in the hadith. The final sign heralding his appearance will be, in an echo of the Cold War, a communist *coup d'etat* in Turkey that will lead through Russian and American intervention to a nuclear Third World War in which six out of seven people will perish. After 90 days the Mahdi and his supporters will land in Qadam, Syria, and usher in a new era of supernatural events, including a miraculous end to the war

---

[30]   For an overview, see David Cook, *Studies in Muslim Apocalyptic* (Princeton, NJ: Princeton University Press, 2002).

[31]   Cook, *Contemporary Literature*, pp. 13–15.

[32]   Furnish, *Holiest Wars*, pp. 60–62.

[33]   Nazim Adil Al-Haqqani An-Naqshband (*sic*), *Mercy Ocean: The Teachings of Mevlana Sheikh Abdullah Ad-Daghistani, Book Two* (n.p., 1980), pp. 198–9.

[34]   Daphne Habibis, 'Millenarianism and Mahdism in Lebanon', *Archives Européenes de Sociologie*, 30 (1989): pp. 221–40.

by stopping the weapons – a triumph over Western materialism. At that time Nazim himself will make the call to prayer in three places at once, conveying his global pretensions: Nelson's column in London, the Statue of Liberty in New York and the Kremlin in Moscow.

After that the Mahdi will travel to Istanbul. Dajjal (the anti-Christ), who is now chained on an island, will appear in eastern Persia. He will conquer the entire world, except for Mecca, Medina and Damascus, while his followers – the Jews and all deniers of God – will assemble in Israel. Contrary to other contemporary apocalyptic writers, though, Shaykh Nazim contends that the Mahdi's camp will consist of believers of all religions, not only Muslims. Then, Jesus will descend on the Umayyad Mosque in Damascus, kill Dajjal and lead a war to exterminate all unbelievers. The *jinn* (spiritual beings) will cleanse the earth of radioactivity and pestilence, and a 40-year period of peace and goodness will ensue under the successive rule of the Mahdi and Jesus. But unbelief will reappear to be followed by the signs presaging the Day of Judgement: the flooding of Egypt and Cyprus, the eruption of a volcano in Turkey and the war of Gog and Magog that will destroy everything. God will then send down a regenerative rain, life will be restored and, when the angel Israfil blows his horn, all humanity will rise from their graves to stand before their Lord.

For his Lebanese followers, the main appeal of Shaykh Nazim's apocalyptic myth lay in explaining the agonising events of the civil war as part of the turmoil anticipating the coming of the Mahdi, and in the hope it gave that salvation was near. Nazim himself saw it in broader terms. To him the end of days promised to dissolve the two major forces that threatened religious belief in the age of modernity: atheist Communism and the materialist West.

Next time we meet Shaykh Nazim's apocalyptic vision is in the mid 1980s in the completely different atmosphere of the Western European spiritual communities. It was actually his hosts in Switzerland who raised the issue.[35] The Shaykh took the opportunity to update the time of the end of days and consciously referred to the Great War by the Christian term 'Armageddon', promising that the West will be victorious and the East will vanish. It would be at the same time a battle between good and evil, in which only God's deniers, the cruel and the envious will perish.[36] In these upcoming events Jesus receives a special role, which mirrors Nazim's disaffection with the (post)modern disorder along with the pursuance of materialistic goals and worldly pleasures.

---

[35]   Muhammd Nazim Adil al-Haqqani al-Naqshbandi, *Mystical Secrets of the Last Days* (Los Altos CA: The Haqqani Islamic Trust for New Muslims, 1994), pp. 21–32.

[36]   Ibid., pp. 53–4, 103–6.

(H)e is coming and he is going to be amongst people like a judge to make everything clear because before he comes everything is mixed up. Truth mixed up with untruth, goodness with evil, believers and unbelievers, dirt with purity. Now that is the case with the whole world, with the Christians, with the Jews, with the Muslims. Everything is mixed up with everything. When he comes, he will put everything in place.[37]

In another talk in Cambridge,[38] Shaykh Nazim maintained that two hindrances were still to be faced before the appearance of the Mahdi, which was now calculated to take place in 1988 when Ramadan begins on Saturday and Israel reaches the age of 40. One was the Soviet invasion of Afghanistan, from where the Russians, as he called them, would continue to Pakistan and Turkey. The second was World War III, which would break out between the Russian armies advancing from the valleys of northern Syria and the American forces stationed in Adana. When the Mahdi appeared, he would use his miraculous powers to make all technology stop functioning. By the mid 1980s Nazim had thus chosen to side with the West, despite its postmodern aberrations, while seeking common ground with Christian apocalyptic prophecies in general and worldwide New Age spirituality in particular.

The Haqqani apocalyptic myth continued to evolve in the 1990s in close relation to worldwide events and with increasing resort to New Age content and language, including the calculation of the last days in the Gregorian rather than the *hijri* calendar. Among the events were the collapse of the Soviet Union, the Gulf War and, most significantly, the advent of the Christian millennium.[39] At the same time, the 'Wahhabi' threat to traditional Islam, and particularly to its Sufi aspect, began to loom large on Shaykh Nazim's eschatological horizon. One of its early expressions was the astounding statement made by Shaykh Hisham that:

Grand Sheikh [Nazim] said that ninety per cent of the Western (European) countries will believe in the Mahdi. Because their hearts are pure and clean. But many of the Muslim countries, most of whom are Arabs, will deny him. Particularly Arabs, the Wahhabis, because of jealousy in their hearts. When the

---

[37]   Ibid., p. 22

[38]   Ibid., pp. 125–9.

[39]   On the Christian millennium in contemporary Muslim apocalyptic literature, see Cook, *Contemporary Literature*, pp. 84–97.

Mahdi comes, he will cut the heads of 7000 Wahhabi scholars. When the Mahdi appears, all Wahhabis are going to tremble.[40]

Shaykh Nazim was confident that the war of the last days would break out before 2000 and that 'the twenty-first century will oppose everything which belongs to the satanic kingdom. It will be destroyed and the heavenly Kingdom will be founded and established'.[41] However, unlike other apocalyptic prophecies of the imminent downfall of the hated America, in the Haqqani scheme the USA will impose global peace before the hour comes. As the millennium approached there were reports of disciples going to Damascus or Lebanon to anticipate the Mahdi, while others took shelter in safe houses in Britain. As nothing happened many followers became disoriented, but the general explanation was that the Shaykh's solicitude on behalf of humanity brought about postponement.[42]

The various elements of the Haqqani apocalyptic myth were assembled in the form of a book published in 2002. Addressed to Western audiences, the book sought to establish the credibility of the Qur'an and *hadith* prophecies of the last days and their alleged prediction of contemporary scientific discoveries.[43] On this basis, Kabbani proceeds to enumerate the signs of the approach of the hour. Some of these signs relate to the imitation of the ways of the unbelievers with bad effects, such as the dissolution of the family, provocative dressing of women and the watching of obscene talk shows on television. Others are about Muslim regimes, most of which are tyrannical and engaged in widespread torture and human rights abuses, and yet others concern religious malpractices such as the issuing of unauthorised *fatwas* on the internet.[44]

The gravest affliction of all, however, is the rise of the Wahhabi–Salafi trend, which has turned religion upside down. At this point, Kabbani's idiom becomes specifically Islamic. The 'Wahhabis' belittle Prophet Muhammad as if he were a mere postman, charge Muslims with *kufr* (unbelief) and *bid'a* (unlawful innovation) according to their misguided opinion, and disdain the traditional system of Islamic knowledge and authorisation.[45] With the advent of Armageddon there will nothing left to be done. The Muslim should better

---

[40] Hisham Kabbani, 'The Peckham Mosque in London, 24 March 1992', cited in Atay, *Naqshbandi Sufis*, p. 216.

[41] Nazim al-Haqqani, *Secret Desires* (London: Zero Publications, 1996), p. 116.

[42] Nielsen et al., 'Transnational Sufism', 106–7.

[43] Hisham Kabbani, *The Approach of Armageddon? An Islamic Perspective* (Washington, DC: Islamic Supreme Council of America, 2002), pp. 37–86.

[44] Ibid., pp. 87–143.

[45] Ibid., pp. 147–80.

sit at home and look after his family, increase his worship and not interfere in religious debates or in politics.[46] Salvation will ultimately come from the West. Westerners, who are gaining knowledge of Islam through books, television and the internet, will convert in droves and bring with them their spirit of calm and patience in the face of tribulation, resourcefulness in solving problems, support of the needy and objection to tyranny.[47]

Studies of Haqqani's apocalyptic vision have tended to focus on its role in his self-declared spiritual mission to the West. Damrel notes that although the symbols used have an Islamic provenance, they are unmistakably familiar to many Western audiences and thus help the Haqqani shaykhs emphasise how Islam and Islamic spirituality are vital to the lives of non-Muslims.[48] Ron Geaves similarly maintains that by referring to the year 2000 Nazim and Hisham invited a generation of European and North American spiritual seekers to discover Islam.[49] Yet, the underlining motivation behind Shaykh Nazim's approach to the New Age culture, and his growing reliance on the West despite its materialist and promiscuous culture, is the militant Islamist threat. His apocalyptic myth thus amounts to a call to the foremost Western powers and especially the USA to join hands with the spiritual forces of Sufism in a common struggle against worldwide 'Wahhabism' and establish, for the eternal time being, a new (age) global order.

Conclusion

The Haqqani apocalyptic–messianic myth articulates the paradoxes inherent in the endeavour to pursue the Sufi tradition in a globalising world. Like other contemporary apocalyptic writers, Shaykh Nazim's references to the end of days reflect a deep frustration with the present condition of Islam in general and its mystical aspect in particular. Acutely sensitive to the formidable modern materialist challenge and to the more immediate militant Islamist threat, this Sufi shaykh has found solace in imagining their miraculous disappearance. As an heir to the activist Naqshbandi tradition, however, Shaykh Nazim was not content with idly waiting for the appearance of the Mahdi. Taking his cue

---

[46]   Ibid., pp. 190–91, 275–8.

[47]   Ibid., pp. 209–16.

[48]   David Damrel, 'A Sufi Apocalypse', *ISIM Newsletter* 4 (1999): pp. 1–4.

[49]   Ron Geaves, 'The Haqqani Naqshbandis: A Study of Apocalyptic Millenialism within Islam', in Stanley E. Porter, Michael A. Hayes and David Tumbs (eds), *Faith in the Millennium* (Sheffield: Sheffield Academic Press, 2001), pp. 215–31.

from his master, Abdallah al-Daghestani, and later following the advice of his foremost deputy, Hisham Kabbani, he has exploited apparently more than any other contemporary Sufi shaykh the new opportunities offered by the present revolution in communications. The Haqqaniyya was established between the local and the global through Shaykh Nazim's constant travel both in the East and the West and through the internet. This has turned him into a global wayfarer and his brotherhood into a virtual network of communities.

Integration into the global cultural economy did not leave the Haqqani apocalypse intact. Shaykh Nazim's mingling with western New Age groups and spiritual seekers who share his revulsion at modern materialist civilisation brought in its wake a conscious effort to explain the Muslim vision of the last days through Christian and universal symbols of the millennium. His growing apprehension at the rising tide of militant Islamism lies behind the unprecedentedly positive role he gives in the upcoming events to the USA and the West in general at the expanse of the Arab and Muslim worlds. As a traditional Muslim Sufi shaykh, Nazim al-Haqqani has remained rooted in the myth of eternal return to the archetypal sites and past heroes of Islam and of his own Naqshbandi brotherhood. But, by emptying the space and time of this myth through constant travelling and the use of the universal calendar, and disembedding it through the erection of a network of virtual communities, Nazim's ever-shifting and ever-expanding vision of the end of days also marks his adoption of an alternative global myth of perpetual departure.

Chapter 7

Shaykh Osama Bin Laden: An Evolving Global Myth

Anne Birgitta Nilsen

Until his death in 2011, Osama Bin Laden was a prominent figure in the world media. Portrayals of him have differed considerably, however, and these differences form the background to my interest in the al-Qaeda leader. They first came to my attention in the spring of 2006, when a text attributed to Bin Laden received particular attention in the Norwegian media. The text contained comments on the publication in Denmark of caricatures of the Prophet Muhammad, and the newspaper articles often presented quotations from the text. Puzzlingly, most of the quotations did not seem to make much sense, and were of poor rhetorical quality. Subsequent study of the original Arabic texts, transcribed and published on al-Jazeera's pan-Arab news website, gave a very different picture, as parts of some of these texts seemed remarkably eloquent,[1] a fact that has also been noted by others.[2] Interestingly, similar findings as to the portrayal of Bin Laden have been discussed by Bruce Lincoln in his studies of American media.[3] These constructions of realities seem to reflect the war on terror,[4] and support Steve

---

[1] Anne Birgitta Nilsen, 'Osama bin Ladens Slagkraft', *Babylon Nordisk Tidsskrift for Midtøstenstudier*, 2 (2008): pp. 40–49; *idem*, 'Osama bin Ladens Retorikk', *Rhetorica Scandinavica*, 51 (2009): pp. 6–24.

[2] See, for example, Abdel Bari Atwan, *The Secret History of al-Qa'ida* (London: Saqi, 2006); Peter L. Bergen, *The Osama bin Laden I Know: An Oral History of al Qaeda's Leader* (New York: Free Press, 2006); Osama bin Laden and Randall B. Hamud, *Osama bin Laden: America's Enemy in His Own Words* (San Diego, CA: Nadeem, 2005); Osama bin Laden and Bruce Lawrence, *Messages to the World: The Statements of Osama Bin Laden* (London: Verso, 2005); Bruce Lincoln, *Holy Terrors: Thinking about Religion after September 11* (Chicago, IL: University of Chicago Press, 2003); Michael Scheuer, *Through Our Enemies' Eyes: Osama bin Laden, Radical Islam, and the Future of America* (rev. edn, Washington, DC: Potomac Books, 2006).

[3] Lincoln, *Holy Terrors*.

[4] Anne Birgitta Nilsen, 'Osama bin Ladens Skjulte Slagkraft', *Norsk Medietidsskrift*, 4 (2007), pp. 298–312.

Tatham's observations on the media's role in times of crisis.[5] Tatham observes that the media 'often become unwitting participants in the sometimes shadowy world of the "Information Campaign" – an intellectual war embracing a series of varying disciplines, waged by governments to win over "hearts and minds" and to demoralise the enemy'.[6] In other words, information about the adversary in the war on terror is withheld from the public. Such censorship not only represents a problem for democracy, but may skew public perceptions of the enemy in a way that may escalate the war on terror. This is not only because consumers of Western media will be left with a biased picture of Bin Laden, but – and this matters more – the censorship also creates a perception among these consumers that Bin Laden's audience is happy to listen to nonsense and is appreciative of poor rhetoric.

As some of the texts attributed to Bin Laden are eloquent they may have an impact. Their potential power lies in their capacity to construct a convincing worldview for his audience and to induce in it an us–them perspective, in which the 'crusaders', represented by the USA and its allies, are attacking the Muslims militarily, economically and culturally. Since some of the texts are rhetorically of high quality, their effect may be convincing, particularly since many of them are directed towards a wide audience. The texts reveal an understanding of the importance of history, and an ability to exploit the memories of a common past by referring to Islamic symbols and myths and re-establishing them in new contexts. Many of the myths, symbols and memories in the texts are of such importance to Muslims that they are potentially extremely emotive, and it is this latter effect that Bin Laden has exploited as he attempts to persuade people of his worldview. This does not mean that al-Qaeda gained many more adherents among the general Muslim population, but possibly that its already convinced adherents were motivated to action. For others the texts may still have had the effect of strengthening the us–them image, thus preparing the ground for a broader acceptance of future actions under the auspices of al-Qaeda.

We do not know the extent to which Osama Bin Laden participated in the production of any of the texts attributed to him – if, indeed, he has done so at all. In the last years before his death it was not even known whether he was still alive, although some viewed every new audio recording with a resemblance to his voice that appeared on the internet as a sign of his survival. Others doubted that he was alive, however, since no convincing live video of him had appeared since 2004. What is beyond doubt is that many people had an interest in keeping

---

[5]   Steve Tatham, *Losing Arab Hearts and Minds: The Coalition, Al-Jazeera and Muslim Public Opinion* (London: Hurst, 2006).

[6]   Ibid., p. 7.

Bin Laden alive – al-Qaeda was in need of a charismatic leader, and the war on terror needed an identifiable enemy.

Whether or not Bin Laden is alive is not in my view particularly relevant when attempting to understand his popularity, since in any event we and his intended audience have had no access to him in person. His audience encountered the discursive Bin Laden, the text-internal Bin Laden, the representations of Bin Laden as a textual participator, as he appeared in the different media. Bin Laden may have been the world's most wanted man, and we have had no means of finding out to what extent the text-internal Bin Laden matches the text-external or the empirically observed Bin Laden. Besides, as argued below, Bin Laden's power in his last years was more in his role as a symbol of resistance and a historical figure than as an actual executive leader.

Since 2002, al-Qaeda's media organisation al-Sahab has played an important role in the staging of Bin Laden through its various productions. We have no information about the people behind it: the only evidence of the existence of the organisation is its logo, clearly visible on all its productions. Without knowing who controls the production of texts attributed to Bin Laden, or even knowing whether he has been involved at all, it makes no sense to describe the texts, as is common in the media, as the speeches or messages of Bin Laden. A better description would be 'texts attributed to Osama Bin Laden'; the agent acting in these texts, orally and/or visually, is a *discursive* Bin Laden. This chapter attempts to illuminate the eloquence of this discursive figure, as well as the ways in which his persona is staged, since an important factor for understanding his rhetoric is the progression of his verbal and visual rhetorical style. Until approximately 2004 Bin Laden was staged as a *mujahid* (a holy warrior), as also argued by Bruce Lincoln,[7] while from 2004 until 2006–07 he appeared as a statesman, also discussed by Peter Bergen.[8] This chapter will agree with Lincoln and Bergen, but argue that subsequently Bin Laden was appearing as a mythical hero, with more of a symbolic function referring to the Muslim past and collective memory. The concept of myth in this article refers to stories of human heroes of the past. The function of these myths is to provide an explanation for current realities by locating the present in the historical continuum and to mobilise for action.[9] Interestingly these myths about Bin Laden are not only for local purposes within al-Qaeda, but are directed towards a broad audience where Bin Laden is staged, through the internet, as a global leader and mythical hero for all

---

[7]   Lincoln, *Holy Terrors*.
[8]   Bergen, *The Osama bin Laden I Know*.
[9]   Emmanuel Sivan, *Arab Political Myths* (Tel Aviv: Am Oved, 1988).

Muslims. The Bin Laden productions have even, in the last few years, appeared with subtitles in English as well as in other languages. Globalisation in this chapter is therefore about the increasing interconnectedness of the world, 'the intensification of worldwide social relations in such a way that local happenings are shaped by events occurring many miles away and vice versa'.[10]

Following general trends in the media, Bin Laden's communications have become increasingly multi-modal in format, exploiting different verbal as well as visual devices in conveying the message. From the audio tapes of the mid 1990s and very early twenty-first century, the communications have developed video recordings to their current form of animated collages with audio commentary. These three stages are not only characterised by the use of different technologies, however, but also by the staging of Bin Laden: first as a *mujahid*, secondly as a scholarly statesman and finally as a mythical hero. The discursive constructions of Bin Laden are important because the character of the speaker – his *ethos*, in rhetorical terms – may also act as a device in the process of persuasion, and are certainly an important aspect of his eloquence and charisma. This chapter will first introduce the content and persuasive goals of the texts, and then present an analysis of the different representations of Bin Laden.

The Political Rhetoric

From the mid 1990s onwards the media regularly reported on texts attributed to Osama Bin Laden. The first text to really catch their attention was the letter in 1996 in which, apparently writing from a cave in the mountains of Afghanistan, Bin Laden declared war on the USA. Randall B. Hamud, an editor of Bin Laden's texts, writes:

> On August 23, 1996, Mr. Bin Laden became an official enemy of the United States of America. On that date he signed a 'Declaration of War' against the United States. The expressed goal of the war was the expulsion of U.S. military forces from the Arabian Peninsula, the toppling of the Saudi 'apostate' regime, and the support of revolutionary Islamic movements worldwide.[11]

Much later, in a text of September 2009, Bin Laden warned the people of Europe against further cooperation with the USA, and told Europeans they would

---

10   Anthony Giddens, *The Consequences of Modernity* (Cambridge: Polity, 1990).
11   Bin Laden and Hamud, *Osama bin Laden*, p. xiv.

understand the causes of the bloody events in London and Madrid if they had seen the gruesome acts perpetrated by Europe's American ally and its helpers in Afghanistan.[12]

The most striking feature of the texts attributed to Bin Laden is that they are always relevant and up to date, discussing issues of current political interest. In a text released just before the invasion of Iraq in 2003, he says:

> We are with great interest and concern keeping watch over the Crusaders' war preparations in order to occupy a former capital of Islam, plunder the wealth of Muslims, and establish a puppet government over you that gets its cue from its masters in Washington and Tel Aviv – just like the other traitorous and puppet Arab governments – all in preparation for the creation of Greater Israel.[13]

Hamud writes:

> The United States provided tangible proof of the new Crusade on March 20, 2003, when it invaded Iraq. Whereas the West focused on the sight of Saddam Hussain's statue being toppled in downtown Iraq a few days after the invasion, the Muslim world focused on the humiliating sight of Christian soldiers occupying Baghdad, which had been the seat of the Abbasid Caliphate.[14]

As shown in the above example, the texts draw attention to political causes not only of well-known perspectives of general interest to many people, but that are also capable of arousing emotions, in this case by referring to Baghdad as a former capital of Islam, alluding to the seat of the Abbasid Caliphate and an era that is often referred to as the Islamic golden age. The Palestinian case and the war in Iraq are examples of other recurring current themes about which many have strong feelings.

In an audio recording of September 2009 Bin Laden is heard taking part in an international political discussion. He states that President Obama is powerless to stop the war in Iraq and Afghanistan and that there will be no real change in US policy during his presidency. This was a response to Obama's Cairo speech, where the President pledged a new beginning between Muslims

---

[12]   Osama bin Laden, 'Osama bin Laden's Message to Europe', 25 September 2009, at http://www.youtube.com/watch?v=NNpAAd-qy7Y, last accessed 19 February 2014.

[13]   Raymond Ibrahim, Ayman Al Zawahiri, Osama Bin Laden and Victor Davis Hanson, *The Al Qaeda Reader* (New York: Doubleday, 2007), p. 243.

[14]   Bin Laden and Hamud, *Osama bin Laden*, p. 197.

and Americans. Bin Laden's texts are typical examples of political rhetoric, arguing against other politicians – in this case the President of the USA – and again in this case, exploiting people's feelings of doubt about a new beginning. Commenting on Bin Laden's knowledge of the enemy, Faisal Devji writes that 'all his pronouncements were an exercise in intimacy. Unlike the foreign and exotic colors in which al-Qaeda is painted in the west, its founder has always spoken of his enemies in the most familiar of terms.'[15] Devji also refers to Bin Laden's comments on the American elections in 2004, writing that Bin Laden

> recognised that an American election was a global event that required global participation. So Bin Laden placed his own organisation alongside the Republicans and Democrats when he concluded his speech by appealing to the American people: 'I say to you in truth that your security lies not in the hands of Kerry, Bush or al-Qaeda. It lies in your own hands, and whichever state does not encroach upon our security thereby ensures its own'.

Many may admire Bin Laden for the political issues he has promoted, and his popularity may accordingly stem from the social and political involvement displayed in the texts. According to Abdel Bari Atwan, the editor of the London-based Arabic newspaper *al-Quds al-'Arabi*, Muslims in favour of Bin Laden feel he is a powerful person who fights their corner.[16] John Esposito says his 'messages and cause resonates with many in the Arab and Muslim worlds'.[17] Many people's attitudes harmonise in certain ways with much of the content of the texts. They are angry with the USA because of its support of authoritarian and corrupt regimes. In a text from 2003, Bin Laden says with reference to such regimes:

> And we should ask ourselves: what is the difference between a Persian Karzai and an Arab Karzai? Who was it that installed the rulers of the Gulf States? It was the Crusaders, the same people who installed the Karzai of Pakistan, who installed the Karzai of Kuwait, the Karzai of Bahrain, Qatar and others.[18]

Many people remember that the USA supported Saddam Hussain throughout the period when he carried out some of his worst atrocities, including the gassing

---

[15]   http://www.opendemocracy.net/conflict-terrorism/osama_3140.jsp, last accessed 19 February 2014.

[16]   Atwan, *Secret History*, p. 50.

[17]   John L. Esposito, *The Islamic Threat: Myth or Reality?* (3rd edn, New York: Oxford University Press, 1999), p. 278.

[18]   Bin Laden, *Messages*, p. 197.

of the Kurds. Obviously there is also anger about US support for the Israeli military occupation of Palestine, now in its 44th year. When Bin Laden states the reasons for his anger, his listeners recognise many of his arguments and the feelings these issues evoke, which may in turn allow these arguments and feelings to gain in strength. There is little sign of the ideology and concrete methods of al-Qaeda in the texts; such references usually take indirect forms – an example is this well-known quotation from 2004: 'You tried to deny us a decent life, but you cannot deny us a decent death.'[19]

Contrary to what appears to be the general belief in the West, the main goal of the texts is not in fact to persuade people into taking violent action but rather to win over a broad audience to a particular worldview, one with a distinctive us–them perspective, and, I believe, to prepare the ground for a broader acceptance of action under the auspices of al-Qaeda.

The Rhetoric of the Crusade

The rhetorical goal of the texts attributed to Bin Laden is to convince people that a crusade is taking place against Muslims, as also noted by others. The crusade is therefore a key concept in the texts whose function is to legitimise a certain worldview – that Muslims are the victims of aggressors in the form of crusaders. In this respect, the concept can be described as a signifier of ideology. According to compiler Hamud, Bin Laden cites the following specific American policies as proof of the new Crusade: support for Israel; support for the autocratic regimes of the Middle East; support for non-Muslim countries outside the Middle East which are either repressing Muslims or battling Muslim insurgencies; the stationing of American military forces in Saudi Arabia and the Gulf States; the American invasions of Afghanistan and Iraq; and exploitation of Middle East oil resources.[20]

One of al-Qaeda's most prominent ideologists, 'Umar Abd al-Hakim, alias Abu Mus'ab al-Suri,[21] whose theories may have informed the conduct of the London and Madrid attacks, describes the 'battle against terrorism' as a crusading campaign against Muslims covered under the slogan 'battle against

---

[19]   http://english.aljazeera.net/archive/2006/09/200841012647537920.html, last accessed 19 February 2014.

[20]   Bin Laden and Hamud, *Osama bin Laden*, p. 203.

[21]   Brynjar Lia, *Architect of Global Jihad: The Life of al-Qaida Strategist Abu Mus'ab al-Suri* (New York: Columbia University Press, 2008).

terror'.[22] In the texts attributed to Bin Laden, the concept is used in similar ways. In an interview with al-Jazeera journalist Tayseer Alouni, Bin Laden referred to a historical continuity, stating that the original crusade brought Richard the Lionheart from England, Louis from France and Barbarossa from Germany.[23] Used in this context, the concept provides a feeling of continuity, potentially strengthening perceptions of the evil nature of the enemy. In the same interview, Bin Laden continues by saying, in what is probably a reference to the establishment of Western forces on the Arabian peninsula in the early 1990s, that the crusading countries rushed to join in as soon as President Bush raised the cross. Subsequently, in a text from 2004, he states:

> I say that the West's occupation of our country is old, yet new, and that the confrontation and conflict between us and them started centuries ago ... There can be no dialogue with the occupiers except with weapons. If we look at the nature of the conflict between us and the West, we find that when they invaded our countries more than 2,500 years ago they did not have a sound religion or ethics.
>
> Their motive was to steal and plunder. Our ancestors in Bilad al-Sham [Syria] remained under occupation for more than ten decades. We defeated them only after the mission of our Prophet Muhammad. It was the true commitment to Islam that reshaped the Arab character.[24]

In the same text, he continues:

> The leader was Salah-al-Din [Saladin], may God bestow His mercy on him, and the approach was Islam, whose pinnacle is jihad in the cause of God. This is what we need today, and should seek to do. Islamic countries in the past century were not liberated from the Crusaders' military occupation except through jihad in the cause of God.[25]

Bin Laden's argument revolves around this key concept. All negative events are explained by reference to the crusades, probably because of the concept's potential impact as a well-known event in the history of Islam. Seen from

---

[22] Umar 'Abd al-Hakim, *Daawa al-muqaawima al-islamiyya al-aalamiyya* (*The Call for Global Islamic Resistance*), (2004), p. 4. Available at http://archive.org/stream/The-call-for-a-global-Islamic-resistance#page/n13/mode/2up, last accessed 14 February 2014.

[23] Bin Laden and Lawrence, *Messages*, p. 127.

[24] Bin Laden and Lawrence, *Messages*, p. 217.

[25] Ibid., p. 218.

an Arab perspective, the crusades are a historical trauma, as illustrated by Amin Maalouf:[26]

> The Franj had taken the holy city on Friday, the twenty-second day of the month of Sha'ban, in the year of the Hegira 492, or 15 July 1099, after a forty-day siege. The exiles still trembled when they spoke of the fall of the city: they stared into space as though they could still see the fair-haired and heavily armoured warriors spilling through the streets, swords in hand, slaughtering men, women, and children, plundering houses, sacking mosques.[27]

The trauma of the crusades was resurrected in the colonial era and again in more recent experiences with Western aggression, making it a useful concept for understanding present conflicts. Accordingly it may function as a *topos*, a general and widespread view of the West and of the relationship between the West and Muslims, and as a common point of departure for the process of convincing an audience of a certain worldview. Such common points of departure are an important factor in all rhetoric, as the process of persuasion must always be based on some initial agreement. Experienced rhetoricians will meet their audience on common ground. The crusades as common ground is visible in school textbooks in Arab schools, as all pupils in schools run by the governments of Saudi Arabia, Jordan, Syria, Lebanon, Palestine, Egypt, Libya and Tunisia are taught about them.[28] In these books the crusaders' greed for the goods and treasures of the Middle East is described, whereas the Muslims and Arabs are described as tolerant and culturally superior, in contrast to the hatred and savagery of the crusaders.[29] Crusade is a concept that is comprehensible to a large number of people sharing the same history and is probably also accepted as a means of legitimising a certain worldview. Jonathan Riley Smith says that 'the Nationalist and Islamist interpretations of crusade history help many people, moderates as well as extremists, to place the exploitation they believe they have suffered in a historical context and to satisfy their feelings of both superiority and humiliation'.[30] Through the

---

[26]   Amin Maalouf, *The Crusades Through Arab Eyes* (Cairo: American University in Cairo Press, 1983).

[27]   Maalouf, *Crusades*, p. xiv.

[28]   Matthias Determann, 'The Crusades in Arab School Textbooks', *Islam and Christian-Muslim Relations*, 19/2 (2008), p. 210.

[29]   Ibid., pp. 206–7.

[30]   Jonathan Riley-Smith, *The Crusades, Christianity, and Islam* (New York: Columbia University Press, 2008), p. 76.

effective use of language, an author can shape or form an audience's perception of reality: Bin Laden's potential power lay in the extent to which he was able to construct a certain understanding of reality for his listeners.

The political content of the texts attributed to Bin Laden typically arouses little controversy, simply because they promote values shared by many in his audience. From one perspective, the texts may be described as a kind of *epideictic* oratory, whose most important function is to strengthen the values and opinions that are being praised. According to Andreea D. Ritivoi, 'epideictic discourse relies on a particular way of constructing the past rhetorically for the purpose of forming and maintaining national identities through an allegiance to values and beliefs grounded in a shared past'.[31] In the texts attributed to Bin Laden it is, however, not a question of forming and maintaining a national identity, but rather a religious identity in the *umma*. While the values and beliefs may not currently be under direct challenge, they may be so in the future. Epideictic oratory is thus intended to prepare listeners for possible coming challenges to their attitudes and opinions, accordingly to function over the longer term and to prepare the ground for the future. The audience is being readied for later action, and made more susceptible to accepting action carried out by al-Qaeda. As we shall see, and as already indicated in the quotations above, references to symbols and myths from Islamic history and to memories of earlier experiences are essential rhetorical devices in the texts, which latter are emotive through their references to crucial issues in people's lives and history. The following discussion will focus on how the texts exploit these references, and will also attempt to explain why they are potentially so powerful, as this may help shed light on Bin Laden's popularity.

Al-Mujahid

Until 2004, the media portrayed Bin Laden as a *mujahid*. This concept (in its definite form *al-mujahid*) and jihad are often translated respectively as 'holy warrior' and 'holy war' (a defensive war). In the texts, Bin Laden emphasises that jihad is to be understood as defence, and a *mujahid* as a defender, against attacks on Muslims and Islam.

A *mujahid* is a person conducting jihad, and the representation of Bin Laden as such is a reference back to the 1980s, when he took part with other *mujahidin*

---

[31]   Andreea Deciu Ritivoi, *Paul Ricoeur: Tradition and Innovation in Rhetorical Theory* (Albany, NY: State University of New York Press, 2006), p. 97.

in combat against the Soviet army in Afghanistan. Bin Laden's participation in the Afghan resistance was an indispensable stepping stone in his rise towards leadership in the Islamic world. He apparently showed no fear of death, and frequently expressed regret at not yet being martyred like so many of his comrades in Afghanistan.[32] This feeling of religious devotion is apparent in a poem included in one of the texts from the early 1990s:

> So let me be a martyr,
> Dwelling in a high mountain pass
> Among a band of knights who,
> United in devotion to God,
> Descend to face armies.[33]

Equally important for understanding the portrayal of Bin Laden as a courageous hero is the outcome of the war in Afghanistan – the Soviet army withdrew in 1989. In the texts attributed to Bin Laden this withdrawal is described as the victory for the *mujahidin*, not only over the Soviet army, but also over the mighty Soviet empire, which was subsequently dissolved.

Another factor in understanding the potential appeal of the portrayal of Bin Laden as a *mujahid* is his family background. He grew up in one of the richest families in Saudi Arabia, and some of the admiration for him probably stems from the fact that he renounced a life of luxury to devote himself to fighting for Muslim causes and to lead a simple life on the battlefield. Atwan describes him as living without running water, electricity or a toilet because he wanted to emulate the Prophet's companions and early Muslims.[34] In the texts attributed to Bin Laden, references to Islamic history feature strongly as rhetorical devices. Hamud writes:

> Mr. Bin Laden repetitively refers to certain landmark battles fought during the early years of Islam. The first was the battle of Badr in 624. This battle was fought in Arabia against a Meccan army intent upon destroying the Prophet (PBUH) and his vastly outnumbered followers. The battle was won by the Muslims and marked the first Muslim victory over an enemy intent upon destroying Islam.[35]

---

32 Atwan, *Secret History*, p. 49.
33 Bin Laden and Lawrence, *Messages*, p. xxiii.
34 Atwan, *Secret History*, p. 53.
35 Bin Laden and Hamud, *Osama bin Laden*, p. ixi.

خاص بالجزيرة

Figure 7.1   Bin Laden and al-Zawahiri in the mountains of Afghanistan

Kepel describes footage of Bin Laden filmed in a mountainous area in Afghanistan, and shown on al-Jazeera on 7 October 2001. He suggests that visual portrayals of Bin Laden also made clear references to the early Muslims and folk memories: the entire scenario – the cave, the outfits, the exhortations – suggested that Zawahiri and Bin Laden were playing out, in full costume, the epic story of the Hijra, or Flight from Mecca, which marked the beginning of the Islamic era in 622 CE.[36] A similar scenario to that described by Kepel is shown in Figure 7.1.

Scheuer writes that Bin Laden had a substantial knowledge of Islamic history, and a strong sense that he was acting out a role in a historical process that had been under way for more than 14 centuries.[37] He also observes that Bin Laden's personality fitted the heroic model in Islamic history, where a cardinal virtue is modesty in appearance and behaviour – such history is not prone to making heroes of men who are brazen, boisterous, boastful and who seek notoriety.[38]

---

[36]   Gilles Kepel, *The War for Muslim Minds: Islam and the West* (Cambridge, MA: Belknap Press/Harvard University Press, 2004), p. 77.

[37]   Scheuer, *Through Our Enemies' Eyes*, p. 75.

[38]   Ibid., pp. 303–4.

Until 2004, the figure of Bin Laden that we encounter in the media was a humble, ascetic *mujahid* with a strong vocation. As well as humility, however, he also exudes self-confidence, declaring war on the United States, apparently from a cave in Afghanistan, just as attacks were starting in 1996 on American forces in Khubar and Riyadh. From then on the discursive Bin Laden is no longer confined to addressing Muslims on the Arab peninsula, but Muslims across the world. Calling for a boycott of Americans goods, and jihad against the 'Judeo-Crusader alliance', Bin Laden exhorts the warriors who fought in Afghanistan and Bosnia not to lay down their swords. 'Cavalry of Islam, be mounted'[39] was a request with clear historical and religious overtones.

Figure 7.2   *Al-mujahid*

The image of a *mujahid* is also found in the images accompanying articles in various media outlets reporting on the texts attributed to Bin Laden. These images are important for understanding Bin Laden's position, for images may

---

[39]   Bin Laden and Lawrence, *Messages*, p. 24.

also function as rhetorical devices. They have a potentially strong appeal, and are realistic in the sense that they may document Bin Laden's appearance, which may give the viewer a sense of seeing an objective representation of reality. Just as listeners may be affected by words that echo those of a *mujahid*, they may be affected by images reminiscent of the *mujahidin*. While verbal description can only indirectly create visual impressions, an image does so directly. Accordingly, images may have a stronger emotional appeal, making them a more important persuasive device in Bin Laden's rhetoric. Lincoln writes that Bin Laden in 2001 presented himself as a *mujahid*, seated on a prayer rug, with a Kalashnikov and Qur'an close at hand.[40] A similar image is reproduced in Figure 7.2, where Bin Laden is shown in a tent, once again with the AK47 close at hand.

There is an authentic feeling to this image – there is no impression of its having been staged in order to affect the viewer. Bin Laden does not look towards the camera, nor does he seem interested in the fact that he is being photographed. The image appears to capture the 'real' Bin Laden, content, ascetic and visionary, dressed in *mujahid* uniform and sitting on the ground in his battlefield tent with a Kalashnikov – the very symbol of resistance – resting inoffensively in the corner; here is a man who has rejected a life of luxury to dedicate himself to the Muslim cause. The image evokes associations with the victory over the Soviet army in 1989. Accordingly, the image's function may be to support Bin Laden's ethos, his character and credibility, by providing proof of his simple lifestyle and his role as a *mujahid*. Seen in a broader context, the image may also function as proof of his well-being and his ability to take action and avoid being captured, in spite of large-scale military efforts to do so.

The Statesman

Referring to a video recording of Bin Laden from October 2004, Hegghammer notes that 'Bin Laden was standing up in front of a desk against a brown background, unarmed, wearing a golden cloak and white headdress, a posture which many commentators described as statesmanlike',[41] for from 2003 Bin Laden starts to appear as a political rather than a military leader. His new role is

[40]   Lincoln, *Holy Terrors*, p. 25.
[41]   Thomas Hegghammer, *Al-Qaida Statements 2003–2004 – A Compilation of Translated Texts by Usama bin Ladin and Ayman al-Zawahiri*, FFI/RAPPORT-2005/01428, Forsvarets Forskningsinstitutt, 2005, p. 65.

as statesman, shaykh and scholarly leader, a role transition that is as clearly visible in his verbal as well as in his visual rhetoric. From 2003, Bin Laden is gradually staged more as a statesman than a *mujahid*. The first and most clear-cut portrayal of him as a statesman is, as mentioned above, in a 2004 video recording, just before the American elections. A still from this video recording is reproduced in Figure 7.3.

Figure 7.3   The shaykh

Both Bin Laden's verbal and visual rhetoric have changed. The latter is evidenced by his physical appearance and surroundings. Instead of a uniformed *mujahid* with the AK47 at his side, we see a dignified figure, apparently in a modern TV studio. Bin Laden now appears as a scholarly leader with both authority and charisma. His refined clothing has religious and political connotations, and his verbal rhetoric is suitable for a political leader. He claims that the real causes of actions are being hidden from the American people by their President and, by arguing against him personally, he positions himself implicitly as the President's counterpart, a mighty global leader, not only of al-Qaeda but of all Muslims – one who speaks on behalf of the Muslim *umma*. Atwan claims that

Bin Laden has filled the contemporary gap created by history for a strong Muslim leader to unify the *umma* in battle against the US and its allies, and to restore the Muslim world to its former glory. This is the way he is perceived by millions. Alive or dead, whether we like it or not, Bin Laden is and will remain one of the key historical figures of our times.[42]

Peter Bergen, journalist and al-Qaeda expert, has commented on Bin Laden's texts:

over the years, Bin Laden's tone becomes more forceful and self-assured. He even has made an attempt to appear statesmanlike from 2004 onwards, offering 'truces' with nations that pull out of the coalition in Iraq and, just before the U.S. presidential, speaking directly to American voters. In recent years Bin Laden has increasingly adopted the role of the Elder Statesman of Jihad.[43]

Sarcasm is also an interesting element now introduced in the texts attributed to Bin Laden, since, as Suleiman Yasir has pointed out, one of the most interesting features of the language of political conflict in the Arabic-speaking world is satire.[44] It is thus interesting to see sarcasm entering into Bin Laden's rhetoric as he takes on the role of political leader, the counterpart of the President of the United States. In a text from 2004, President Bush is compared to Saddam Hussain and referred to as a foreign thief: 'It is true that Saddam is a thief and an apostate, but the solution is not to be found in moving the government of Iraq from a local thief to a foreign one.'[45] This description of the American President might well be perceived as amusing, especially since President Bush became increasingly unpopular in the Arab world before and after the invasion of Iraq in 2003. Another example of the use of satirical language, in a text dating from 2003, also exploits people's dislike of President Bush by naming him as the pharaoh of the age:

Then when they saw the gang of criminals in the White House misrepresenting the truth, whose idiotic leader claims that we despise their way of life – although the truth that the Pharaoh of the age is hiding is that we strike them because of

---

[42] Atwan, *Secret History*, p. 251.

[43] Bergen, *The Osama bin Laden I Know*, p. 369.

[44] Yasir Suleiman, *A War of Words: Language and Conflict in the Middle East*, Cambridge Middle East Studies (Cambridge: Cambridge University Press, 2004) p. 2.

[45] Bin Laden and Lawrence, *Messages*, p. 225.

their injustice towards us in the Islamic world, especially in Palestine and Iraq, and their occupation of Saudi Arabia – the mujahidin decided to overcome this obfuscation and to bring the battle right into their heartland.[46]

Many have noted Bin Laden's references to historical heroes, whom he compares to the heroes of today, although of course this is not typical only of Bin Laden. The history of Islam is important for many Muslims, and the fact that the former presidents of Egypt, Jamal Abdel Nasser, and of Iraq, Saddam Hussain, have both compared themselves to Saladin may serve as an illustration. What is typical of Bin Laden's rhetoric, however, is the reference to war, his choice of heroes and the images he chose to represent the enemy, and also that he included an enemy in the associations he made with the past. The references to these well-known anti-heroes may have been intended to indicate knowledge and creativity and to strengthen Bin Laden's position as a leader. This is particularly true when the references have satirical features, such as when George W. Bush is referred to as the 'pharaoh of the age'. For Bin Laden's audience the concept of a pharaoh would not only allude to the building and construction of the pyramids and other impressive buildings, as well as excessive wealth, but also to tyrannical heathen leaders who were also self-styled gods. The stories of these beings are well known from the Qur'an and the stories of the Prophets (*Qisas al-anbiya*).

The Mythical Hero

After 2006 the construction of texts attributed to Bin Laden once again changed significantly, as did his portrayal. Some of the texts now had subtitles in other languages, probably indicating that they were aimed at a broader global audience. Many of the texts appeared on the internet as part of multi-modal collages and with an accompanying commentary. Bin Laden himself had a ghost-like appearance, indicating his power as an invisible but strong enemy, whose invisibility is its strength. He was portrayed as an immortal, strong leader who avoided all attempts to capture and kill him. He represented the irreproachable symbol of resistance, an invincible hero. These more recent texts might even have alluded also to Bin Laden as a possible *mahdi*, the 'rightly guided one' who will appear near the end of time. Furnish writes that 'of all the charismatic leaders in all the cities and towns in all the Sunni Islamic

---

[46]   Bin Laden and Lawrence, *Messages*, p. 193.

world, the one most likely to be considered or to consider himself Mahdi material is undoubtedly, at this juncture in history, Osama Bin Muhammad Bin Laden'.[47]

Whether Bin Laden was still alive no longer seemed relevant, and this was reflected in how he was portrayed. He now appeared as a mythical hero, in a way already occupying a seat in history, to have entered the folk memory, sometimes taking the role of a shaykh (a scholarly leader), although of an increasingly mythical nature, as seen in the collage dating from 2007 shown in Figure 7.4.

Figure 7.4   The mythical shaykh

In this multi-modal collage, Bin Laden is dressed as a mighty shaykh and appears against a dark background that alludes to our ignorance of his whereabouts. He seems to be placed on the edge of the globe, a supernatural being above ground raising his index finger to warn the people of Iraq against aligning themselves with the crusaders. In the collage, the contours of the map of Iraq are vaguely visible, with a light area to the south-west of Iraq, in the direction of the two holy

⁴⁷   Timothy R. Furnish, *Holiest Wars: Islamic Mahdis, Their Jihads, and Osama bin Laden* (Westport, CT: Praeger, 2005), p. 156.

cities, Mecca and Medina, representing hope in religion. In the background, Bin Laden's voice is heard discussing the situation in Iraq.

On other occasions Bin Laden was portrayed once again as a *mujahid*, but now as a mythical rather than a practising *mujahid* in the field, as in Figure 7.5, from 2008.

Figure 7.5   The mythical *mujahid*

In this image, viewers again see a Bin Laden dressed in white, the colour of innocence and cleanliness, with a shaykh's robe over his shoulders to emphasise his role as a leader. The Kalashnikov is back, alluding to resistance, to Bin Laden's participation in the battles in Afghanistan, and to the victory over the Soviet army. The other weapon, the spear, points to victories in the Muslim golden age, in centuries past. The collage can be read as a narrative, read from right to left, as it presents a continuum of battles from the time of the Prophet Muhammad, represented by the spear, to the current day and age: a prolonged war in which Bin Laden is the final hero. As in other texts attributed to Bin Laden, a prominent feature is the exploitation for emotive effect of historical symbols and myths. Memories of the distant past are linked to modern events in an attempt to bring people hope through references to victories and through putting Islamic symbols and myths into new contexts. Despite this emphasis on the past, the texts are still of current interest, as in this text where Bin Laden addresses his enemies: 'How it saddens us that you target our villages with your bombing: those modest mud villages which have collapsed onto our women and children. You do that intentionally and I am witness to that.'[48]

Bin Laden adds in a reference to the reprinting of the caricatures of the Prophet: 'Then came the publishing of these drawings, which came in the framework of a new crusade in which the Pope of the Vatican has played a large, lengthy role. And all of that is confirmation on your part in the continuation of the war.' He continues: 'This is the greater and more serious tragedy, and reckoning for it will be more severe.' The crusade referred to here probably derives from an incident in 2006 when the Pope cited a mediaeval text in which Islam was described in harsh words. Clearly the crusade once again is an important recurrent concept that through its flexibility may also explain the Pope's position.[49]

Conclusion

In this chapter I have argued that Bin Laden's portrayals seemed increasingly staged. From the *mujahid* of the 1990s, he evolved, via a period as a political leader, to become the symbolic mythical hero of 2009 – virtually a historical figure or a phenomenon from the Islamic past. Rather than a participant in current news events, his actions were part of history. Indeed, this historical role seems in line with the general perception of Bin Laden, since there seems to have been much doubt about his well-being before he was killed in May 2011. Periodically the media had reported claims that Bin Laden was dead, and against that background the collages might well have contributed to strengthening the view of Bin Laden as a figure from the past. From a strategic perspective, al-Sahab's motivation for portraying the al-Qaeda leader as a historic hero and leader may well be that the organisation wished to prepare for his death – stealing a march by pre-emptively establishing a post-mortal image. Intentional or not,

---

48 Osama bin Laden, 'Shaikh Usama bin Ladin Audio Message, 20 March 2008', at http://www.youtube.com/watch?v=MiCck0xYe-Q, last accessed 19 February 2014.
49 Ibid.

the establishment of Bin Laden as a historical figure may have had a striking effect on people's perception of him. Nonetheless, it remains to be seen to what extent the construction of his image has contributed to his being accepted as a symbolic historical figure beyond the circles of al-Qaeda.

PART III
Preaching, New and Old

Chapter 8

The Postmodern Reconstitution of an Islamic Memory: Theory and Practice in the Case of Yusuf al-Qaradawi's Virtual *Umma*

Uriya Shavit

Yusuf al-Qaradawi's rise to prominence began in 1961, when he was invited to teach at Qatar's newly established College for Higher Education. At that time Qaradawi, born in 1926, was a little-known religious scholar at al-Azhar and a member of the Muslim Brothers, then effectively suppressed. The tiny Gulf emirate was a safe haven for the intellectually promising young Islamist, who had just published his book on *al-Halal wa'l-Haram fi al-Islam* (*The Legal and the Prohibited in Islam*), a guide on religious law directed to Muslims living in the West.[1]

In the half century to follow, Qaradawi's list of accomplishments has been exceptional: *al-Halal wa'l-Haram* became one of the most popular publications in its genre, and was followed by dozens of other books; Qaradawi established the faculty for Shari'a and Islamic studies at Qatar University; became a spiritual leader of Muslim Brothers movements all around the world, albeit rejecting an official role in them; was recognised as the leading scholar of the socio-legal Islamic school *Wasatiyya*; established in 1997 the European Council for Fatwa and Research (*al-Majlis al-Urubbi li'l-Ifta' wa'l-Buhuth*), which he has headed ever since; and initiated in 2004, again heading it ever since, the International

---

[1] On al-Qaradawi's early career, relations with al-Azhar and with the Muslim Brothers, see Jakob Skovgaard-Petersen, 'Yusuf al-Qaradawi and al-Azhar', in Bettina Gräf and Jakob Skovgaard-Petersen (eds), *Global Mufti: The Phenomenon of Yusuf al-Qaradawi* (London, 2009), pp. 27–53; Husam Tammam, 'Yusuf Qaradawi and the Muslim Brothers: The Nature of a Special Relationship', in ibid., pp. 55–83; Samuel Helfont, *Yusuf al-Qaradawi: Islam and Modernity* (Tel Aviv, 2009), pp. 35–8; Akram Kassab, *al-Manhaj al-Da'wi ind al-Qaradawi* (Cairo, 2006), pp. 281–4.

Union for Muslim Scholars. Following the ousting of Egyptian president Husni Mubarak, Qaradawi returned to Egypt and gave a Friday sermon on 18 February 2011 to hundreds of thousands of supporters who gathered at Tahrir Square, the heart of the Egyptian revolution. The speech signified his special moral status in Egypt, and in the Arab world at large.

Notwithstanding all these achievements, arguably one of Qaradawi's lasting legacies will be his conceptualisation and utilisation of advanced media technologies in promoting the resurrection of a universal Muslim nation, or in striving to transform the myth of the *umma* into reality. The *umma* is, of course, not a myth in the narrow sense of the word; while often idealised by some Muslims, it nevertheless belongs to history rather than to legend. I apply the term here in a broader sense, implying 'ideology in narrative form'.[2]

Since the mid 1990s, Qaradawi has been involved in a variety of satellite-television and internet operations. These are not appendices to his mission; rather, they are part of a broader approach, which is pioneering in its comprehension of the merits which advanced media technologies provide for the Islamist religious-political vision, and in particular for its ambition to constitute the mythicised *umma* as a viable – even if imperfect and only gradually evolving – political force. As such, they add another layer to the tangled Islamist correspondence with modernity.

The Muslim Brothers movement was founded in 1928 as a response to the modernist project that the West had introduced into Muslim societies from the late eighteenth century onwards. Modernisation of Middle Eastern societies involved four main transformations: a) substituting the political framework of the Ottoman Empire, which was based on religious affiliations and represented an ambition for Islamic global hegemony, with nation-states based on territorial affiliations; b) substituting religious law and religion-based social organisations for non-religious laws and organisations; c) substituting the principle of God's sovereignty for that of the People's sovereignty and d) substituting metaphysical scholarship for empiricism and rationalism.

Hasan al-Banna, the founder and first leader of the Muslim Brothers, challenged the modernist project by basing his agenda on the call for the reconstitution of religious-political Muslim unity and of Islam as the sole framework for all aspects of life.[3] However, he did not reject modernity, or the

---

[2]   Bruce Lincoln, *Theorizing Myth* (Chicago, IL, 1999), p. 207.

[3]   Hasan al-Banna, 'Bayna al-ams wal-yawm', in *Majmu'at Rasa'il al-imam al-Shahid Hasan al-Banna* (Beirut, 1965), pp. 220–55; 'Risalat al-mu'tamar al-khamis`, in ibid., p. 244; 'D'awtuna fi tur jadid', in ibid., p. 73.

West, at large, but rather attempted to assimilate some of its technical aspects into his programme. Following the road taken by Jamal al-Din al-Afghani and Muhammad 'Abduh's reformism (and continued by al-Banna's mentor on Muslim–Western relations,[4] Muhammad Rashid Rida), al-Banna Islamised scientific and technological advancements using theological as well as historical arguments that were based on idealisations of the Muslim past;[5] he believed that interpretations of the meaning of the Qur'an must be linked scientifically, socially and morally to aspects of modern life.[6] The modernist aspect of his approach also manifested itself in his modified acceptance of Western political norms and institutions and in his belief in mass, popular mobilisation as the means to enhance a complete transformation from a broken, harsh reality to an ideal, Islamic one. S.N. Eisenstadt further argues that the crucial aspect that makes this type of fundamentalism a product of modernity is its appropriation of some central aspects of the political programme of modernity, particularly of various – especially Jacobin – participatory, totalistic and egalitarian orientations.[7]

At the core of the Islamist idea is a belief that the modernist order can be challenged through reinterpreting modernity. Yusuf al-Qaradawi's activities during the past two decades suggest a new type of correspondence with modernity: he challenges the modernist order by reinterpreting postmodernist innovations. Qaradawi has become the conscious standard-bearer of an Islamist appreciation that, just as agents of modernity can be interpreted and applied in multiple ways other than the Western ones, so can agents of postmodernity. This appreciation rests on analysis of global media as crucial components of Islamic resurrection and universalism. Qaradawi, who distinguishes between Islamic universalism as a desired objective and Western globalisation as an enemy, believes that advanced media technologies are the most useful tool of our times in promoting the resurrection of the Muslim nation and in bringing non-Muslims to Islam. He regards satellite television and the internet as the pillars of the Muslim past's desired return to the future.

This chapter explores the relation between Qaradawi's vision, the modern nation-state and postmodern advanced media technologies. Its first section deals with Qaradawi's ideology; the second analyses his interpretation and facilitation

---

[4]   Hasan al-Banna, *Mudhakarat al-da'wa wa'l-da'iya* (Cairo: Dar al-Kitab), pp. 49–50; Richard P. Mitchell, *The Society of the Muslim Brothers* (New York and Oxford, 1993), p. 5.

[5]   Al-Banna, 'Bayna al-ams wal-yawm', pp. 218–19.

[6]   Brynjar Lia, *The Society of the Muslim Brothers in Egypt: The Rise of an Islamic Mass Movement 1928–1942* (Reading, UK, 1998), p. 76.

[7]   S.N. Eisenstadt, *Fundamentalism, Sectarianism and Revolution: The Jacobin Dimension of Modernity* (Cambridge, 1999), p. 91.

of satellite television and the internet; the third (based in part on a one-year field study in five Arab mosques in Frankfurt am Main, Germany) analyses some limitations that Qaradawi's ambitions to transform a myth of the *umma* to a political reality encounter.

Yusuf Qaradawi's Religious-Political Programme

The distinction between radical and moderate Islamists, when applied in broad brushstrokes, oversimplifies the religious-political programmes of movements and individuals. Qaradawi is one example. An understanding of his ideas and activities calls for a distinction between a) Qaradawi the Islamist intellectual; b) Qaradawi the political leader and c) Qaradawi the religious-legal authority.

Qaradawi the intellectual echoes the main concerns of Hasan al-Banna, who was, according to Qaradawi's own testimony, his teacher in his first year at university and the source of the inspiration for his joining the Muslim Brothers.[8] As did al-Banna, Qaradawi emphasises in his writings the need for the re-establishment of an Allah-abiding united religious-political community, with a united leadership, in which Islam will be the comprehensive framework for all aspects of life; he accepts that in contemporary times the myth of the ideal, united *umma* can be realised in different ways; a federation, a confederation and a commonwealth.[9]

Directly inspired by al-Banna,[10] Qaradawi asserts that the Muslim world is a victim of a well-planned and collective Western socio-cultural attack, far more dangerous than any military or political campaign. This attack is aimed at stripping Muslims of their faith and their appreciation of Islam's all-encompassing nature. It is an attack which has been using a variety of means, from orientalists and missionaries to Western-oriented schools and mass media.[11] According to Qaradawi, the triumph of the attack over the Muslim mind is the primary explanation for the failures of the Muslim nation, including the Arab defeats against Israel, for it had distanced Muslims from what had granted them victory in the past – their faith in Islam, their acceptance of God's laws as a sole

---

[8]   Yusuf al-Qaradawi, *Nahnu wal-gharb: as'ilah sha'ika wa-ajwiba hasima* (Cairo, 2006), p. 124.

[9]   Yusuf al-Qaradawi, *Ummatuna bayna al-qarnayn* (Cairo, 2000, repr. 2002), pp. 148–51.

[10]   Al-Banna, 'Bayna al-ams wal-yawm', pp. 218–25.

[11]   Yusuf al-Qaradawi, *Al-hulul al-mustawrada wa kayfa janat 'ala ummatina* (Beirut, 1971, repr. 1974), pp. 15–46; *idem, Ummatuna*, p. 77.

point of reference, and their unity with other Muslims.[12] Therefore Qaradawi believes that a Muslim renaissance requires a re-Islamisation of Muslim societies. Secular and infidel notions that became hegemonic must give way to Islamic principles and Islamic laws. A true Muslim state must be established. This state will have the Qur'an as its constitution and will be universal.[13] It will be led by a *khalifa*, a second Salah al-Din, an able leader whose primary goal will be to lead the united nation in *jihad*.[14]

How is the objection to Western hegemony reconciled with the quest for Islamic world domination? In one of his explanations, Qaradawi distinguishes between two terms: Western *'awlama* (globalisation) and Islamic *'alamiya* (universalism). The former is a coercive process in which the United States aims to force on the world its political, economic, cultural and social hegemony. The latter sees all human beings as equals and distinguishes between them only in relation to their piety.[15]

While his writings clearly define him as al-Banna's student and admirer, Qaradawi does not follow him blindly, openly declaring that he is not committed to the former's opinions.[16] In relation to parliamentary democracy, for example, he follows his own path. Al-Banna responded to a broken liberal-democratic political reality, which he did not utterly reject, but was deeply suspicious of, while Qaradawi has responded from the 1960s onwards to autocratic political realities, amidst speculation that fair and secret ballots will lead his camp to power. Therefore, while carefully distinguishing the Islamic conception of electoral politics from the Western, Qaradawi puts great emphasis on Islam's democratic underpinnings, manifested by the principle of *shura* (consultation).[17] He overrules al-Banna's rejection of political parties, possibly because of his understanding that this could weaken the Brothers' political leverage. He strongly defends this position, contending it has foundations in the times of the righteous *khulafa* as well as in the reality of contemporary Muslim societies. He compares a plurality of parties in politics to the plurality of schools in Islamic law; but he also cautions that embracing plurality does not imply embracing disputes and contradictions, and that plurality is legitimate so long as the people

[12]   *Idem, Durus al-nakba al-thaniyya: limadha inhazamna ... wa kayfa nantasiru* (place of publication not mentioned, repr. 1969), pp. 30–40; *idem, Ummatuna*, pp. 131–3; *idem, Ta'rikhna al-muftara 'alayhi* (Cairo, 2005, fourth repr. 2008), pp. 15–25.

[13]   *Idem, Min fiqh al-dawla al-muslima* (Cairo, 1997, third repr. 2001), pp. 30–4, 90.

[14]   *Idem, Durus,* pp. 112–15; *idem, Ummatuna*, pp. 148–51.

[15]   Ibid., pp. 229–38.

[16]   *Idem, Nahnu wal-gharb*, p. 125.

[17]   *Idem, Durus,* p. 107; *idem, Min fiqh*, pp. 35–7.

stand as one in regard to crucial issues such as Muslim existence, Muslim faith, Muslim law and the Muslim nation.[18]

In Qaradawi's capacity as a political leader, his actions fail to match his rhetoric. While he did not plan on settling down in Qatar when he sojourned there in the 1960s,[19] the oil emirate has become his refuge, and allows him a great measure of freedom in writing and preaching. But this comes at a price: Qaradawi is banned from harming the emirate's strategic interests. This explains why, throughout most of his career in Qatar, much of his writing in relation to the required political revolution in the Muslim world has been abstract, avoiding reference to specific conditions or leaders; it also explains why his support for the uprisings in the Arab world during 2010 and 2011 fell short of an endorsement of political reforms in Qatar, one of the Arab world's most autocratic countries. Qaradawi's very presence in Qatar has given the emirate legitimisation which, judging from his own ideology, it is unworthy of. Qatar does not apply the principle of *shura* as Qaradawi demands; it is as distant from the Islamic principles of social justice which Qaradawi endorses as any country can be; it is a strategic ally of the United States, and is deeply influenced by Western culture; and it has normalised relations with Israel more than any other Gulf state, a normalisation which Qaradawi strongly opposes. It is not clear how influential Qaradawi is within Qatar's circles of power, but it is clear that he has not been able to turn even his own direct sphere of influence toward his religious-political goals. The failure on May 2012 of the independent Islamist contender for Egypt's first free Presidential elections, 'Abd al-Mun'im Abu al-Futuh, whom Qaradawi supported, demonstrated that Qaradawi's direct political influence is also perhaps more limited in Egypt than he would like to believe.

Qaradawi attempted to institutionalise his call for Muslim unity by establishing, on 11 March 2004, the pan-Muslim International Union for Muslim Scholars. The major objective of this organisation is to 'persistently strive to preserve the Islamic identity of the Muslim *umma* so that it retains its *wasati* stance and lofty goals of enjoining what is good and forbidding what is evil'. Among the Union's minor objectives are to 'alert the whole *umma* to the new weapons being used under the guise of carefully-tailored terms like globalization and modernity' and to 'unify the ranks of Muslim scholars'.[20]

---

[18]   Ibid., pp. 151–60.
[19]   *Idem, Nahnu wal-gharb*, p. 124.
[20]   International Union of Muslim Scholars: Union Goals (n.d), at http://iumsonline.net/english/topic_04.shtml, last accessed 1 May 2007.

Since its establishment, the Union has exemplified the prospects for Shiite–Sunni cooperation, but it has not become an independent force to be politically reckoned with.

Qaradawi, a veteran of Nasser's jails and an admirer of Sayyid Qutb's earlier writings, knows all too well the price that can be paid for upsetting those who hold a monopoly on the use of force, and is thus in opposition to Qutb-inspired Islamist *jihadism*.[21] In attempting to reconcile the gap between his radical rhetoric and moderate political actions, he explains that a quest to replace a corrupt government by force is justified only if the challengers can prevail. If they cannot, they should remain patient and wait until they muster sufficient power, and in the meantime should advocate change by speaking and writing.[22] This explanation vindicates Qaradawi's practical cooperation with the Qatari and other regimes, but creates a paradox: the Islamic revolution can only take place when the time is right, but how will the time ever be right, if one has to wait for it to be so?

Thirdly, as a religious-legal authority Qaradawi has become the champion of the socio-legal school of Wasatiyya (the harmonising middle path approach). Wasatiyya, which is a general approach to the essence of Islam applied in the field of jurisprudence, suggests that Islam is a golden mean, bringing notions into harmony which are seemingly contradictory: rights and duties; continuity and change; materialism and spiritualism; revelation and rationalism; communalism and individuality; private ownership and public ownership. Wasatiyya holds Islam to be a religion of firm principles, but also one that leaves much leverage for addressing changing realities. It seeks to find, where possible, practical and flexible solutions to problems faced by Muslims, to make their lives easier, and to make them fond of their religion. To achieve these goals, Wasati scholars do not commit themselves to any one of the four religious-legal schools (*madhhabs*). They also resort in generous measure to the loosely defined principle of *maslaha* (safeguarding a principle objective of the shari'a).[23]

Wasatiyya's main adversaries in Muslim-Arab societies are religious scholars who are contemporarily referred to as *salafis* – that is, scholars who endorse

---

[21] Al-Qaradawi, *Nahnu wal-gharb*, p. 125.
[22] *Idem, Min fiqh*, pp. 118–28.
[23] *Idem, Al-Halal wal-haram fi al-islam* (Beirut, 1973), pp. 17–39; *idem, Ummatuna*, p. 171. For an overview of Wasatiyya, see Sagi Polka, 'The Centrist Stream in Egypt and its Role in the Public Discourse Surrounding the Shaping of the Country's Cultural Identity', *Middle Eastern Studies*, 39/3 (July 2003), pp. 39–64; Bettina Gräf, 'The Concept of Wasatiyya in the Work of Yusuf al-Qaradawi', in Bettina Gräf and Jakob Skovgaard-Petersen (eds), *Global Mufti: The Phenomenon of Yusuf al-Qaradawi* (London: 2009), 213–38.

complete devotion in religious practice and a literal reading of the Qur'an and the *hadith* in establishing religious law. *Salafis* are less inclined to assimilate aspects of modernity into Muslim societies.[24] Being the chief protagonist of Wasatiyya, Qaradawi is thus, among those advocating practical and modern religious-legal decisions, the leading voice in the Arab Sunni world.

The multiple dimensions of Qaradawi's message – the radical intellectual, the pragmatic politician and the moderate jurist – are all combined in his approach to the Muslim minority in the West. Qaradawi is the single most influential Arab scholar in addressing the cultural and religious-legal challenges Muslim immigrants face (while, as will be demonstrated below, his influence is narrower than his ambitions).

In terms of ideology, Qaradawi has been the leading voice in a broad agreement reached in Islamic-Arab jurisprudence during the past 30 years as to the identity and duties of Muslims living in the West. This broad agreement aims to actualise the myth of the *umma* in the lives of Muslim minorities. It involves five points: first, a greater Islamic nation exists of which Muslims are members wherever they live; secondly, while living in a non-Muslim society is undesirable, it might be legitimate on an individual basis if the immigrant acts as a model Muslim; thirdly, it is the duty of a Muslim in the West to reaffirm his religious identity and to distance himself from anything contrary to Islam. Hence, he should help establish and patronise mosques, Muslim schools, cultural centres and shops; he must also unite with his fellow Muslim immigrants, regardless of ethnic, national and linguistic affiliations. Fourthly, Muslims in the West should champion the cause of the Muslim nation in the political as well as the religious sphere, for there should be no distinction between the two; and lastly, Muslims

---

[24]   The contemporary usage of the term 'Salafiyya' is confusing as a description, since it is ascribed to various groups, including several contesting ones; see Thomas Hegghammer, 'Jihadi Salafis or Revolutionaries? On Religion and Politics in the Study of Militant Islamism', in Roel Meijer (ed.), *Global Salafism: Islam's New Religious Movement* (London, 2009), pp. 248–51. In contemporary academic scholarship it is commonly used to describe 'imported wahhabiyya', e.g. individuals or groups outside Saudi Arabia directly or indirectly inspired or financed by Saudi organisations; Muhammad Ali Adraoui, 'Salafism in France: Ideology, Practices and Contradictions', in ibid., p. 369; Hasan b. 'Ali al-Saqqaf, *al-Salafiyya al-Wahhabiyya* (Beirut, 2005), pp. 13, 19–20; Juan Jose Stemman, 'Middle East Salafism's Influence and the Radicalization of Muslim Communities in Europe', *Middle East Review of International Affairs*, 10/3 (September 2005), available at http://www.e-prism. org/images/MIDDLE_EAST_SALAFISM_-_1-9-06.pdf, last accessed 19 February 2014; Febe Armanios, 'The Islamic Traditions of Wahhabism and Salafiyya', *Congressional Research Service Reports* (December 2003), available at http://fas.org/irp/crs/RS21695.pdf, last accessed 19 February 2014.

in the West should spread Islam in the declining, spiritual void of Western societies.[25] Regarding this final duty, Qaradawi elaborates:

> Muslims in the West ought to be sincere callers to their religion. They should keep in mind that calling others to Islam is not only restricted to scholars and *shaykhs*, but it goes so far as to encompass every committed Muslim. As we see scholars and *shaykhs* delivering *khutbas* and lectures, writing books to defend Islam, it is no wonder to find lay Muslims practising *da'wa* while employing wisdom and fair exhortation.[26]

Qaradawi sought to institutionalise his call for Muslim migrants' unity in purpose and action by establishing, in London on 29 March 1997, the Dublin-based European Council for Fatwa and Research. The council's mission is to address in uniformity questions relating to Muslims in Europe[27] – and thus to encourage uniformity in their conduct. Following Qaradawi's Wasati orientation, the council has introduced practical solutions to a variety of dilemmas faced by migrants. The most controversial of these, which caused an outcry even among some Wasatis, was the decision to allow Muslims in the West who do not own a home to take out mortgages, although both charging and paying interest are forbidden in Islam. This decision, which considered mortgages in the context of living in Europe a need (*haja*) that can be regarded as a necessity (*darura*), exemplifies Qaradawi's sensitivity to the special conditions of migrants.[28]

The New Imagined Community and the Universal *Umma*

The main tools through which Qaradawi has diffused his agenda since the mid 1990s are his weekly television show on the Qatari al-Jazeera news channel, *al-Shari'a wa'l-Haya*, and the internet portal which he supervised (until his dismissal by the board of directors in 2010), IslamOnline.net. Though he already

---

[25] For an overview, see Uriya Shavit, 'Should Muslims Integrate into the West?', *Middle East Quarterly*, 14/4 (autumn 2007), pp. 13–21; Uriya Shavit, 'The Wasati and Salafi Approaches to the Religious Law of Muslim Minorities', *Islamic Law and Society*, 19/4 (autumn 2012), pp. 416–33.

[26] Yusuf al-Qaradawi, 'Duties of Muslims Living in the West' (7 May 2006), available at http://www.quranforall.org/fatawaa/duties.htm, last accessed 19 February 2014.

[27] *Idem*, 'Taqdim', in *Qararat wa-Fatawa al-Majlis al-Urubbi lil-Ifta' wal-Buhuth* (Cairo, 2002), pp. 5–10.

[28] *Idem*, *Fi fiqh al-aqalliyyat al-muslima* (Cairo, 2007), pp. 154–90.

enjoyed a formidable scholarly stature before the 1990s, it is his media operations that have elevated him to the rank of a world-renowned religious authority. The initiation and use of these media operations are not incidental – rather, they reflect Qaradawi's articulated proposition that advanced media technologies should be interpreted and facilitated as agents for challenging the premises of the modern nation-state and for promoting the rise of a united Muslim nation and an Islam-based society.

An appreciation of Qaradawi's theory and practice in the field of global media calls first for an analysis of the challenges satellite television and the internet pose to modern nation-states at large. To do so, Benedict Anderson's theory of modern nation-states as imagined communities will be of use.

In analysing the gradual development of national consciousnesses in the Spanish-administered regions of South America, Anderson suggested that a role was played by gazettes distributed in these regions and which first appeared as mere appendages of the market. According to Anderson, it was through these gazettes that large groups of people gradually developed a sense of familial belonging, a mutual belief in common political fates that in time turned into conceptualisations of themselves as nations.[29] Anderson's imagined national communities are the result of an affinity between territories and media contents absorbed simultaneously, primarily and on an ongoing basis by people residing in these territories – and *only* by them. They are inseparable from a benchmark of modernity: the development of mass media which, while massive, has nevertheless been limited in its geographical scope. While Anderson focused on print media, the introduction in the twentieth century of terrestrial television broadcasting fits well with his theory: until the beginning of the 1980s, these broadcasts, numerous as they were, largely coincided with national boundaries.

The rise of advanced media technologies broke the almost exclusive affinity between territorial boundaries and mass-media consumption that was at the heart of Anderson's theory. Satellite television and, later, the internet, reached a global potential audience. During the 1980s and 1990s, theories of media globalisation suggested that global media networks such as CNN International (launched in 1985), which produced 'global' news and aspired to a global audience, constructed a global sphere which replaced, at least to some extent, national spheres, and thus potentially shattered national identities.[30]

---

[29]   Benedict Anderson, *Imagined Communities* (London and New York, 1991), p. 62.
[30]   Stig Hjarvard, 'News Media and the Globalization of the Public Sphere', in Stig Hjarvard (ed.), *News in a Globalized Society* (Gotborg, 2001), p. 20.

However, from the 1990s onwards the endurance of national imageries in a global, postmodern reality became questionable. The strong national affiliations of media organisations which claimed to be global were exposed and debated, while audiences around the world demonstrated a desire to consume news and entertainment along the national lines they were accustomed to. Rather than appeal to a 'global' audience as CNN International continues to do, media organisations have been increasingly focusing since the late 1980s on localised global operations. The British Sky network, established in 1989, is an early example for what later became a trend: while broadcasting via satellite to a potentially global audience, its content and orientation are firmly based on the imagined British community. Becoming a global phenomenon in the mid 1990s, most of the internet's operations also focused on national audiences, albeit using a global tool.

This transformation in the application of advanced media technologies dissipated the 'global' assault on the modern nation-state, but also created new challenges: imagined communities are today extended outside their territorial boundaries. For the first time since the rise of modern nationalism much of the images and texts crucial to the imagination of communities as nations can be consumed far away from the homeland, almost as if consumed in that territory. There is no longer a need to reside in the geographical realms of one's nation-state in order to consume much of its media: one can do so simultaneously, primarily and on an ongoing basis, with one's compatriots while residing thousands of miles away. Thus, rather than a global village created by satellites and the internet, there are many contesting national villages which operate on a global scale. This development poses far-reaching challenges to traditional concepts of nationhood, and particularly to the relations between immigrants and both their original and new nation-states. It complicates already complex concepts such as integration, dual citizenship and transnationalism.[31]

The potential of global media operations to encroach on traditional territorial limitations, and the prospect of their redefining nationality, was not lost on some Islamic scholars; but they interpreted global media in a very different context. From the 1990s onwards, some Muslim scholars realised that advanced media technologies allowed them to appeal to potentially any of their co-religionists wherever the latter were living in the world, or (in even more ambitious terms) any person anywhere in the world. The resurrected *umma* they

---

[31]   For a discussion of these issues, see Uriya Shavit, *The New Imagined Community: Advanced Media Technologies and the Construction of National and Muslim Identities of Migrants* (Brighton, Portland, OR and Vancouver, 2009), pp. 1–97.

had long envisioned, that is, the myth of a united Muslim nation, encompassing all Muslims wherever they lived, was no longer a purely theoretical concept. Through advanced media technologies, a sermon given in Mecca or an edict issued in Riyadh could immediately and simultaneously be read in Ottawa, London, Cairo and Karachi. For a Muslim nation which does not recognise the territorial boundaries of nation-states, the internet and satellite television meant indifference to boundaries; for a nation seeking to resurrect a memory of unity and to join all its members into one dedicated religious-political community, modern telecommunications systems provided Muslims everywhere with the same imagery, simultaneously and on a daily basis.

Religious scholars have become aware of the parallelism between the conceptualised universal *umma* and the global reach of advanced media technologies. In the most radical interpretation, such technologies were regarded as proof of Islam being the true religion. The logic was simple: if the nation of Islam was meant to be universal, then the appearance of universal media could not be a coincidence. Thus advanced media technologies were perceived as Allah's gift to the *umma* – a means designed to connect all believers, and to enhance the spread of Allah's word. Ja'far Shaykh Idris (b. 1931), a Sudanese scholar who was involved in *da'wa* activities in the United States between 1974 to 2004 on behalf of Saudi Arabia, wrote that only Allah could have known that a time would come when the world would be turned into a single global village. Therefore, only Allah could have known that there was no need to send many prophets out to many peoples – one final prophet, bringing his message to all humanity, would suffice. Ever since Muhammad began his prophetic mission, countries have come closer together, a process that has reached its peak in our times, and this development could only be interpreted as corresponding with the heart of Muslim belief.[32]

The internet had one more specific merit that raised its appeal for religious scholars and preachers of all trends: it empowered them on an individual basis. On internet sites, a whole world could revolve around scholars where their biographies, sermons, religious edicts and reflections on current affairs could reach the public with immaculate cohesion and order. Websites dedicated to the life and works of individual religious scholars include those who held a formidable status before the internet ever existed (for example, the Saudi 'Abdallah ibn Baz), but also scholars of a less formidable stature (for example, the abovementioned Idris).

---

[32]   Ja'far Shaykh Idris, 'al-Da'wa wa wasa'il al-ittisal al-haditha', *al-Bayan*, 148, available at http://www.jaafaridris.com/Arabic/aarticles/dawa.htm, last accessed 10 April 2006.

Qaradawi is an example of a scholar who was well-known and influential before the time of advanced modern technologies, only to have become more prominent and influential by utilising the new media. No single scholar has done more than he to Islamise, in theory, advanced media technologies and effectively to use them as agents for his ideas. His weekly television show *al-Sharīʿa waʾl-Haya*, in which he discusses questions relating to diverse aspects of Islamic law, has been broadcast since the early days of al-Jazeera, which was launched in November 1996. Millions of Muslims around the world watch the programme. According to Qaradawi himself, it is broadcast on Sundays, at 19:05 GMT, because that is the most convenient time for Muslims living in Western countries.[33] On the internet, Qaradawi operates a personal site; the European Council for Fatwa and Research and the International Union of Muslim Scholars also maintain sites. Qaradawi's major online operation was the portal IslamOnline.net, established in June 1997 by the al-Balagh Cultural Society. According to Gräf, the idea of constructing the portal was initiated by Maryam al-Hajari, an information technology specialist who in 1996 attended a course given by Qaradawi on alms tax (*zakat*); Qaradawi gave the portal his endorsement and agreed to serve as chairman of al-Balagh and head of IslamOnline.net's supervising committee. After IslamOnline.net was established, he promoted it in his televised appearances. While his role in the portal was largely honorary,[34] it still represented his views and chronicled his activities with great respect. On March 2010, a dispute between al-Balagh and the portal's Egyptian office, which latter had produced most of its contents, led to Qaradawi's dismissal from the board of directors. Egypt-based workers argued that the Qatari management was seeking to transform the portal from wasatiyya to salafiyya, and to curb its strong anti-Israeli agenda. On August 2010, former members of IslamOnline.net launched, with the endorsement of Qaradawi, a new portal, with a very similar name, structure and contents to those of IslamOnline.net – onislam. net; ranking data, provided by Alexa.com, an internet ranking company, on 1 February 2013, suggests it has become more popular than IslamOnline.net, but also that none of them match the popularity attained by IslamOnline.net before Qaradawi's dismissal.

Under Qaradawi, IslamOnline.net had a small administrative office in Qatar's capital, Doha; its content was managed from Cairo, where some 100

---

[33]   Ehab Galal, 'Yusuf al-Qaraḍawi and the New Islamic TV', in Gräf and Skovgaard-Petersen (eds), *Global Mufti*, p. 158.

[34]   Bettina Gräf, 'IslamOnline.net: Independent, interactive, popular', *Arab Media & Society* (January 2008), available at http://www.arabmediasociety.com/index. php?article=576&printarticle, last accessed 19 February 2014.

employees worked full-time. IslamOnline.net's declared mission was to 'create a unique, global Islamic web portal'; its goals were to 'work to uplift the Islamic nation specifically and humanity in general', 'to reinforce values and morals on the individual, family and community levels', and 'to expand the circle of introducing Islam'. Its content was presented in both Arabic and English.[35]

Qaradawi theorised on several occasions on the relations between advanced media technologies and the diffusion of his interpretation of Islam as a universal religion. Speaking about the success of his satellite television show, he said:

> No one imagined that it [the *al-Shari'a wa al-Haya* weekly programme] would be as popular as it is, but Allah willed that it be a run-away hit, and people from all over the world watch it. Anyone who understands Arabic watches – East or West, in places like America, Australia, Japan, Indonesia, all of these countries, and of course the Arab world ... Al-Jazeera has provided me with millions of viewers; where my audience was once numbered in the thousands or tens of thousands, they are now in the millions. I never go to a country now where people do not know me through Al-Jazeera ... Books allow you to delve deeply into an idea, to organize things and place them in sequence, and so on. But how many people read books? They have a limited audience. Meanwhile, the mass media have a very wide audience.[36]

Qaradawi's writings about the internet are even more audacious – he suggested that it and satellite television allow Muslims to turn Islam's conceptual universality into reality,[37] and described his portal IslamOnline.net as the '*jihad* of the era', which enables Muslims to promote *da'wa* globally without relying on armed force,[38] and without enjoying the cooperation of governments.[39] Qaradawi praised web activities as the most important contemporary agent for promoting the global ascendance of Islam. The mission of Islam, he wrote,

35   IslamOnline.net, 'About Us' (n.d), available at http://www.islamonline.net/English/AboutUs.shtml, last accessed 1 May 2007.
36   'Abdallah S. Schleifer, 'Interview with Sheikh Yusuf al-Qaradawi', *Transnational Broadcasting Studies*, 13 (Fall 2004), available at http://www.tbsjournal.com/Archives/Fall04/interviewyusufqaradawi.htm, last accessed 19 February 2014.
37   Yusuf al-Qaradawi, *Hajat al-bashriyya ila al-risala al-hadariyya li-ummatina* (Cairo, 2004), p. 85.
38   Idem, *Ummatuna*, p. 172.
39   Imam Muhammad Imam, 'Khidmat al-islam 'ibr al-intarnat ... jihad hadha al-'asr' (interview with Yusuf al-Qaradawi), *al-Sharq al-Awsat*, 12 November 1999, p. 18.

is universal. It is a mission that is relevant to all the nations in the world. It must be brought to all of humanity in the language of the day and not in the languages of the past, so that Muslims can justify themselves before God when their time comes. In order to do so, there is a need to use all the tools of our times – from print to radio to satellite television to the 'great modern tool called [the] internet', so that Islam can be brought to non-Muslims and so that Muslims can be taught the right Islam. That, he concluded, was the reason behind the initiation of IslamOnline.net.[40]

Qaradawi's assimilation and conceptualisation of new media is all the more impressive when taking into account his poor childhood in the 1930s in the Egyptian Nile Delta village of Saft Turab, as described in his autobiography. There was no running water, no electricity. Only one newspaper, the government's *al-Ahram*, was available. Life centred on the village's five mosques. When radios were first introduced they were greeted with excitement, but most villagers were too poor to purchase one. To listen to the news or readings from the Qur'an, villagers would gather in the local café.[41] Yet perhaps it was in that café that Qaradawi first appreciated the power of the media to unite people into one community with a shared political consciousness.

Qaradawi's combined advanced media operations allow his speeches, initiatives and articles to reach a global audience immediately. Also available globally are any legal opinions he issues, or that are issued by the councils he heads. Muslims anywhere in the world can simultaneously access any *fatwa* that has been issued, as long as they have an internet connection. The accumulation of *fatwa*s is building up a comprehensive guide for Muslims, exemplifying the notion that no aspect of life is outside the jurisdiction of the shari'a. The questions they answer relate mainly to everyday life. Is a Muslim allowed to participate in fancy-dress parties? Can a Muslim go to a mixed summer camp? What can a person do to control sexual desires when away from his wife? How much nudity is allowed during intercourse between a husband and wife? Does Islam allow surrogate mothers? What can one do to give up homosexuality? Must diabetics fast?

One intriguing aspect of the legal opinions expounded on IslamOnline.net (and also those issued by the European Council for Fatwa and Research) was the mention of the inquirer's first name and country of origin. Localities stretched from the United States to Germany and from Egypt to Fiji. While the very rationale of the council and of Qaradawi's school is the adaptation of rulings to

---

[40]   Yusuf al-Qaradawi, *Ummatuna*, p. 172.
[41]   *Idem*, *Ibn al-qarya wal-kuttab* (Cairo, 2002), pp. 15–30, 84–90.

localities, a Muslim reading the opinions can realise that the dilemmas he faces are shared by other Muslims too. The Muslim nation gained validity as a binding legal-religious entity. A similar effect resulted from the forums taking place on IslamOnline.net, where users worldwide address questions to an invited scholar on a certain issue.

One other common quality of these legal opinions was that, when relating to everyday problems, they were enhanced by human interest. Users got fascinating glimpses into human weakness, confusion, misfortune and redemption. In this respect they are no different than the 'Dear Abby' personal advice columns in Western newspapers, only here the fabric of society is not of a nation-state, but of the Muslim nation.

While the *fatwa* bank and other Islamic indoctrinations featured in the portal can be regarded as postmodern transformations of traditional *da'wa*, perhaps the more innovative aspect of IslamOnline.net (which onislam.net has continued) was its concept of covering world news from the perspective of the *umma*. While most news websites maintain the customary hierarchies of national and international news, Qaradawi's portal evaluated and mediated news in terms of each item's perceived importance to his concept of the global Muslim nation. This editorial decision manifested Qaradawi's belief in the universality and viability of the *umma*, and constituted an attempt to reestablish it as a community imagined by its members through global media.

News stories in IslamOnline.net under Qaradawi were concerned with Muslim states, Muslim minorities and Islam in general. For example, on 9 January 2007, its reports highlighted the growing number of Indonesian provinces and districts adopting new regulations for the implementation of shari'a; American strikes on al-Qaeda targets in Somalia; and new awareness training for US airport officials on how to approach Muslims travelling to Mecca for the *hajj* pilgrimage. To use Anderson's terminology on the role of gazettes in constructing national sentiments, what connects these Indonesian provinces, American attacks and new airport regulations is that they all concern members of the *umma* in different parts of the world. The aim is to infuse Muslims with a sense that they share a common fate. An unfolding sphere of events is created in which Muslims all over the world can share simultaneously.

This sphere was not restricted to religious-political issues. IslamOnline. net's news pages also covered culture, science and sports in Muslim societies around the world. In these pages, what connected a certain exhibition, book and football club was that they were perceived to be reflective of, or of interest to, the *umma* as a whole. For example, when the site featured a 10-year-old Turkish wunderkind playing football for Barcelona, the purpose was not to headline a world sporting event, something the site did not routinely cover, but to stress the boy's Muslim identity.[42]

Qaradawi's internet portal paid special attention to issues which reflect the unity of Muslims. For example, the site picked up a story from the American press concerning the Sunni–Shiite Montgomery Muslim Community School in Montgomery, Washington. There, 125 students from 18 countries were 'bridging a divide fuelled by the violence in Iraq', which is seen as evidence that Muslim Shiites and Sunnites in fact share the same morals and values, and therefore separation and antagonism is senseless. In this context the report mentioned a 'high-profile meeting between the Sunni and Shiite scholars, Sheikh Yusuf al-Qaradawi, president of the International Union for Muslim Scholars (IUMS), and Akbar Hashemi Rafsanjani, head of Iran's influential Expediency Council', in which the two 'recently urged Muslims world-wide to act in unison to face the challenges ahead'.[43]

The portal's news coverage and Qaradawi's activities complemented each other. Qaradawi graced the portal with his prestige and authority, and the portal magnified him by characterising his words as representing the Muslim world – a characterisation whose purpose was to create a reality rather than reflect it. For example, in September 2006 the Danish *Jyllands-Posten* newspaper published cartoons of the Prophet, and a Norwegian paper reprinted them, eliciting protests and threats of retaliation in Europe and Muslim countries. The portal highlighted Qaradawi's International Union's statement demanding that officials in both countries take a firm stand 'against these repeated insults to the Muslim nation and the Prophet followed by 1.3 billion people across the globe', or it would 'be forced to urge millions of Muslim across the world to boycott all Danish and Norwegian products and activities'.[44]

---

[42]   Al-Amin Andalusi, 'Turkish Muhammad ... Next Ronaldinho' (27 March 2007), available at http://www.islamonline.net/servlet/Satellite?c=Article_C&cid=11730879151 42&pagename=Zone-English-News/NWELayout, last accessed 27 March 2007.

[43]   IslamOnline.net staff, 'US School Bridges Sunni-Shiite Divide' (8 March 2007), available at http://www.islamonline.net/servlet/Satellite?c=Article_C&pagename=Zone-English-News/NWELayout&cid=1173364084003, last accessed 8 March 2007.

[44]   Adel Abd al-Halim, 'Scholars Threaten Boycott over Anti-Prophet Cartoons' (21 January 2006), available at http://www.islamonline.net/English/News/2006-01/21/article06.shtml, last accessed 21 January 2006.

Is the *Umma* Being Resurrected?

In an interview he gave for the German news magazine *Der Spiegel* on September 2005, Qaradawi was asked whether Muslims need a central authority such as the Catholic Pope. He answered that in Islam there was no pope, but did not neglect to mention that '[m]ost Muslims would like such a central authority, to avoid constant debate over contradictory and extremist scholarly opinions.'[45] An exploration of Qaradawi's ideology and activities reveals not only that the unity of the nation, the spread of Allah's final revelation and the constitution of religion as the sole framework of life are at the core of his agenda, but also that Qaradawi seeks for himself a pivotal role in enhancing this agenda, and that he considers advanced media technologies as his most effective weapons.

To what degree has Qaradawi been successful? While a period of less than two decades of using such technologies is too short a time to pass judgment, three inherent limitations can be identified.

First, while Qaradawi addresses a global audience, his media operations still function from a clearly defined national/territorial basis. To appear on al-Jazeera, Qaradawi cannot cross red lines set down by the Qatari regime. There are few limitations on what Qaradawi can say, but his capacity for political recruitment and mobilisation is restricted mainly to rhetoric. Furthermore, his dramatic dismissal from IslamOnline.net demonstrated that, despite his personal popularity and the success of the portal, the final word in any business initiative is reserved to the shareholders rather than the employees.

Second, while media can be an effective tool for political mobilisation, they are not sufficient in and by themselves. In the affair of the Danish cartoons, for example, Qaradawi was vociferous in regarding the controversy as an opportunity to unite the *umma*, in rejecting appeals for dialogue so long as an explicit apology from the Danish government was not forthcoming, and in attacking Muslims (such as the popular satellite preacher 'Amr Khaled) who dared to suggest otherwise.[46] His anti-Danish crusade, channelled through his various media, gained much publicity; but Qaradawi was in no position to transform his popularity into binding political decisions, or even long-term

[45]   Volkhard Windfuhr and Bernhard Zand, 'God Has Disappeared' (interview with Yusuf al-Qaradawi), *Der Spiegel*, 27 September 2005), available at http://www.spiegel.de/international/spiegel-interview-with-al-jazeera-host-yusuf-al-qaradawi-god-has-disappeared-a-376954.html, last accessed 19 February 2014.

[46]   Lindsay Wise, 'Amr Khaled vs. Yusuf al Qaradawi: The Danish Cartoon Controversy and the Clash of Two Islamic TV Titans', *Transnational Broadcasting Studies* 16, 2006, available at http://www.tbsjournal.com/wise.htm, last accessed 25 February 2014.

popular protests. The crisis illustrated the power, but also the limitations, of calling into being, through global media, a conceptualised political community which has no territorial base and holds no actual governing power.

Third, there is reason to doubt the extent to which Muslim media consumers develop a sense of sharing their political fate with an *umma* created in the virtual sphere. This doubt draws on a year's field research I conducted during 2007 in five mosques in Frankfurt am Main on the impact of advanced media technologies on the construction of Islamic identities. The five mosques were the Islamische Information und Serviceleistungen, which is German-speaking and serves many second-generation migrants, and the North-African-dominated and Arab-speaking Abu Bakr, Tariq Ibn Ziyad, Taqwa and Bilal mosques. I interviewed 17 first- and second-generation migrants and conversed in a less formal manner with several dozen others. My interviewees and partners in conversation originated from Egypt, Lebanon, Morocco, the Palestinian Authority territory and Tunisia. Interviews were conducted in English, German or Arabic, and at times in a combination of all three.

In the interviews I found that Islamic global media operations, including those of Qaradawi, have an effect in enhancing feelings of pride in Islam as a universal, powerful religion. One of my interviewees, Hasan, a 20-year-old high-school student and a second-generation migrant from a Moroccan family, who testified to having discovered his Islamic roots in the months before the interview through searching Islamic websites, said the following:

> Life here is hectic. There is so much to study, so much work. Then there is the time that we sit together in the living-room and watch Iqraa [a satellite religious channel, part of the ART network] during Ramadan. It's a special feeling – a feeling that we are all together, as a family, but also part of 1.2 billion Muslims all around the world.

While advanced media technologies promote a sense of Islamic universalism, I found no evidence that a sense of belonging to a global, viable, religious-political *umma*, imagined through the internet and satellite television, was evolving among any of my interviewees. More specifically, my field study did not suggest that Qaradawi's advanced media operations effectively promote either his vision for a resurrection of a united *umma* or his vision of providing a role for Muslim migrants in that *umma*.

Several limitations count against Qaradawi's ambitions. Some second-generation Muslim immigrants with whom I spoke, including the above-mentioned Hasan, had no idea who Qaradawi was. A serious obstacle is the language gap: Qaradawi's message is spread mainly in Arabic and English, two languages many of them do not speak.

Older, first-generation migrants, fluent in Arabic, presented ideological concerns about Qaradawi's project. They told me of the great respect they have for the Qatar-based scholar, but expressed resentment at his political interpretations of Islam and objected to the prospect of non-local jurists impacting their communities; they consider Qaradawi's concept of the *umma* as unrealistic, as well as undesirable in terms of their interests as Muslims in Germany. While some of the first-generation interviewees reported using IslamOnline.net as a source for learning of events in their homelands and the Arab world at large, none defined the portal as recounting the chronicles of 'the *umma*' and none hinted at sharing a political fate with Muslims worldwide.

Ahmad, a 44-year-old Moroccan school teacher, one of the community leaders in the Abu Bakr mosque, said:

> What is the *umma*? It doesn't mean much to me. There are states. There is Sudan. There is Saudi Arabia. There is Kuwait. If I want to visit Saudi Arabia, I need a visa. I cannot define the *umma*. I am a Muslim with German citizenship. I have my duties and my rights as a German. I never had a conflict between these duties and rights and being a Muslim.

Several first-generation migrants said that they reject the use of the internet for Islamic education, fearing it could misguide the young and undermine the authority of local community leaders. 'Abdallah, a 59-year-old unemployed Egyptian-German who was one of the founders of the Islamische Information und Serviceleistungen mosque and organises religious seminars for second-generation migrants seeking to learn more about their religion, argued:

> There's a difference between information you can trust and information you can't trust. Books, you know who wrote them. What's on the internet – you don't know who wrote it. How can I know if Qaradawi really controls his site? When you buy a book, you know whom you buy it from. And there's so much information on the internet, I don't like that. Also, I don't like to read on a screen.

Not only ideology matters; boredom is another reason for the limited effect of Qaradawi's global media. Qaradawi's – and others' – advanced media operations offer mainly 'heavy' religious and political content; the community they encourage to imagine provides very little relaxation. Several of my interviewees expressed their desire, after a hard day's labour, to watch television or read more entertaining online content. Satellite dishes provide ample alternatives, including some in Arabic – from cartoons to pornography; so does the internet. Muhammad, an unemployed 44-year-old and al-Azhar graduate who has lived in Germany since 1985, used to watch Qaradawi's television show frequently (on al-Jazeera), but in time lost interest. He explained:

> They speak about the same things. They now have nothing to attract you. For me, it is interesting to get Muslims to be active, to get them to return to morals, that they don't cheat. But it's not interesting to discuss whether I should or I shouldn't shake a woman's hand. That's not important.

Conclusion

A clear distinction should be drawn between imagined communities and the concept of a Muslim nation imagined globally through the media. Anderson's nation was an imagined community based on an affinity between territory and mass media. Advanced media technologies allow for modern imagined national communities to extend to some degree beyond their traditionally defined boundaries. However, the *umma* mediated through advanced media technologies is neither a modern imagined community nor an extended, postmodern, new imagined community. In fact, it is not an imagined community at all, but a *virtual* community. The two should not be confused. Qaradawi's *umma* does not have a territorial basis, nor even a symbolic one. There exist no government of the *umma*, no central bank, no military, no football team. Being a mere abstract manifestation of a religious-political ideology that finds its way to a global audience through global channels, this 'nation' can attract interest and emotions, and to some extent reinvigorate the myth and memory of Islamic unity. But the imagined Muslim *umma* lacks an essential linkage between the tangible and the imagined, without which an imagined community cannot be transformed into a politically viable force. Thus, while advanced media technologies endow Qaradawi with greater respect and influence, they fall short of enhancing his religious-political hope of meaningfully promoting global Muslim unity. The contribution of these media to diffusing religious law globally should also not be overstated.

Hasan al-Banna attempted to challenge the modern political order through modernist means. Yusuf al-Qaradawi, the most renowned of his disciples, found shelter in Qatar as a result of the failure of that challenge. For the past two decades Qaradawi has been attempting to challenge the modern political order through postmodern means. Ambitious and even resounding as his endeavours have been, in the final account they too may fail to transform myth and memory into reality.

Chapter 9

The Rating of Allah:
The Renaissance of Preaching
in the Age of Globalization

Shosh Ben-Ari

Preaching Islam has always attracted the attention of individuals and states, both Muslim and non-Muslim.[1] This interest became significantly greater following the September 11 events in the United States, and researchers are now focusing more than ever on the ways in which religious leaders spread their beliefs. In this chapter I will attempt to shed light on preachers' activities that are aimed towards those who are already Muslim—where there is no intention to convert them, but rather to strengthen their ties to Islam and, if they have gone astray, to bring them back to the faith. A better understanding of the preachers and their methods will surely help us to understand the vast numbers of those who follow them.

Preaching at the Beginnings of Islam

As with many other Islamic institutions, the origins of story-telling and preaching are controversial.[2] From the first Islamic century, we meet story-tellers and preachers in the city square, next to the mosques and in the public markets, telling stories and answering questions concerning ritual and right behavior posed by members of their audience.[3]

Let us join one of these preachers in the city of Basra. In the space of the mosque, at midday, seeking a brief respite from their daily toil and an escape

---

[1] See Thomas Walker Arnold, *The Preaching of Islam* (Lahore, 1961); Mustafa al-Tahhan, *Sifat al-Daʿiya al-Muslim* (Kuwait, 2000).

[2] See Khalil ʿAthamina, "Al-Qasas: Its Emergence, Religious Origin and Its Socio-Political Impact on Early Muslim Society," *Studia Islamica*, 76 (1992), pp. 53–74.

[3] Jonathan Porter Berkey, *Popular Preaching and Religious Authority in the Medieval Islamic Near East* (Seattle, WA, 2001), pp. 23–6.

from the sun beating down, a group of poor hard-working Muslims are seated. This is the time of day when they will listen to the story-teller, whose tales carry a promise of a better future, a day when the righteous will enjoy good fortune, evil will be punished and justice will prevail. The stories also help as a relief, an outlet from the burden and distress caused by a ruler that nobody dares to criticize.

Here is the story-teller standing and revising his tale; it is well known, as are the other stories he will tell to elaborate it. Most of the listeners are familiar with them down to the minutest detail. To stimulate the audience's attention and encourage them to participate actively in the story-telling, he engages them in a dialogue; with dramatic gestures he asks: "What was the name of the wolf that swallowed Yusuf?"[4] Among the generally ignorant listeners, who try to guess the name, there is by chance an educated person, a knowledgeable man who has read or recited the Qur'an. He calls out, saying that in the original story there was no wolf that swallowed Yusuf, and his brothers made up this story. "So if this is so," the story-teller persists, "tell me, please, what was the name of the wolf that did not swallow Yusuf?" He goes on, "Ya'qub, who refused to believe that Yusuf was dead, summoned the king of the wolves of Israel, and as he knew his language, asked him if he or his friends had swallowed Yusuf. 'Don't you know that God forbade us to eat prophets' flesh?' answered the king of the wolves."

Clearly, in the oral telling of the tale there were supplements and additions: the story-teller would frighten his audience in the marketplace or the mosque area with a vivid description of the wolf, his claws, and so on, and he might make his voice sound like an animal to imitate the way the wolf howls.[5] One may wonder why the venerable men of religion included this fantastic street-story in the canonical compilations of the "Stories of the Prophets";[6] it is probably because this anecdote serves to explain the text of the Qur'an, which implies that Ya'qub knew that his son had not been devoured.[7]

---

[4]   See Adam Metz, "The Lies of the Story-tellers," in *al-Hadara al-Islamiyya fi al-Qarn al-Rabi' al-Higri* (Beirut, 1967), Vol. 1, p. 429; Ramzi Na'na'a, *al-Israiliyyat wa-Aatharuha fi Kutub al-Tafsir* (Dimashq, 1970), p. 72.

[5]   The interaction between the story-teller and his audience contributes to the changes, and therefore we find several versions of the same story. See Julius Germanus, "Legacy of Ancient Arabia," *Islamic Culture*, 37 (1963), pp. 261–9; James Monroe, "Oral Composition in Pre-Islamic Poetry," *Journal of Arabic Literature*, 3 (1972), pp. 1–52; Malcolm Cameron Lyons, *The Arabian Epic and Oral Story-telling* (Cambridge, 1995), pp. 77–127.

[6]   The best known are those of al-Kisaai and al-Tha'labi, both termed *Qisas al-Anbiya*.

[7]   Usually there was a tendency to delete fictional elements, or at least to cover them with realistic facts, mainly in edifying literature. See Zaki Mubarak, *al-Nathr al-Fanni fi l-Qarn al-Rabi'* (Cairo, 1934), pp. 246–57; Albrecht Noth, *The Early Arabic Historical Tradition: A Source-Critical Study* (Princeton, NJ, 1994); Andras Hamori, "Exemplum, Anecdote and

The story-telling and preaching started as an individual's initiative, and became a part of a widespread network which contributed to the spread of the elaborated stories of the Qur'an as well as to the slow process in which the Islamic law took shape. In order to understand it we should try to understand the origins of the preaching and story-telling.

"The Stories of the Prophets" (*qisas al-anbiya*)

The genre named "The Stories of the Prophets" is defined in Arabic literature according to its subject matter, and varies between popular and formal religious literature (applied by the story-tellers, *al-Qusas*). Among the written genres, it can be placed alongside Qur'an commentary (*tafsir*) and the oral law—reports about Prophet Muhammad (*hadith*). There was undoubtedly a reciprocal influence between the written genres and the needs and style of those who told stories in public, the preachers, and so on. This is not a form of popular literature but rather a kind that simultaneously inhabits both formal literature and the street.

We do not have written versions in the style intended for the crowds, but we may infer such a style from clues occasionally appearing, from the enriching influence of the formal text, and from criticism of the lies and additions of the oral story-tellers, at least regarding material that invoked the formal religious elite and sparked its attacks, as we shall see.[8]

A writer is influenced by many factors, all centering on him, and he alone shapes his story. By contrast, the oral story is shaped by many effects that alter its nature and leave their mark. Oral story-tellers are the representatives of the people, obeying their listeners' demands and satisfying their needs. The version which reaches us at the end is shaped and moulded by the many transmitters who have passed the story down from generation to generation and from one place to another; unrestricted by any copyright, they have not held back from

---

the Gentle Heart in the Text of al-Gahshiyari," *Asiatische Studien*, 50 (1996), pp. 363–70. Nevertheless, literature which was also meant to entertain was less influenced by the urge to eliminate pure fiction. See Stefan Leder, "Conventions of Fictional Narration," in Leder (ed.), *Story-telling in the Framework of Non-Fictional Arabic Literature* (Wiesbaden, 1998), p. 41; Berkey, *Popular Preaching*.

[8]   Angelika Neuwirth attempted to trace some narrative elements that had undergone metamorphosis in the process of reading/listening. See her "Quranic Literary Structure Revisited: *Surat al-Rahman* between Mythic Account and Decodation Myth," in Leder (ed.), *Story-telling*, pp. 407–15.

changing the story. Despite the mutual feedback between the clerics and the religious story-tellers, many of the latter deviated from the norm, invented miraculous stories and exaggerated, to meet the expectations of the crowds in the street and the marketplace. Most of these tales were condemned by religious leaders; they were censored, and excluded from the written compilations of "The Stories of the Prophets."

The Growth of Oral Literature in Islam

In Islam, as in Judaism, popular literature was always accompanied by written literature. There was at no time a vacuum in which pure creativity could work without the influence of previous writings. The Islamic legends were inspired by the Jewish *midrashim* (commentaries) and by Christian stories, which were widespread in the Arabian peninsula before the emergence of Islam. But they also evince the influence of Arab culture in respect of style, formulation, and original motifs.

The oral tradition, particularly in pre-Islamic times (*jahiliyya*), was tightly bound up with the image of the poet, whose language and sayings in times of war were no less important than the bravery of the tribesmen, while in times of peace his words could undermine the tribal order or give rise to exploits, raids of revenge, or looting. The poet was also the tribe's historian, genealogist, and spokesperson. His status was elevated because his poetry faithfully reflected the entire tribal folklore and way of life. Initially, the carriers of the cultural heritage passed it on orally, which implies that in fact the flowering of story-telling and preaching dates back to pre-Islamic times.[9]

"The Stories of the Prophets" came into being as a part of the commentary on the holy book and as background to the events described in it. Popular literature drew on the Qur'an, but the most important element in its shaping was the dynamics between the story-teller and his audience. As most of the stories were religious, preaching was the main element.[10] The religious stories were a combination of fables, legends related to the reality of nomadic life, allegories, heroic stories, miracle tales, mythological stories, and the like; they were told

---

[9]   See Shawqi Dayf, *al-Fann wa-madhaahibihi fi al-Adab al-Jahili* (Cairo, 1960), p. 48.

[10]   In oral literature the art of using the voice is as important as the text itself. Sometimes changes in the tone or the rhythm of speech, body language, and expressions replaced the verbal contents. The story-teller could choose the words, idioms, actions, and metaphors that would provoke reactions based on the cultural values of the listeners and their norms of behavior.

on the days of the pilgrimage to Mecca, at the public baths, on the nights of Ramadan, and so on.

The Preaching Literature (*mawaʿiz*)

The preaching literature (*mawaʿiz*) is a sub-genre that developed against the background of bringing people back to religion. Ibn al-Jawzi (d. 1201) is a good example of a very productive writer who preached and wrote about preaching. His preaching attracted masses of listeners. In one of his books he wrote that his talks caused hundreds of Jews and Christians to convert to Islam and thousands of Muslims to repent.[11] The Andalusian traveler Ibn Jubayr (twelfth century) describes one such session:

> Afterwards we attended his second morning session of Thursday at the gate of Badr in the square of the Caliph's palace ... We woke early in order to see him and sat until this superb speaker came and stepped up onto the podium and the readers of the Qur'an formed rows before him. They saw what they wanted and enjoyed it and very soon their eyes started shedding tears ... He wended his way with preaching, and connected his sayings to verses from the holy book which had been recited by the Qur'an readers before, in the same session. The eyes shed tears and the souls exposed their deep secrets and people confessed their sins and repented.[12]

This was also the final will of Ibn al-Jawzi to his son: to continue propagating the religion in order to return people to Islam.[13]

In his books, Ibn al-Jawzi writes about religious matters such as prayer, charity, alms-giving and the like; other writings are on education, such as the need to take an interest in literature.

The preaching books deal with moral issues, but also with daily concerns such as parent–child relations and agriculture. Naturally, this kind of literature was meant to entertain the listeners/readers and to stimulate their interest, and not to burden them with recitation of the religious commandments and prohibitions.[14] Accordingly, it is akin to "The Stories of the Prophets" in content,

---

[11] Ibn al-Jawzi, *Laftat al-Kabid* (Beirut, 1987), p. 37.

[12] Ibn Jubayr, *Rihlat ibn Jubayr* (Beirut, 1974), p. 196.

[13] al-Jawzi, *Laftat al-Kabid*.

[14] One example of such a situation is described by Ibn al-Jawzi as follows: A preacher named Ardashir ibn Mansur al-ʿAbbadi stopped in Baghdad on his way home to eastern Iran after fulfilling the pilgrimage to Mecca, in the year 486/1093, and started preaching

though it clings more closely to the religious form: the chain of transmitters (*isnad*) appears in full throughout the story. This feature may be intended to affect the listeners/readers psychologically and to enhance the authenticity of the characters in the stories.[15] Ibn al-Jawzi wrote many books about the art of preaching, devised some rules, and offered advice to preachers.

As mentioned above, the story-tellers did not feel obliged to repeat the traditional stories exactly as they had heard them, and felt free to change and tailor them to suit their audience. One prominent feature was to add elements in order to dramatize the religious material, so as to intensify the effect on the listeners. Many parts of the stories were modified according to economic circumstances, national-religious needs, and the hidden desires of individuals in each and every generation. As already mentioned, the public needed to find an outlet for daily pressures and suffering, while disguising their criticism of the rulers and being unafraid to do so.

The folklorist Knappert gathered stories he had heard in Muslim countries such as Indonesia and Malaysia that are still popular today.[16] The purpose of the stories was to spread the knowledge of the right way, the way of Muhammad and his friends, who are the prototypes for the ideal way of life. Knappert's work was basically anthropological research aimed at collecting all the stories told in the mosques in order to reconstruct what he called "the popular religion." In the Middle Ages, the aim of the stories was to teach the younger generation the principles of Islamic doctrine in a pleasant way.

A basic rule in Islam is that all the prophets were Muslims and preached for Islam. Together with the ancient Arab messengers, they are included in the Muslim tradition of pre-Islamic world history. Another feature of "The Stories of the Prophets" is the inclusion of commentary and explanations, elaborate

---

in the Nizamiyya *madrasa* in the city. His sessions were very popular, and crowds filled the courtyard, the building and even the roof. Eventually the number of attendees reached 30,000. Al-'Abbadi had a strong influence on his listeners and probably also a profound dramatic sense, as "this man was more silent than not," as described by Ibn Jawzi. Once he finished his sermon the crowd would shout aloud, some abandoning their occupations in order to obey his call to piety, young men cut their hair and began to spend their days in mosques, while others roamed through the city's streets, spilling jugs of wine and smashing instruments. See Ibn al-Jawzi, *al-Muntazam fi tarikh al-muluk wa-al-umam* (Hyderabad, 1359h), Vol. 9, pp. 75–6; Abu Muzaffar Yunus Sibt ibn al-Jawzi, *Mirat al-zaman fi tarikh al-a'yan,* (Hyderabad, 1951–52), Vol.1, p. 5.

[15]   On the importance of these chains, see Julia Ashtiany, "*Isnamads* and Models of Heroes," *Arabic & Middle Eastern Literature,* 1(1), (1998).

[16]   Jan Knappert, *Islamic Legends: Histories of the Heroes, Saints and Prophets of Islam* (Leiden, 1985).

descriptions of Qur'anic events, and a complementary account of the original story. For this reason these stories are wholly dependent on the Qur'an. Berkey elaborates on the social and political context of preaching, but as it is not the main goal of this chapter I do no more than refer to it here.[17]

The Story-teller (*al-Qass*)[18]

At a very early stage, the need for simplification of the text of the Qur'an became quite clear, as its language, for the common people, was not always transparent, particularly in the case of vague allusions and esoteric verses. Narration was obviously an act of free will by the story-teller, as opposed to the strict authority of the religious elite (*'ulama*). Here the story-teller also showed his personal talent, embellishing the Qur'an's sayings and nurturing among the masses hope, faith in God, and visions of a better life in future.

This process reflects the gradual growth of an educational semi-elite consisting of story-tellers (*qussas*) and Qur'an readers (*qura'*), who included all the religious material in their preaching, and sometimes replaced the *'ulama*, thanks to the social or religious approval they received. The formal religious leaders at first tried to block the path of story-telling and preaching, because it involved the uncontrolled spread of material of other religions (mainly *Isra'iliyyat*[19]); also, at times, the story-tellers preached on issues with political and religious connotations. But the religious leaders' resistance was in vain, and a new class developed: the story-tellers.

Already in the first century of Islam the story-teller is mentioned as the person whose role in the mosque was to quote and elaborate the stories of the Qur'an. In the Qur'an itself there is an explicit instruction to tell the ancient forefathers' stories, because one of the purposes of the holy book is to make believers aware of their history: "We have brought upon you inspiration, just as we have done with Noah, Jonas, Aaron and Solomon; and to David we have

---

[17] For further information, see Berkey, *Popular Preaching*, ch. 3, pp. 53–69.

[18] The first to take note of the historical importance of the *qass* was Goldziher. See Ignaz Goldziher, *Muslim Studies* (London, 1971), Vol. 2, p. 150.

[19] On *Israiliyyat*, see Georges Vajda, "Isra'iliyyat," *Encyclopedia of Islam*, 2nd edition, Vol. IV, pp. 211–12; Louis Cheikho, "Quelques légendes islamiques apocryphes," *Mélanges de la faculté Orientale, Université Saint-Joseph*, 4 (1910), pp 5–56; Roberto Tottoli, "Origin and Use of the Term *Israiliyyat* in Muslim Literature," *Arabica*, 46 (1999), pp. 193–221; Jane Dammen McAuliffe, "Assessing the *Israiliyyat*: An Exegetical Conundrum," in Leder (ed.), *Story-telling*, pp. 345–64.

given the book of Psalms and messengers about whom we have already told you and other messengers about whom we have not yet told you."[20] The evident goal is to use these stories as a model and a tool to teach the righteous way. Some of the stories were meant to encourage patterns of conduct, others to serve as warnings—a lesson for all to see.

The verb *qassa* originally means "bringing news": "We will tell you [*naqussu*] from his news,"[21] and "to follow the footsteps": "... and he returned following their footsteps [*qassa*]."[22] Only later did *qassa* become synonymous with narration generally. The story-teller apparently also became an orator (*khatib*), Qur'an reader (*qari*), and the leader of the community in prayer (*imam*).[23] But his main role was to stir up the masses by telling semi-didactic stories.

Al-Maqrizi[24] differentiated between the personal and the formal story-teller—the latter was a functionary established by Mu'awiya. His main purpose was, after the Morning Prayer, to curse all the infidels and enemies of Islam, and on Friday, after the sermon, to interpret the Qur'an. The sermon (*khutba*) became an integral part of Friday prayers, festivals, and special events such as the eclipse of the sun or a drought, under Umayyad rule (661–750). However, it is already Muhammad who is mentioned as preaching so as to exhort the warriors before battle and on festivals (here we might find a Jewish influence of prayers on holy days, or the Christians' Sunday sermon).[25]

The first generation of story-tellers in the mosque were still tightly bound up in religious studies. At first the stories were taken from the Qur'an unchanged, together with interpretation and commentary; the story-tellers sat in the

---

20   *Surat al-Nisa* (4), 163.

21   *Surat al-A'raf* (7), 101.

22   *Surat al-Kahf* (18), 64.

23   See Johannes Pederson, "The Islamic Preacher," *Goldziher Memorial* (1948), Vol. 1, p. 232; *idem*, "*Khatib*," *Encyclopedia of Islam 2*, Vol. IV, pp. 1109–11.

24   Taqi al-Din Ali ibn al-Maqrizi (1364–1442) was an Egyptian historian. Although he was a Mamluk-era historian and himself a Sunni Muslim, he is remarkable in this context for his unusually keen interest in the Ismaili Fatimid dynasty and its role in Egyptian history. See Paul Walker, *Exploring an Islamic Empire: Fatimid History and its Sources* (London, 2002), p. 164.

25   While Becker is inclined to connect the *khutba* to the Christian mass, Mittwoch connects it to the reading of the Torah by the Jews, mainly because of "The Stories of the Prophets," which are told in it. See Carl Heinrich Becker, "Die Kanzal um Kultus des altan Islam," in Carl Bezold (ed.), *Orientalische Studien Theodor Nöldeke ... gewidmet* (Giessen, 1906), p. 331; Eugen Mittwoch, "Zur Enstehungsgeschichte des islamischen Gebets und Kultus," *Abhandlungen der koniglich-prrussischen Akademie der Wissenschaften* (1913), pp. 1–42.

mosques and plied their craft there. Initially, their activities did not bother the rulers; only when the stories became more like the preaching of religious zealotry, conveying political messages or supporting new religious doctrines that sprang up every now and then, did they begin to anger the authorities.

Opposition to the Story-tellers

From the beginning of the eighth Islamic century, resentment towards, reservations about, and criticism of the story-tellers increased.[26] They were giving free rein to their imagination and inclined more and more to street stories, intended to attract their listeners' attention through fantastic inventions and an embroidered style of telling. Soon, the opposition began spreading to the religious establishment; the clerics did not necessarily oppose the content of the preaching per se, because as long as it served religious purposes, the formal Muslim leadership could tolerate it. But anger really began when story-tellers argued with educated people and turned serious religious matters into fun and entertainment, using piquant etymologies and charlatanism disguised as serious debate. Biblical and Qur'anic stories were decorated with all kinds of anecdotes, which became the main content of the stories. The formal claims against them may be categorized into four groups:

1. Story-telling was not a common practice (*sunna*) in the time of the prophet, and so should be stopped.
2. The story-tellers distracted the listeners from the important occupation of religious studies, and therefore should be banned.
3. Many stories contained elements which might corrupt believers' morals.
4. Most story-tellers were uneducated and ignorant.

Apart from their in-principle resistance, it is probable that the authorities were concerned more at the growing status of the story-tellers than at the content of their stories. The story-teller himself was gaining prominence and his popularity becoming more widespread, far more than his story-telling. He was displacing the orator and acquiring a position among the masses, who began to turn to him for advice on all aspects of life, and almost sanctified his sayings. This phenomenon was loathsome to the ruling circles. They were afraid of the

---

[26]　See Johannes Pedersen, "The Criticism of the Islamic Preacher," *Die Welt des Islams*, 2 (1953), pp. 216–31.

formation of an organized opposition, with the story-tellers at its head; and more than once, story-tellers used the framework of their stories to criticize and even attack the rulers.

At a certain stage, the authorities started issuing explicit prohibitions against telling stories. The increasing numbers of formal punishments mentioned in the history books create the impression that the prohibitions were ineffective: even if the story-tellers were expelled from the mosques, they most probably continued reaping success among uneducated audiences, and drawing crowds that were more vivid, interested and numerous than the audiences of the religious leaders (*'ulama*)—this sounds familiar in the age of TV—or those of the legal theologians (*fuqaha*), who tried to generate contempt for the story-tellers.

Justifying Story-telling

The reasons given by the story-tellers to justify their occupation were compiled at an early stage by Abu 'Abdallah ibn Muhammad Munif al-Kinani, one of the earliest collectors of "The Stories of the Prophets," if not the first. He insisted that the importance of the tales lay not necessarily in their historical accuracy but in their emphasis on moral concerns. Talking about the wisdom of the stories, he quoted the verse: "We are telling you the stories of the messengers, everything that can strengthen your heart; and by this you will learn the truth and it will be for you a lesson and a reminder."[27] He lists five arguments in favor of story-telling:

1. The importance of story-telling lies in emphasizing the moral aspects of the stories about the prophets. Historical accuracy is less relevant.
2. The examples taken from the stories prior to Muhammad constitute a moral support to the prophet himself and to the way he preached.
3. These stories prove the predominance of the nation (*umma*) of Muhammad.
4. The stories help to improve the nature and education of the people. Most of them talk about heavenly rewards as well as the punishment of the infidels, and all the listeners are able to derive moral benefits by thinking about and scrutinizing the meaning of the stories.
5. The stories serve as a model to be imitated, by describing characters which are prototypes of holy men, righteous and good believers.

---

[27]   *Surat Hud* (11), 120.

The rulers' turning against the story-tellers became increasingly aggressive until eventually it caused the latter to become no more than poor beggars. Thus, from being a popular interpreter of the holy book, the story-teller became a clown. He exchanged edifying stories for jokes and twisted stories about biblical and Qur'anic figures, who he presented as ridiculous. It was the lack of integrity linked with their name that brought about the change: the story-tellers considered to hold a high-status position as serious preachers were replaced by less formal tellers, and the content of the stories lost its didactic goals and became amusing, and serving political purposes.

In spite of the war waged on them by the religious leaders, such stories were widespread, and a few compilations were written in the fourth century of Islam. This genre survived in small circles in all the Muslim countries, but the preachers were considered to be telling stories for didactic purposes, mainly for children. Let us now turn to the twenty-first century.

The Popularity of Religious Preachers Today

After centuries of being kept away from religious and political life, present-day preachers are regaining their status. The Islamic resurgence of the past few decades, accelerated by globalization trends and influences, has contributed to a gradual growth of the educational elite of televangelists and online preachers, who have replaced traditional religious leaders thanks to the social or religious approval they receive.[28]

The New Preachers emerged in Egypt at a time when the violent radical Islamist organizations of the mid 1990s were either fading away or changing course. The Muslim Brotherhood was embargoed in the political arena, and radical groups like al-Jama'a al-Islamiyya were reworking their philosophies, renouncing violence as a means for political action and change.[29] While Egypt stagnated politically and economic growth remained slow, neo-liberal reforms

---

[28]   Lutfi Wa'il, in his *Dawlat al-Du'aa al-Judud* (Cairo, 2007), claims that the easiest way to define the New Preachers is by their appearance, which differs from that of the old preachers mainly in the way they dress and in the language they use. See ibid., pp. 13–14. See also Patrick Gaffney, *The Prophet's Pulpit: Islamic Preaching in Contemporary Egypt* (Berkeley, CA, 1994).

[29]   About the Jama'a, see: Caryle Murphy, *Passion for Islam: Shaping the Modern Middle East: The Egyptian Experience* (New York, 2007), p. 65; Lawrence Wright, *The Looming Tower: Al Qaeda and the Road to 9/11* (New York, 2006). See also at <http://www.cdi.org/terrorism/algamaa.cfm>, last accessed 15 October 2012.

nonetheless created new business opportunities. In this milieu, the New Preachers emerged as one of the most important socio-religious phenomena in Egyptian society.[30]

The phenomenon began with a few isolated celebrities, and was led primarily by two young preachers, 'Amr Khalid and Khalid al-Jundi,[31] who transformed the new religious cadre into a formidable social force. This evolution coincided with the decline of veteran Islamic preachers such as Muhammad al-Ghazali, Shaykh Abdel Hamid Kishk, and Shaykh Muhammad Mutawali al-Sha'arawi, leaving a vacuum to be filled by younger stars.

The New Preachers' reliance on the mass media and new media is the first thing setting them apart from the old guard. Many of the New Preachers rose to prominence by using non-traditional outreach methods. Instead of conducting public religious instruction exclusively in mosques they offered lessons in elite upper-class clubs and five-star hotels; one of the New Preachers even gave lectures in Dreamland, an Egyptian up-market housing development with a golf course. These non-traditional gatherings were instrumental in introducing the preachers to the media, which in turn made them into superstars, with popular programs and legions of fans. The media's attention added to the preachers' perceived charisma, and later translated into huge profits, as will be explained below.

One of the distinguishing characteristics of most New Preachers is their use of new media technologies, which allow them to address larger audiences and to demonstrate their compatibility with the computer age. Some preachers use email and chat rooms for online prayer and religious instruction, but other mass-media tools are equally important. Whereas in the year 709 the preacher used to sit next to the mosque with his poverty-stricken listeners, the modern Muslim preachers (*al-wu'az al-judud* or *al-du'a al-judud*) of the early twenty-first century are drawing hundreds of young people who are hungry for religious teaching by moderate preachers—or should that be socio-economically smart preachers?

'Amr Khalid,[32] who started preaching in the mosque he used to attend, had to move to a bigger mosque in another neighborhood, but due to the traffic jams (surely an excuse?) which were created by the hundreds of followers who came

---

[30]   Lindsay Wise, *Words from the Heart: New Forms of Islamic Preaching in Egypt*, unpublished MPhil thesis, Oxford University, 2003, available at http://users.ox.ac. uk/~metheses/WiseNoImages.pdf, last accessed 20 February 2014; Hossam Tammam and Patrick Haenni, "Chat Shows, Nashid Groups, and Lite Preaching: Egypt's Air-Conditioned Islam," *Le Monde diplomatique* (English edn), September 2003.

[31]   Wa'il, in his *Dawlat al-Du'aa al-Judud* (pp. 15–22), tells the stories of two preachers who paved the way for these New Preachers: Yasin Rushdi and Umar abd al-Kafi.

[32]   For a biography of Khalid, see Lutfi Wa'il, *Dawlat*, pp. 35–95.

to listen to him, he had to move nearly 20 miles to the west of Cairo, to a yet bigger mosque. However, his move did not stop buses packed with thousands of young people from arriving every week, not only from Cairo but also from Alexandria and Port Said. His fans filled the streets and the rooftops around the mosque. Many others came with their cars, the newest models on the market, to listen to sermons which lasted up to five hours non-stop.

Many of 'Amr Khalid's followers grew up in traditional rather than extremely religious families. They heard his sermons, saw him on television, or heard about his lectures from friends. 'Amr Khalid was different from any religious speaker they had ever heard. He was not an *imam*; in fact he had no official religious credentials at all. He is young, and dresses in stylish European suits or polo shirts rather than robes. He speaks literary Arabic (*fusha*) but peppers his sermons with spoken dialect and slang. He tells the same "stories of the prophets" that often conclude with simple and satisfying morals, together with a list of practical lessons to apply in the week ahead. Unlike traditional Muslim religious leaders, Khalid does not parse the finer points of Islamic law or go too deeply into political questions, emphasizing that he is not qualified to speak on either. He talks instead about how to be successful and happy and how to enjoy life while avoiding sin.

Though 'Amr Khalid built his ministry in Egypt, he began to turn his attention towards a new audience—second-generation Muslims in Europe. The ballrooms of Paris, London, Vienna, and the other big European cities where he lectures are crowded with educated young people, often fluent in English, well-off and worldly, who have become more religious than their parents. His unique blend of conservative Islamic belief and Western style has become popular at the moment when governments and scholars from Washington to Cairo are wrestling with the question of whether religious Islam is compatible with democracy, Western culture, and globalization.

'Amr Khalid is only one of a new breed of moderate Muslim televangelists who are challenging Islamic fundamentalists in preaching with a blend of piety and modernity over the airwaves of satellite TV. Mu'iz Mas'ud, Ahmad al-Shugairi, Sallah al-Gumal, Khalid al-Jundi, and many others are met with a rock-star welcome whenever they appear on stage. They stand in stark contrast to the most respected and popular Muslim figure on television and the internet, Yusuf al-Qaradawi, who appears on al-Jazeera and is widely considered to be a spiritual leader of the Muslim Brotherhood, and thus one of the key figures of Islamism. Even though he is totally different from the New Preachers, his activities are another example of the globalization of Islamic preaching. Since he constitutes a link between the traditional preacher and the New Preachers, I will try to give a brief description of the relevant views of Qaradawi, who is the exception that proves the rule: an *'alim* who has partly reinvented himself as a popular preacher.

Shaykh Yusuf al-Qaradawi[33] is the co-founder and president of the International Association of Muslim Scholars and of the European Council for Fatwa and Research. He has his own Arabic-language website and supervises the popular site Islam Online, which is bilingual (English and Arabic). His website describes him as the most prominent voice of moderation in Islam (*wasatiyya*), bridging the gap between traditionalists and modernizers. He gained global fame through his regular appearances on the religious program *al-shari'a wa-l-hayat*, broadcast by al-Jazeera, but even before that Qaradawi had been identified as one of the key figures of Islamism, capable of drawing crowds reaching over a quarter of a million.[34]

Qaradawi resents being categorized as a traditionalist, and insists that he has always been a reformer. Nevertheless, he carefully cultivates the image of a shaykh, and always appears in public wearing a traditional dark robe and a white turban wrapped around a red cap. He is keen to preserve the *'ulam*'s control of religious affairs: during the crisis over the Danish cartoons, for example, he attacked 'Amr Khalid for taking part in a conference in Denmark to promote an interfaith dialogue, deeming it "a departure from the *'ulama*'s consensus." Indeed, Qaradawi stresses that "reform of [the Muslim] religion must be carried out from within, using its legal instruments, according to the way of its people and its *'ulama*."[35] Qaradawi argues that the adaptation of Islam to the modern world should be based on the legacy of the past, an immense wealth of jurisprudence illuminating the way for contemporary jurists to build a legal framework that draws on its logic, spirit, basis, directives, and interpretations to treat the problems of this age, while taking into account changes in time, place, and the human condition.[36]

Qaradawi is a fierce critic of globalization, which he characterizes as

---

[33]   For a detailed biography of Qaradawi see "Al-Sira al-Tafsiliyya lil-Qaradawi," al-QaradawiNet, 24 November 2004; Bettina Gräf and Jakob Skovgaard-Petersen (eds), *The Global Mufti: The Phenomenon of Yusuf al-Qaradawi*, London, 2009); Ana Belén Soage, "Shaykh Yusuf al-Qaradawi: Portrait of a Leading Islamist Cleric," *Middle East Review of International Affairs*, 12/1 (March 2008); Uriya Shavit, Chpter 8, this volume.

[34]   See Raymond Baker, "Invidious Comparisons: Realism, Postmodern Globalism, and Centrist Islamic Movements in Egypt," in John Esposito (ed.), *Political Islam: Revolution, Radicalism or Reform?* (Cairo, 1997), p. 125.

[35]   Yusuf al-Qaradawi, *Thaqafatuna Bayna al-Infitah wal-Inghilaq* (Cairo, 2000), p. 54.

[36]   *Idem, Ummatuna Bayna Qarnayn* (Cairo, 2000), p. 225.

The imposition of the political, economic, cultural, and social hegemony of the United States over the world ... It does not mean a relationship of fraternity, such as that favoured by Islam, or a relationship of equality, such as that favoured by the free and the noble all over the world. It means the relationship between the master and the slave, the giant and the dwarf, the arrogant and the meek.[37]

The new preacher A. Shugairi says about Qaradawi: "He should understand that Islam is an excellent product that needs better packaging." Shugairi is a rising star in a new generation of "satellite shaykhs" whose religion-themed television shows have helped fuel a religious revival across the Arab world. Shugairi and others like him have succeeded by appealing to a young audience hungry for religious identity but deeply alienated from both politics and the traditional religious establishment, especially in the fundamentalist forms of the latter now common in Saudi Arabia and Egypt.

In part, that is a matter of style: a handsome, athletically built 35-year-old, Shugairi effortlessly mixes deep religious commitment with hip, playful humor. He earned an MBA during his years in California, and sometimes refers to Islam, as remarked above, as "an excellent product that needs better packaging." But his message of sincere religious moderation is tremendously powerful: for young Arabs, he offers a way to reconcile a world painfully divided between East and West, pleasure and duty, the rigor of the mosque and of a desk-bound working life. Shugairi's main TV program, *Khawatir* ("thoughts"), could not be more different from the dry lecturing style of so many Muslim clerics. In one episode on literacy, the camera follows him as he wanders through Jeddah asking people where to find a public library (no one knows). In another, he pokes through a trash bin, pointing to mounds of rotting rice and hummus that could have been donated to the poor. He even sets up *Candid Camera*-style gags, confronting people who pocket a wallet from the pavement and asking them if the Prophet Muhammad would have done the same. Inevitably, hard-line clerics dismiss Shugairi as a lightweight who toadies to the West, while on the other hand some liberals lament that Shugairi and the other satellite shaykhs are Islamizing the secular elite of the Arab world.

Part of his inspiration, Shugairi says, came from the terrorist attacks of 11 September 2001, which hit him especially hard, as someone who spent his formative years in the United States. "Many of us felt a need to educate youth to a more moderate understanding of religion," he said, during an interview in

---

[37] Ibid., p. 232.

a cafe. Yet his approach to Islam, as with most of the other satellite TV figures who have emerged in the past few years, is fundamentally orthodox. He says that women should wear the *hijab*, and he talks of the Qur'an as a kind of constitution that should guide Muslim countries.

Shugairi's own life—and especially his struggle with the poles of decadence and extreme faith—is an essential feature of his appeal to many fans. Born in the USA in 1973 to a wealthy, cosmopolitan family, Shugairi went to college at age 17 in Long Beach, California. By his own account, he completely stopped praying. He chased women in clubs, and he even—for a year—drank. In 1995 he got married, and the pendulum swung toward a severe Islamism, as he angrily renounced the freedoms of his student life. He moved back to Saudi Arabia to manage his father's importing business, but his wife did not share his turn toward extremism, and the marriage soon ended in divorce.

It was then that he began studying with a cleric, 'Adnan al-Zahrani, who exposed him to the idea that Islam's greatest strength comes from its diversity and its openness to new ways of thinking. For the first time, Shugairi found a way to balance the warring forces in his life, his American self and his Saudi self. For much of his young audience, this synthesis is the key to his appeal. These young Muslims have inherited a world painfully divided between what they hear from the clerics and what they see on satellite television and the internet. This is especially true in Saudi Arabia, with its powerful and deeply conservative religious establishment. In his shows, Shugairi mixes deep religious commitment with playful humor, gaining the admiration of thousands of young Muslims. Most of them admit that they are not fans of religious programs, but Shugairi excels in attracting them.[38]

The picture will not be complete without mentioning Tariq Ramadan. Though he is not one of the New Preachers, as his main goal is to bridge the gap between Islam and the West, yet there are many similarities between his way of establishing contact with his followers and that of the New Preachers, and like them he is a by-product of globalization's influences. He claims that his main target is to help Muslims integrate into Western societies, and so introduce liberal Islam to the West.

From before the beginning of the twenty-first century, the Arab world has been increasingly open to globalization and its projections. Some Muslims have reacted by adopting extreme fundamentalist interpretations of Islamic law and ways of conduct, while others have turned secular. The New Preachers offer a

---

[38]   At http://www.islamonline.net/servlet/Satellite?c=Article_C&pagename=Zone-English-News/, last accessed 17 October 2010.

middle-ground solution, balancing religious devotion with an acceptance of modern life.[39]

Preaching—A Source of Income

The tremendous sums of money which flow into the pockets of the preachers are discussed in the media, and though the media as a source are not always reliable, their conclusions can be based on certain evidence and the balance of probabilities.[40] Apparently, there is also a full-scale industry growing up alongside the preaching. Contemporary preachers are up-to-date in the entertainment industry of our times, just as the early Islamic preachers were up-to-date in their own day. One might also wonder to what extent the phenomenon is being produced by media and travel executives rather than the preachers themselves.[41]

Much tourism revolves around it: organized trips to shows by preachers, mainly for young men and girls. 'Amr Khalid the Egyptian and Tariq Suwaydan of Kuwait are two popular preachers who travel all over the world, and organized groups fly to their performances.[42] Travel agencies which arrange tours to football games or popular tourist attractions are now offering deals to attend these shows. Groups of 50–200 participants buy tickets for the shows in advance, spend a few days in whatever country the preacher is appearing in, and then return home. These groups contain both men and women, and this causes agitation in circles that suspect that the purpose of the tour is not exclusively religious.[43]

---

[39] Samantha M. Shapiro, "The Telegenic Face of Conservative Islam," 28 April 2006, http://www.nytimes.com/2006/04/28/world/africa/28iht-muslimweb.html, last accessed 20 February 2014.

[40] Al-Sayed Zaied, "Da'wa for Dollars: A New Wave of Muslim Televangelists," at http://www.arabinsight.org, last accessed 16 October 2010; Patricia Backora, "Scriptural Truths Waved Aside by Covetous Preachers," 11 May 2011, at http://www.nairaland.com/nigeria/topic-665220.0.html#msg8301278, last accessed 20 February 2014.

[41] Patrick Haenni, "Islamisme, management et vidéoclips," *L'Expansion*, 1 April 2005, available at http://www.lexpansion.com/art/134.0130015.0.html, last accessed 16 October 2010.

[42] See http://www.facebook.com/group.php?gid=131811948746, last accessed 12 January 2013.

[43] It should be noted that the need for a "respectable" environment which educated girls can enter freely, especially to meet potential marriage partners, is a very urgent one, if only because it avoids having someone "suitable" found by the family. This is a dynamic that seems to underlie a great deal of religious activity, and even perhaps the burgeoning of coffee shops.

However, the tour organizers insist that they check each and every passenger thoroughly; the putative participants on the tours must be vetted in a personal interview with the tour guide to "prove" that they are genuinely interested in the religious preaching, and do not intend to use the trip for immoral purposes. There are strict rules to determine the morality of each person by his or her appearance, and the way he or she talks helps to judge the potential traveller's purpose: to change oneself positively, by listening to the preacher, or merely to enjoy oneself.

The preachers do not receive any payment from these groups, but they do earn a large commission from the hotels in which the groups stay. The costs of such tours are not small, as the youngsters usually come from wealthy families; even a short trip of this sort can cost US$3,000 or more.

The commercials which promote the tours state that the young people are destined to inhabit the centers of economic power in their countries, and therefore must be guided down the right path. The meaning of this "right way" is a source of debate between religious leaders, who see any transformation of religion into entertainment as a serious matter, particularly when the knowledge of these preachers is questionable. The discussions are almost the same as those which revolved around the activities of preachers in the first days of Islam. The arguments for and against them have also changed little: they are being attacked for their lack of a deep Islamic education. The emphasis today is on their ignorance, their inclination towards Western culture, and their greed.

Authority's attitude towards the New Preachers becomes more ambivalent the bigger their popularity. Arab regimes across the Middle East have attempted to use centralized control of television, cinema, print, and radio to manipulate nationalist discourse and impose their own definitions of Arabism, Islam, and modernity on the public consciousness. Religious content in the state-controlled media has ranged from calls to prayers and Ramadan programs to sermons and talk shows.[44] At the beginning it seems that the Egyptian government could not decide whether to promote the preachers actively, to ignore or simply tolerate them, or to fight their growing popularity.[45]

'Amr Khalid, for example, began getting "visits" from the Egyptian police, who imposed new conditions on his lectures, followed him, and slashed his car's tyres, until he was ordered to stop preaching in Egypt and was forced to

[44] See Gilles Kepel, *The Prophet and Pharaoh: Muslim Extremism in Egypt* (London 1985), p. 173.
[45] Armando Salvatori has talked about this dilemma in connection with Mustafa Mahmud and other New Preachers. See his "'Public Islam' and the Nation-State in Egypt," *ISIM Newsletter*, 8 (September, 2001), p. 20.

emigrate, first to Lebanon and later to London. In Saudi Arabia the authorities seem to prefer the rush of youngsters towards popular preachers to their listening to radical extremist preachers or surfing their internet sites. Their attitude would seem to be that if the style of the New Preachers helps the young generation to observe religious teachings while maintaining their modern way of life—then let it be so. It also counterbalances the image of Islam created by the fundamentalists, by saying that Islam is international, modern, and tolerant.[46]

Preaching on Television

The new Muslim televangelists are riding a satellite TV boom that began after the Persian Gulf War in 1991, when the region's elites were shocked by the power and reach of CNN. The Middle East at the beginning of the second decade of the twenty-first century has at least 370 satellite channels, nearly triple the number there were in the end of the twentieth century, according to Arab Advisors Group, a Jordan-based research firm. Among channels that offer news, movies, and music videos, at least 27 are dedicated to Islamic religious programs, an increase from only five channels two years ago, and the numbers are still growing.[47]

Liberal preachers, who appear dressed in Western apparel and without beards, contribute to the prosperity enjoyed by the religious stations in the last few years. Such success is evident from about 250 religious programs broadcast daily to over 350 million viewers. On the religious channels, some funded by governments and others by wealthy investors, voices such as Mas'ud's still compete with extremists for attention.

Who will improve the ratings of a certain religious television station: the modern preacher 'Amr Khalid[48] or three preachers from the conservative stream, the *'ulama*, with their long beards, who recently decided to leave that station

---

[46] Howeidy has suggested that the effectiveness of the government's media monopoly has been eroded over time, especially with the new media technologies and the internet, which facilitate a more pluralist and participatory discursive authority. See Fahmy Howeidy, interview by the author, 16 December 2002, quoted in Lindsay Wise, *"Words from the Heart"*, p. 39. On the new public sphere, outside formal state control, which is emerging in Muslim communities across the globe, see Dale Eickelman and Jon Anderson, "Redefining Muslim Publics," in: Eickelman and Anderson (eds), *New Media in the Muslim World: The Emerging Public Sphere* (Bloomington, IN, 1999).

[47] See online updated reports on this group, available at http://www.arabadvisors.com/publishedreports.htm, last accessed 20 February 2014.

[48] http://www.amrkhaled.net/news/details.php?id=141, last accessed 12 January 2013.

and join its rival? This has been the dilemma before the Saudi businessman Mansur ibn Karsa, owner of the station al-Nas,[49] as its ratings have fallen dramatically of late. The station started in Egypt two years ago in an old, small office building, under the slogan "The station of the people for the people." At first it was operated by volunteers, who performed all kinds of services without payment. There were dream-interpreters, tax consultants, match-makers, and even wedding photographers. Most of the income was from mobile phone calls and text messages that reached the editorial desk.[50]

The change occurred when the owners decided to turn al-Nas into a religious station. They hired the services of three popular conservative preachers, gave them unlimited air-time, agreed to their religious demands—to fire all the women who worked at the station and to have female visitors cover their heads, as well as totally to eliminate music. And the money started pouring in. The preachers brought their adherents with them from their previous stations, and many viewers called in, filling the al-Nas coffers.[51] This "Stories of the Prophets" replaced many television series, and its variations started appearing in prime time.

This success was followed by the music station al-Khalijiyya[52] being turned into a religious station. The preachers explained that it was not proper for the owner of such a station to disseminate corrupt Western culture, but this caused resentment and angry responses among many viewers, who opposed the takeover by the clerics. Meanwhile, the station's existing slogan was replaced by "The Screen that Will Lead You to Paradise," and it flourished. So much so, that when the station manager brought in a Sufi preacher, the conservative preachers delivered an ultimatum demanding his removal. Furthermore, they insisted on establishing a Sharia committee in the station, which would decide who was allowed to speak and who was not a true representative of God. The manager, however, decided not to give way to this, believing that a variety of preachers would contribute to ratings. The three preachers thereupon resigned, and moved to the rival al-Rahma station, also owned by a Saudi businessman. The issue that infuriated them most, even to the point of rejecting the offer to double their share of the profits, was said to be the station's intention to grant

---

[49]   On this channel and its programs, see http://www.alnas.tv, last accessed 12 January 2013.

[50]   al-Nas had to abandon SMSs and premium-priced calls after people got their six-monthly telephone bills and discovered to their horror how much their children (and sometimes they themselves) had run up in phone charges. The government was then forced to change the rules about premium-rate calls.

[51]   On this station today, see http://anaraby.net/122, last accessed 1 December 2012.

[52]   http://www.khkh.tv, last accessed 1 December 2012.

a great deal of air-time to 'Amr Khalid, the liberal preacher who appeared in Western dress, had no beard and dealt with everyday matters, and whose live audience consisted of men and women, seated together. He was also one of the richest preachers, and required a special studio to suit the style of his preaching. This last demand was approved after a popularity poll gave his appointment the viewers' sweeping support. The television ratings of the New Preachers soared, while the religious stations' burgeoning prosperity over the past few years has been paralleled by the growing share in it which the New Preachers earn from their television programs.

'Amr Khalid posted on his website the list of lectures he would deliver during the month of Ramadan; the main theme was to be Qur'anic stories. Nevertheless, he emphasized that he did not mean the genre "The Stories of the Prophets," but only the stories told in the holy book. He also asked for feedback from surfers on his website. The question is why he thought fit to make this artificial division between genres of stories. The answer might lie in his desire to differentiate between his activities and those of the old preachers, in order to deflect the accusations made against the latter.

The New Preachers—Good for Islam?

With the New Preachers rising to fame by using Western neo-liberal methods to preach sacred Islamic values, the controversy over the group is unsurprising. Modern global communications have lent themselves well to these individuals, allowing them, in true neo-liberal, capitalist, American fashion, to rise from merchants to superstars. Ultimately, "*da'wa* for 27 dollars" (one of the advertisements promoting lectures by preachers), commercialization, and mass dissemination of Islamic preaching can be construed as either positive or negative. Regardless of whether or not their rise to fame is a boon or a detriment to Islam and its practitioners, however, the New Preachers' popularity is a striking trend, and warrants continued examination.

The new moderate preachers are emerging in the midst of an Islamic religious revival, especially among the poor, that has seen mosque attendance boom and fundamentalist imams become increasingly popular, with their promises of a better after-life while preaching rigid morality and a paranoia about other faiths. Experts disagree on the impact of the moderate preachers in the face of fundamentalism. Khalil Anani, a scholar with the Cairo-based al-Ahram Institute, thinks that they are a temporary phenomenon because they have no organizational or institutional bodies. "I think that the main task of this new preacher phenomenon is to spread tolerance and the values of coexistence and being civilized in one's way of thinking," Anani has said. "This is the most important benefit now, to decrease the tension between the West and Islam." But Abdallah Schleifer, of the American University in Cairo, strongly disagrees. Mas'ud, he claims, has a message that meets the concerns of the growing mainstream: "He is in rapport actually, now with television, with millions, and will be in rapport with still greater millions and this is not a passing fad. This is part of the transformation of Arab society."[53]

Two anecdotes illustrate the tremendous impact of the New Preachers at the present time. In 2007, *Time* magazine carried out a survey on who readers thought should be on the list of the hundred most influential people of the year; over 200 candidates were to be given a rating between 1 and 100. 'Amr Khalid came in ahead of Barack Obama, Angela Merkel, and Warren Buffet. The *Foreign Policy Journal* issue of July/August 2008 asked readers to rank the world's top 20 public intellectuals; 'Amr Khalid was sixth, ahead of Noam Chomsky, Bernard Lewis, and others.

Conclusion

The New Preachers' activities today are essentially no different from those of preachers during the first centuries of Islam, in such major respects as content and provocativeness, and in their popularity as compared to those of religious leaders. True, technical facilities have improved and the context of a mosque at noon[54] is replaced by an air-conditioned room with a television set. But there is no doubt that the motives for story-telling, the power which it brings to the story-tellers, given their mass support, and the authorities' attitude towards them (even if they are religious leaders) have all remained little altered over time. This change in media also creates a change in essence, though the goals remain the same. This is because the rulers are still oppressive, the people are still indigent, and the need to find relief for their frustrations without being arrested produces

---

[53]   See Kate Seelye, "Religion news: New Muslim Televangelists Spread a Message of Moderation," at http://pewforum.org/news/display.php?NewsID=16012, last accessed 12 January 2013.

[54]   Richard Antoun describes the mosque as "a place of asylum, a place to discuss important public matters including preparations for collective defense, a school, a resting place for travelers and a place for worship"; see his *Muslim Preachers in the Modern World* (Princeton, NJ, 1989).

a preaching literature which is very similar to the old one, dating back to the first years of Islam, and based on sources which are very similar, if not identical. There are exceptions, and this is not substantiated in terms of the stories 'Amr Khaled and his coterie actually tell, but most of the televangelists fit this description.

Television ratings are no doubt very important, but so is the image. This is probably another reason for 'Amr Khalid's differentiation between "The Stories of the Prophets"—a genre which might be related to fantasies and inventions—and stories about prophets from the Qur'an which are presented as authentic and original. In fact, 'Amr Khalid elaborates his commentary, adding fragments, episodes, and chapters from the "The Stories of the Prophets" in order to spice up his stories and make them more interesting. The nights of Ramadan in the twenty-first century differ from those of the tenth century only in the setting—the glow of the TV set, in some places even the whirring of an air-conditioning system, replace the floor of the mosque with its heat and overcrowding. The content of the stories remains much the same. It is too soon fully to gauge the long-term impact of the youthful New Preachers, but interviews with viewers as well as analysts of religion and the media make it evident they are clearly a rising force.[55]

---

[55] Kevin Sullivan, "Younger Muslims Tune in to Upbeat Religious Message," *Washington Post Foreign Service*, 2 December 2007; Kate Seelye, "Muslim Televangelists," at http://uscmediareligion.org/theGet/528/>, last accessed 12 January 2013; *idem*, "New Muslim Televangelists Spread a Message of Moderation," at http://stage.pewforum.org/Religion-News/New-Muslim-Televangelists-Spread-a-Message-of-Moderation.aspx, last accessed 15 December 2012; Jeffrey Fleishman, "Preachers Repackage Islam with Beaches, BBQ and Quran," *Los Angeles Times Daily Herald*, 2 January 2009, available at http://www.heraldextra.com/lifestyles/article_81a36dbe-bedc-59f4-940c-28381df0643a.html, last accessed 20 February 2014; Richard Antoun, "Modern Muslim Preachers," at <www.islamonline.net/servlet/Satellite?c=Article_C&pagename=Zone-English-News/...>, last accessed 12 January 2013.

Chapter 10

The Reception of Islamic Prophet Stories within Muslim Communities in Norway and Germany

Gerd Marie Ådna

The Islamic Prophet Stories, *Qisas al-anbiya'*, are found in the Qur'an, and also elsewhere. They are included and expanded in collections of narratives of the prophets' lives, found in many versions up to the present day. In most of them the life story (*sira*) of Prophet Muhammad is included at the end of the collection. Many stories are also referred to in exegetical literature (*tafsir*). Of the highest importance in Muslim tradition, the prophet stories are both well suited to and highly valued as narrative to be recounted to children in the context of family, school and mosque. As the central figures of such stories, the prophets obviously constitute an important part of the tradition exposed to 'memory and forgetfulness' among Muslims.

Hence, a 'colourful carpet of narratives' might be an appropriate metaphor for what this study wants to explore with regard to childhood memories and to the reception- and transmission-practice of the prophet stories in some Muslim communities and among individuals in Berlin, Germany and Stavanger, Norway. The main research question is: to what extent has this heritage of narratives been preserved or changed from the time and space of origin to a new geographical setting?

The qualitative in-depth interviews and follow-up talks that form the basis of this chapter were undertaken with Muslims from various backgrounds, but predominantly with those from Arab, Turkish and Kurdish communities. Further, I informally observed several gatherings in Muslim settings – prayers and teaching in mosques, and other meetings arranged by Muslim organisations. I spoke with several Muslims in different informal settings and regularly interacted with families in Berlin during a period of more than three years; I met with some families in Stavanger over a period of almost 10 years. I also discussed the issue of prophets with a group of women in Stavanger whom I met during the course of a year. Additionally, I carried on an email correspondence with some of these Muslims.

This chapter is a presentation of a continuing project and a preliminary assessment of its results. It will not go into all childhood memories but only those linked to the transmission of histories of the prophets, and the role these may have played in their spiritual life; nor will it compare memories from members of one and the same family, but rather randomly choose Muslims who have been living in either Berlin or Stavanger for some years.

To some extent, the questions covered are related not only to the *Wirkungsgeschichte* of the Qur'an and the *Qisas al-anbiya'* but also to the dreams and ideals for transmission of valuable narratives. The central issue is whether the histories of the prophets belong to the *active* chain of memory, to use the term on which the French sociologist Danièle Hervieu-Léger has reflected in her *Religion as a Chain of Memory*.[1] Her considerations about *structural* connections between memory and religion inspire an assessment of how Muslim individuals try to maintain their inherited prophet narratives in a new geographical and social context. Being situated in a European environment, Muslim immigrants find moral direction and positive links to their family's place of origin through these narratives. Moreover, as Hervieu-Léger emphasises, 'The differentiation of a specialized religious field, the gradual pluralization of institutions, communities and systems of religious thought historically – and exactly – correspond to the differentiation of total social memory into a plurality of specialized circles of memory.'[2] Informants in Berlin and Stavanger seem to be bound to circles of memory that are connected to the narratives of the prophets, and to rituals and material objects connected to the latter. This memory is more or less connected to the institutional memory of the prophets – that propagated by the mosques – even if this wider context will be only slightly touched upon in this chapter.

Further, the effects of personal memories will be discussed in the context of literature on memory and forgetfulness and of the extended term 'cultural memory' introduced by Maurice Halbwachs, Jan Assmann and Aleida Assmann, and by some specialists in the field of Islamic narratives.[3] In other words, the

---

[1]   Danièle Hervieu-Léger, *Religion as a Chain of Memory* (Cambridge, 1993/2000), pp. 124–7.

[2]   Ibid., p. 129.

[3]   Maurice Halbwachs, *On Collective Memory*, trans. and with an introduction by Lewis A. Coser (ed.) (Chicago, IL, 1941/1952/1992); Jan Assmann, *Das kulturelle Gedächtnis: Schrift, Erinnerung und politische Identität in frühen Hochkulturen* (Munich 1992/2005);

chapter tries to verify Jan Knappert's claim that 'the old oral literature of the Islamic peoples, [is] still a living tradition which has not yet been extinguished by radio, television and other luxuries'.[4]

Islamic Prophet Stories and the Issue of Memory and Forgetfulness

Prophet stories recounted in the Qur'an and early Islam constitute an important object for religious and Islamic studies.[5] The *Qisas al-anbiya'* genre has developed from oral and written sources.[6] In many countries and traditions such stories are retold and integrated into different strings of local narratives. This process has not ceased, but so far Muslims' attitude towards their heritage from the *Qisas al-anbiya'* has not played any significant role in research on religious life and memory among Muslims in Europe. In this chapter I therefore investigate whether and how these prophets' lives and their narratives have been transmitted and are still alive.

The prophets are mentioned both in the longer Qur'anic narratives (the Yusuf story is the longest one, found in the eponymous *sura* 12), and in 'some of the

---

Jan Assmann, *Religion and Cultural Memory: Ten Studies* (Stanford, CA, 2000/2006); Aleida Assmann, 'The Religious Roots of Cultural Memory', *Norsk Teologisk Tidsskrift*, 4 (2008), pp. 270–92.

  [4] Jan Knappert, *Islamic Legends: Histories of the Heroes, Saints and Prophets of Islam* (Leiden, 1985), p. xi.

  [5] Brannon M. Wheeler, *Prophets in the Quran: An Introduction to the Quran and Muslim Exegesis*, sel. and trans. Brannon M. Wheeler (London and New York, 2002). To place the genre of prophet stories in a wider literary context, see Tarif Khalidi, *Arabic Historical Thought in the Classical Period* (Cambridge, 1994), especially pp. 68–73. Khalidi has also convincingly shown, in the introduction to his *The Muslim Jesus: Sayings and Stories in Islamic Literature* (Cambridge, MA and London, 2001), that the prophet Jesus has an immense influence on Islamic literary and thus on Muslims' lives, on those who read this literature, on those who live in the periphery of these texts, and even more on Muslims who live an ascetic or mystic life. Some of these narratives are analysed historically and structurally in Gerd Marie Ådna, *Muhammad and the Formation of Sacrifice*, (Frankfurt a.M., 2014).

  [6] Al-Tabari's works served as a significant source for the important later *qisas* work *Ara'is al-majalis* of al-Tha'labi (d. AD 1036), much expanded by the addition of different tales, most of them about many more prophets, including others from non-Qur'anic sources. See William M. Brinner, 'Noah', in Jane Dammen McAuliffe (ed.) *Encyclopaedia of the Qur'an*, (Georgetown University, Washington DC, 2009), at Brill Online, available at http://referenceworks.brillonline.com/entries/encyclopaedia-of-the-quran/noah-COM_00134, last accessed 20 February 2009.

shorter more poetic *suras*, grouped in the latter part of the Qur'an'.[7] Joseph Bell underlines the difference between the two genres, stating: 'The stories of the past prophets and nations named in the sacred text undoubtedly play a certain rhetorical role, but in general they have a recognizably more didactic place in the Prophet's message.'[8] This element of education connected to the history of the prophets is to be seen in Q 12:111 where the annals of the prophets 'point to a moral for men of understanding'.[9] However, the poetic *suras* presenting the prophets are, according to Bell, additional 'examples of use of the evocative technique'.[10] In other words, we are reminded that the names of the prophets in the Qur'an were used to evoke memories and feelings among the listeners.[11]

The fact that the 'People of the Book ... are called *ahl al-dhikr* (Q 16:43; 21:7)',[12] and that they will 'confirm the truth of the Qur'anic allusions to them',[13] is an interesting aspect of the dialogue between Muslims, Jews and Christians, which we may experience in the contemporary European context. Michael Sells emphasises that 'the Qur'anic revelation is nothing but a "reminder to all beings" (Q 38:87; 81:27)'.[14] Hence, the prophets and their message point to the essential fact that this remembrance is not only one of the prophets but a *dhikr* of and a love for God;[15] and the Prophet Muhammad, according to Q 87:9–15, is the principal reminder. In post-Qur'anic writings the terms *dhikr* and *qur'an* are often synonymous, and 'the *dhikr* in the Qur'an can be seen as a *dhikr li'l'nas*,

---

[7]   Joseph Norment Bell, '"Say it Again and Make Me Your Slave": Notes on al-Daylami's Seventh Sign of Man's Love for God', in Farhad Daftari and Josef W. Meri (eds), *Culture and Memory in Medieval Islam: Essays in Honour of Wilferd Mandelung* (London and New York, 2003), p. 191.

[8]   Ibid., p. 191.

[9]   *The Koran*, trans. N.J. Dawood (London, 1994), p. 174.

[10]   Bell, '"Say it Again"', p. 191.

[11]   Sachiko Murata and William C. Chittick (in *The Vision of Islam* (St. Paul, MN, 2006), p. 147) underline this aspect, writing that 'God sent the prophets in order to remind the people of the covenant ... [and] people should respond to the prophets by remembering God.'

[12]   Ibid., p. 147.

[13]   Uri Rubin, 'Prophets and Prophethood', in Andrew Rippin (ed.), *The Blackwell Companion to the Qur'an* (Malden, Oxford and Chichester, 2009), p. 234.

[14]   Michael A. Sells, 'Memory', in Jane Dammen McAuliffe (ed.), *Encyclopaedia of the Qur'an* (Georgetown University, Washington DC, 2012). Brill Online, available at http://referenceworks.brillonline.com/entries/encyclopaedia-of-the-quran/memory-SIM_00276, last accessed 20 February 2014.

[15]   Bell, '"Say it Again"', pp. 191–2.

"memory for the people".[16] Therefore, I propose that there is not one single chain of memory in Islam, but, according to Hervieu-Legér, two such chains, with God, the prophets, the Prophet Muhammad and the Qur'an forming the first chain, and the place and rituals connected to these narratives forming the second.

As we have seen, the Arabic term *dhikr* may be translated 'remembrance' or 'mention'. The pre-Islamic prophets are an important part of Islamic cultural memory. They may even be called the 'memory of the Muslim group', according to the sociologist Maurice Halbwachs and the historian and specialist on ancient Egyptian culture Jan Assmann. Halbwachs clearly distinguishes between the individual's and the group's memory, but maintains that the two are created in dialogue with each other.[17] The individual memory cannot grow without communication with the group. Hence, the opposite of memory, cultural *forgetfulness*, is a phenomenon that depends not only on the individual but on the wider group, for example family or community.[18] 'One remembers only what is communicated,' writes Assmann, and he continues, 'the memories build each single one an independent system which elements reciprocally support and decide both the individual and the group.'[19] As for individual feelings and experiences connected to memories, they are unique, but the memory becomes a collective memory. Crucial in the creation of memory are the two elements of repetition and contemporary realisation (*Vergegenwärtigung*).[20] In a religious context, this is seen in performance and rituals.[21]

Cultural memory then, according to Assmann, is first a mimetic memory of acts; secondly a memory of objects; thirdly a memory of language and communication; and fourthly a memory of rituals in which the first three of these memories are combined in different patterns and with internal emphases.[22] Thus the repetitive calendar of any religious or civic group may be formed to

---

[16]   So Jean Butler, 'Tidlig islamsk historie i mnemohistorisk belysning – Et case-study af *sûrat al-kâfirûn*', *Religionsvidenskabeligt Tidsskrift*, 52 (2008): p. 59. Toshihiko Izutsu, *Ethico-Religious Concepts in the Qur'an* (Montreal, 1962/2002), pp. 193–4, understands *dhikr* in the light of *huda*, 'right guidance' (Q 20:123–4).

[17]   Halbwachs, *On Collective Memory*, pp. 52–3.

[18]   Assmann, *Das kulturelle Gedächtnis*, p. 37. Aleida Assmann ('The Religious Roots', pp. 270–92) has discussed the issues of tradition, transmission, cultural memory and forgetfulness, canonisation and text. One of her main points emphasises 'what is transmitted cannot be disconnected from those who transmit' (p. 283).

[19]   Assmann, *Das kulturelle Gedächtnis*, p. 37, my translation.

[20]   Ibid., pp. 16–20.

[21]   Ibid., p. 18.

[22]   Ibid., p. 26.

keep, to forget or to suppress elements from the past.[23] The festival calendar in Islamic cultures is essential for people's own understanding; it stands for the repetition – and as a reminder – of the common heritage and rituals, often connected to the two sacred cities of Mecca and Medina and to various narratives about the prophets' actions when they visited Mecca.

Jacques Waardenburg points out that 'one way is to ask people what religious data and religions are or were significant to them, in what situations, and in what sense ... Another way is to ask people how they interpret and apply their own religion.'[24] My material, together with its interpretation, is a combination of these two approaches. It joins with Waardenburg's third approach, which sees religious studies as

> the construction of religious phenomena ... as an ongoing process. It takes place
> around a tradition with a mysterious origin and in a community that identifies
> itself through mysterious parameters from other communities. The believers
> themselves, however, tend to view and interpret their tradition as a continuum and
> their community as distinct. Both the tradition and the community are shaped,
> of course, according to practical needs and interests, but also in accordance with
> orientations and intentions of the people themselves, or their leaders.[25]

Hence, when Muslims are interviewed about their relation to the prophets, they seem to presume that prophet stories have a character or uniqueness which makes them particularly well suited to transmission. The narratives suit the goals (often not very clear) of education and the formation of Islamic values. They are simply 'pure' entertainment or a pleasant activity in its own right, with no specific need of justification, but constitute an essential part of the Islamic heritage to be passed on to children, as it was to themselves when they were young. A lady with Kurdish-Turkish roots, 35 years old, well educated and living in Norway, said the following, when I asked about Ibrahim and Isma'il in her childhood narrative and religious world:

> I come from a small place in East Turkey. There, the sacrificial lamb was
> bought some days before the *'id al-adha*, and it was grazing in the garden of my

---

[23]   Ibid., pp. 20–21. See also Roy A. Rappaport, *Ritual and Religion in the Making of Humanity* (Cambridge, 1999), who emphasises the power of embodied ritual in the collective work of creating belief and traditions within a group.

[24]   Jacques Waardenburg, *Muslims as Actors: Islamic Meanings and Muslim Interpretations in the Perspective of the Study of Religions* (Berlin and New York, 2007), p. 369.

[25]   Ibid., p. 370.

grandparents. On the very day the slaughterer arrived and slaughtered the animal in the garden. Then we heard how prophet Ibrahim did not need to sacrifice his son. In many homes there was a picture on the wall where Isma'il (with a blindfold around his eyes) was kneeling with his head on a stone and Ibrahim with a knife in his hand and an angel standing behind with a sheep.

Afterwards she sent me a similar picture taken from the internet. The memories of the narrative and of the practised ritual were becoming one and the same, and were imprinted in her mind. When she mentioned (in an email) the now forbidden practice of slaughtering at home, she added a 'smiley' emoticon, telling me that in this case Turkey and Norway have the same rules. This means that (religious) slaughtering practices have changed, due to communal cleanliness and health rules. But the image of the prophet Ibrahim with the knife and the angel with the lamb is seemingly not subject to change.

The new communications media help her to stay in touch with the place and religion of her origin, and to negotiate between her childhood memories and her need for knowledge about the same prophets today; she is therefore, geographically and in her imagination, connecting these two worlds. It has become a 'journey of the mind', which in this case is not to Mecca but to a local sacred place, sometimes connected to certain rituals only performed in that particular village, and hence important for the group of migrants from it. It includes 'an imaginary connection ... that has a significant impact on notions of religious belonging over distance, collective identity with those elsewhere, and ritual practice that is both universal and localized'.[26]

Muslim Communities of Stavanger and Berlin

The city of Stavanger and the county of Rogaland in which it is located lie in the south-western part of Norway. So far no scholarly research has been undertaken on specifically religious aspects of Muslims in this region. Of Norway's c.150,000 Muslims, 98,953 were registered as members of particular mosques in 2010. Some 6,565 individuals were registered in Rogaland,[27] but exact numbers are difficult to find, given the fact that membership of religious communities,

---

[26] Dale F. Eickelman and James Piscatori (eds), *Muslim Travellers: Pilgrimage: Migration and the Religious Imagination* (London, 1990), p. xii.

[27] See at http://www.ssb.no/trosamf/tab-2010-12-13-02.html, last accessed 20 February 2014.

on the one hand, as opposed to a group's ethnic background/religious beliefs, on the other, is not always clear-cut, in spite of the systematic surveys undertaken by Statistics Norway (SSB, Statistic Sentralbyrå).

Stavanger is Norway's fourth largest city, with some 125,000 inhabitants; altogether the area around Stavanger and its neighbouring communes have around 265,000.[28] Most Muslims live in this part of Rogaland, but there are some living in the city of Haugesund and also in the villages. The main groups are Turks, Kurds, Palestinians, Iraqis, Moroccans, Sri Lankans and Somalis, together with Pakistanis, who were the first to come to Norway at the beginning of the 1970s.

In the present project I concentrate on the Arabic- and Turkish-speaking groups, without excluding the others. Most of these groups are organised, as far as religion is concerned, in seven or eight mosques in Stavanger and Sandnes and some three or four in the rest of Rogaland. They also have an umbrella organisation, the Rogaland Muslim Society. Three of the imams in the city have a solid education, gained in Egypt, Syria, Malaysia, Turkey or Saudi Arabia. The Councils in the bigger mosques are energetic, taking responsibility for many activities; some run Qur'an schools. The biggest of these latter is moderate Sunni, located in a former office building and with about 90 pupils at seven levels. All *tarbiya* (Islamic education) takes place in the Norwegian language, whereas the teaching of Arabic takes place in that language. The schools meet on Saturdays at noon, and sometimes gather for recitals of the Qur'an or songs with Islamic content. Some of the most respected Muslim leaders, men and women, offer their free time for this form of education.

Some adult Muslims in Stavanger have acquired higher education, and some have important posts in the oil industry. Others are employed in professions such as kindergarten and school teachers, or as taxi drivers and cleaners, while some remain unemployed. The first group of Muslims, who came to Stavanger in the 1970s and 1980s, are now reaching old age, and have their own needs for health and social care, but are often living with their extended families.

The so-called Muslim Women's Group has been very active, initiating courses in Eastern dance, swimming, rhetoric, social relations, religious education and so forth, and has established good relations with non-Muslim women and with public offices such as the city council. There is, particularly among young Muslim girls aged between 16 and 25 (from several ethnic groups), an overall high-spiritedness and a strong desire to achieve influential positions in society. A few converts to Islam have taken positions of responsibility in this group.

---

[28]   See at http://www.ssb.no/en/befolkning/statistikker/folkendrkv/kvartal/2011-05-19, last accessed 20 February 2014.

Berlin, since the Wall fell in 1989, has become an increasingly international city with more than 180 different ethnic groups. In the Mitte and Neu-Kölln districts more than half the population consists of people from a non-German background. Among Berlin's 3.4 million inhabitants one of the biggest religious minorities is the Muslim group (some 7 per cent); within this, by far the biggest sub-groups are the Turkish- and the Kurdish-speaking communities, Alevis included. About 25 per cent of all citizens with a foreign passport are of Turkish origin,[29] but many other Muslim groups (more than 50 nationalities) are also represented, from North African and various other Arab countries, and from Iran.[30]

The first Islamic community in Berlin was founded in 1922, and the oldest mosque has existed in Wilmersdorf since 1925. Today, 125 mosques are registered, but there are probably more. The biggest mosque, Sehitlik, at Colombiadamm 128 in Neu-Kölln, is owned by the Turkish DITIB (Diyanet Isleri Türk Islam Birlig/Türkisch-Islamische Union der Anstalt der Religion e.V., or Religious Organisation of the Turkish-Islamic Union), which also runs 11 other mosques in the German capital. The second biggest is 'Umar al-Khattab, close to the Görlitzer Bahnhof, which since its opening in June 2010 has collected a rather large community of moderate Sunni Muslims.

The so-called White Mosque (a fictive name), where I have spent many Saturday hours listening to teachings on ethical, religious and linguistic issues, is one of the moderate Sunni mosques where the role of Ibrahim is retold and interpreted for children just before the *'id al-adha*. Obviously, this mosque is preoccupied with fulfilling its teaching task. One woman of Moroccan origin maintained that 'the mosque is neither Wahhabi nor Salafi; it is not extreme in any way', and thus a safe place to which to entrust her own as well as others' children.

Memories of Home in Childhood

The lives of Muslim immigrants in Berlin or Stavanger are clearly influenced by their experiences before migration to Europe. Categories like the role of home,

---

[29]   See at <http://www.statistik-berlin-brandenburg.de/produkte/jahrbuch/jb2010/ JB_BE_2010_Kap-01.pdf>, last accessed 25 June 2011.

[30]   Different statistical approaches are used (e.g. Amt für Statistik Berlin Brandenburg, *Berlin in Zahlen*), and it is not known exactly how many Muslims live in Berlin, given the differences between organisational models. Umbrella groupings such as the German Islam Conference (*Deutsche Islamkonferenz*) do not cover all German Muslim communities.

school and mosque, not least the role of the family in the transmission of the prophet narratives for migrant Muslims, will be presented and discussed in what follows, as will knowledge about the prophets and their significance in the lives of these contemporary Muslims.

'Before 1981 we had no electricity and therefore no television set. At that time we told each other stories.' A man from a Jordanian background did not seem to have experienced at home any transmission of stories about the prophets: 'You know, we had to work hard and we were tired after a long day of labour.' Even in a middle-class Egyptian home there was seldom or never any mention of the prophets. Another man with an Iraqi background maintained that his mother did not tell prophet stories, perhaps only other stories that were not religious. 'She had no education. Nobody in her family was educated.' Hence, the level of education seemed to play a role, as it did also for a man from a Syrian background: 'My mother was illiterate and did not know the prophets' histories.' He repeated this three times, but was clearly ashamed of the admission.

However, a woman in her mid-thirties with Moroccan roots, living in Berlin, proudly told me that in her childhood her mother had been the very best of story-tellers. She 'told me the story about Yusuf, the very beautiful man. This is the most important story about the prophets in the Qur'an to me; then come Ayub and then 'Isa.' In her opinion, this has led to her strong identity as a mother to her children, putting great emphasis on their civil and religious education. A Kurdish woman from Stavanger seemed to have forgotten those prophet stories that were not directly connected to the annual feasts; her childhood stories were overlain by many new stories and events, so that the earlier narratives were at least temporarily forgotten.

For all informants, most school teachers seemed to have been wonderful story-tellers – this at least is the impression they retained. 'He taught us Arabic and told us the stories about the prophets in these lessons; it was part of the curriculum, I think.' Further, an informant with a doctoral degree said: 'The school teachers taught us very systematically about the prophets.' A third man remembered his teacher as the 'most important person to communicate this knowledge'. Others added that their older siblings were taught at school, boys and girls alike, and on their return to the family home after the long school day they retold the stories to the younger ones. Thus the schools' and siblings' role in transmitting the prophet stories was important for most of my informants. However, it would need more research and evaluation to delve into the role of schools in the countries presented here. This short look into the memories of some selected individuals gives an impression of gratitude towards teachers who were good story-tellers, and therefore made the colours in the carpet a little brighter.

The mosques are, like the schools, important places for the transmission of religious narratives. For some the combination of school, mosque and home is the evident transmission chain, and it leads us into the world of the 1970s in Iraq:

> The story about Yusuf was told to us in the mosque and at home in the evenings. I was perhaps eight years old and I listened to the radio where the Egyptian Qur'an reciter 'Abd al-Basit was reciting surat Yusuf in Arabic with his very beautiful voice. My older brothers explained the meaning to me in Kurdish. They spoke Arabic very well. My Arabic was not so good. We heard about all the prophets in the Qur'an.

For some of the informants the mosque was in another village, and not so easily accessed. But statements like 'I went with my father' tell us that this going to-and-fro between home and mosque meant a tightening of family bonds, and probably pride. Sometimes fatigue or excitement was part of the complex feelings. 'I cannot remember what we were taught there on the festival days, but the Yusuf story I remember was told quite early in my childhood.' This informant – an Iraqi man in his mid-forties – continued: 'In the mosque the imam told *all* the stories about the prophets. It was very important.' The female informants never mentioned the mosque in connection with their childhood experiences, but I do not interpret this too generally as indicating total non-attendance.

The Most Important Prophets

It is probably not possible to rank the prophets, although the impression given is that to all informants Muhammad is unique among them.[31] The man with an Iraqi background made a list of the five prophets he was most impressed by: Muhammad, Ibrahim, Musa, 'Isa and Yusuf. He explained why: 'Number one is my direct Prophet, peace be upon him; number two, three and four have, according to my opinion, lived a sublime life; and Yusuf is an example from within the family (*dakhil al-'a'ila*); he showed tolerance.'

This man, who has been living in Berlin for a few years, continued, commenting on the term 'prophet stories': 'I am thinking of the stories in the

---

[31]   Rubin ('Prophets and Prophethood', p. 236) reminds us that the Qur'an itself makes a ranking. See, for example, Q 17:55 and Q 2:253.

Qur'an and in the Israelite writings. We Muslims declare that the *hadith* says: "You can learn from the Israelite writings. You should show respect towards the *isra'iliyat*, and show respect towards the other prophets, to Musa and 'Isa!'" A Norwegian Kurdish woman was also eager to tell me that respect for the prophets is essential to all Muslims. And when in an email she wrote something that could be misunderstood as putting Muhammad second, she rephrased it and sent it a second time. Here, I realised that I, the researcher, being a non-Muslim, was seen differently than a fellow-Muslim would have been, and that this difference applied also when talking of the prophets. Presumably, I heard more statements about respect for 'Isa than I probably would have if I had been a Muslim, because the informants wanted to show respect for my Christian background.

Apart from Muhammad, the other prophets are not hierarchically systematised in my material. Still, Yusuf (e.g. Q 12:1–101; 40:34) is mentioned so often that I had to ask what it is about this figure. His attractiveness is commented on many times. How can he be as handsome as so many suggest? His beauty is mentioned in the *hadith*: '[The gate] was opened for us and I saw Yusuf (peace of Allah be upon him) who had been given half of the [world's] beauty. He welcomed me and prayed for my well-being. Then he ascended with us to the fourth heaven.'[32] Also Ibn Kathir's narrative about the Night Journey of Prophet Muhammad states: 'I passed by Joseph and he had been given half the goodness.'[33]

Hence, in the new context of Europe, Yusuf's beauty seems to have become a positive link between the traditional tales from childhood and the personal ideal of being good-looking and showing the moral attitude of patience. 'Though being betrayed by his brothers and enduring pain in the ditch, he was patient and quiet', one informant said empathically. Suffering is a human experience everyone understands, and Yusuf's nearly mythological existence seems to have brought comfort to many. An elderly Turkish man enthusiastically told me the whole story of Yusuf. He himself had two sons, with whom he had had difficulties; it was as if the 60-year-old was intertwining his own and Yusuf's biography – his sons' loyalties should have taken shape like Yusuf's, manifested in his good intentions towards his brothers, and the practical help he offered them: 'He was patient and he was sweet-tempered ... he was a person of great uniqueness.'

An imam from a Palestinian background, now living in Berlin, wanted to use Yusuf's story in a film and call it *Muwadda*, 'being close to each other'. It would show 'forgiveness, reconciliation, the relations in the family, and peace'. From what he told me on another occasion, Yusuf's qualities are a role model for the

---

[32]   Muslim, *Sahih*, Kitab al-iman, p. 309.
[33]   Ibn Kathir, in Wheeler, *Prophets in the Quran*, p. 135.

imam himself and for his work in the mosque and in society. Thus the prophets' positive qualities can be a source of inspiration for moral lives.

The aspect of man as being a 'guest in the world' was the reason for one informant to be patient, just as he showed much empathy with people in need today: 'Man's goal is to live together with God in the world.' Further, he said that 'the prophets were all poor, but they showed patience and forgiveness.' From another remark I understood that he struggled to earn enough money for daily expenses. Finally, he underlined that 'Yusuf was both patient and tolerant. These are traits that I want to hand on to others. I am a calm, tolerant and patient person.'

A Jordanian academic, in his mid-thirties and living in Berlin, eagerly explained how Yusuf was freed from Pharaoh, and how the narrative was told on the *'ashura* day when he was small. 'On this day we were fasting; I do it still today. I am no Shi'ite, but I fast on this day and in the evening we eat tasty food. This day is very special.' When we discussed this topic in a small group, he emphasised that he fasted on the very day of *'ashura*, but not the days before and after as some Muslims do. 'We are fasting because Prophet Musa was fasting. We do so in remembrance of him. We do not fast in remembrance of Hussein, like the Shi'ites are doing.' Hence, the *'ashura* day, which is a memorial day for Hussein among Shi'ites, becomes a memorial day for Musa to some Jordanian Sunnis living outside the Middle Eastern context.

An educated woman with an Egyptian background told me enthusiastically about prophet Yusuf: 'So when people learn about the prophets at school, they also learn Yusuf's story. It is the most moving one and is a literary pearl in the Qur'an. Everyone knows it.' Her statement supports this model role of Yusuf. Exceptionally, one characteristic, mentioned by an Iraqi, was seen as negative: 'When we say "like Yusuf", it means a man who goes to prostitutes; it is a negative quality, he is a light person (*insan khafif*).' Such negative qualities were never mentioned in connection with other prophets. I would have expected this to be a characterisation of Musa, but no, this Iraqi meant Yusuf.

The memory of Yusuf's life and patience makes him a figure that one could easily identify with, mostly for good. He was simply a human being who created new possibilities for his family. The negative memory mentioned above points to the fact that memory is not an idyllic recollection in all matters, but also a realistic one, creating a critical attitude.

According to all informants, Ibrahim (e.g. Q 2:124–140) was always connected to Mecca and the pilgrimage. His role in the *hajj* rituals seems to be known to everybody. 'Ibrahim gives Prophet Muhammad his family tree.

He is the father of our prophet, and this is important! It gives us the feeling of belonging', an imam from a Palestinian background told me. This is also what I observe in *khutba*s and informal dialogues; Ibrahim is not merely a *hanif*, one who shows existentially the oneness of God, but he is next to Muhammad in importance, theologically and ritually.

In gatherings in the *madrasa*s and in the *khutba*s in the mosques before and during *'id al-adha* the story about the near-sacrifice of Ibrahim's son was mentioned, but not necessarily in an extensive way. This means that his name and his willingness to sacrifice were mentioned, but few of the details that are found in the Qur'an and even more so in the *qisas al-anbiya'* were ever transmitted. Everyone agreed that the event recounted had taken place in Mecca, and not in Jerusalem, as some early exegeses propose. Al-Tabari refers also to the idea that the intended sacrifice could be Ishaq and not Isma'il,[34] but this was never mentioned by my informants.

A Palestinian mentioned Ibrahim's tomb in Hebron (al-Khalil) as an important place, when we were talking about geography and holy places. To him this city meant a blessing, even more so because his grandmother had visited this place before the Six Days War in 1967: 'She brought gifts for my family, and especially oil from al-Khalil.' This gift was a concrete expression and thus a memorial symbol underlining the oral story being a part of this family.

I would have expected the role of Adam (e.g. Q 2:30–39) to be associated with the original rituals in Mecca,[35] but only one informant (male, of Lebanese origin) mentioned Adam and then connected him to Jerusalem. 'The al-Aqsa mosque in al-Quds was long before Muhammad. The al-Aqsa mosque was built by Adam. There was no temple there, neither by Solomon nor by Herod. These temples are not proved to have existed there. They are fictions created by the Jews. The *hadith* says so.' Utterances like these were rare. I would also have expected more political ideas connected to the issue of Isma'il (e.g. Q 19:54–55)

---

[34]   Al-Tabari [d. AD 923], *The History of al-Tabari* (*Ta'rikh al-rasul wa al-muluk*): *An Annotated Translation.* Vol. 2, *Prophets and Patriarchs* (Bibliotheca Persica), trans. William M. Brinner (Albany, NY, 1987), p. 82: 'The earliest sages of our Prophet's nation disagree about which of Ibrahim's two sons it was that he was commanded to sacrifice. Some say it was Ishaq, while others say it was Isma'il. Both views are supported by statements related on the authority of the Messenger of God. If both groups of statements were equally sound, then – since they both come from the Prophet – only the Qur'an could serve as proof that the account naming Ishaq is clearly the most truthful of the two.'

[35]   For instance in Ahmad ibn Abu Ya'qub al-Ya'qubi [d. c. AD 905], *Ta'rikh al-Ya'qubi* (2 vols, Beirut, 1960), Vol. 1, pp. 27–8; and in Sahib al-Kisa'i, *The Tales of the Prophets of al-Kisa'i*, trans. Wheeler M. Thackston Jr. (Boston, MA, 1978), p. 161.

as the intended sacrifice according to the Muslim view and teaching, and Ishaq as the intended sacrifice of Jewish and Christian teachings, based on Genesis 22, but none of my informants seemed to emphasise this.

Why is patience such a virtue among modern Muslims? As Yusuf is connected to *sabr*, so also are Isma'il, Idris and Dhu'l-Kifl (Q 21:86), Dhu'l-Nun (Jonah; Q 21:87), Zakariya (Q 21:89–90), but first and foremost it is Ayub (e.g. Q 21:83) who is seen as the patient prophet par excellence, and hence the common saying *sabr Ayub*. This saying seems to be equally used by non-Arab Muslims. Both my Kurdish and Turkish informants knew it and seemed to understand it. Almost all informants mentioned Ayub's name in connection to an attitude of patience when faced with pain and other challenges. The rest of his biography, however, seems to be of little importance for these Muslims, but 'he was a nice man', said a young Muslim student, smiling brightly.

Scott C. Alexander points to the similarities regarding patience in the Bible and in the Islamic tradition, but he also spells out the dissimilarities: Ayub in the Qur'an never questions God's existence and hence he is *accepting* suffering.[36] This may well be one of the reasons why Muslims today mention the *sabr* of Ayub when they point to injustice and other problems in their own lives. Allah is not to be blamed.

'Nuh is important for us at the Feast of Sacrifice and we read or tell the story about him and the big boat', a Kurdish woman told me in Stavanger a few years ago. This has not been confirmed by other Kurds, so it is difficult to know whether this is a single experience or found in other families. I have also asked several Muslims of Arab origin in Stavanger and Berlin, but nobody else has connected Nuh to this feast. However, a second Kurdish woman in Stavanger told me: 'I cannot remember anything special about Nuh except when people in my village in East Turkey made a dish called *ashure* and sent it to as many persons as possible. *Ashure* is a type of food that consists of many ingredients, at least seven different ones.' This was kept in her memory as one of Nuh's many blessings for people (cf. Q 11:48). Other informants have told me that *ashure* is one of the main sweets during the sacred month of Muharram. But the belief that seven is a sacred number, linked to the seven persons who believed in God,[37] and further to the seven *tawaf* of the Ka'ba, and hence to the ark's seven orbits

---

[36]   Scott C. Alexander, 'Trust and Patience', in Jane Dammen McAuliffe (ed.), *Encyclopaedia of the Qur'an* (Georgetown University, Washington DC, 2012), Brill Online, available at http://referenceworks.brillonline.com/entries/encyclopaedia-of-the-quran/trust-and-patience-COM_00209, last accessed 20 February 2014.

[37]   'A'mash: "Only a few believed with him" means there were seven: Noah, three daughters-in-law, and three of his sons', in Wheeler, *Prophets in the Quran*, p. 60.

around the Ka'ba after it landed at mountain Judi,[38] was not mentioned by any of my informants.

It would have been interesting to discover how Nuh connects to *'id al-adha*. In fact, in internet videos (which have been deleted since I saw them) he seems to be linked to Ramadan celebrations. Is this an example of religious knowledge and a practice that is about to disappear or change, like the celebration of Zakariya?[39] A Palestinian imam said that he saw a clear connection: 'Nuh's son was disobedient to God; Ibrahim's son was not. Therefore, these two stories are connected on the *'id al-adha*. Hence we must be obedient, like Ibrahim's son. Faith (*iman*) is conviction.' For another man, from a Kurdish background, Nuh was also a symbol of long life.

In Q 7:137 Musa is connected to patience, but none of my informants mentioned this virtue in his context. 'Musa, first and foremost, is the one who could make magic,' said an imam. Another man with a Kurdish background underlined that Musa is used in the saying 'he is like Musa'. That means, according to him, that 'he is brave or strong'. If Musa, according to classical views of the prophets, is the most important prophet after Muhammad, he does not seem to play much of an active part in these informants' lives. In fact the 'minor' prophet Joshua was mentioned more frequently, and especially by one man from Jordan: he pointed to a ritual practice connected to the tomb of Joshua that he regretted being forgotten and not in use: 'His tomb was in my village.'[40]

A further narrative about Joshua is not mentioned in the Qur'an, but the Muslim biographer Ibn Ishaq (d. 761) writes that prophethood passed from Musa to Joshua at the end of Musa's life.[41] Therefore, the *perception* of the prophets' lives in a European context seems to have been turned in a new direction by different chains of *qisas al-anbiya'*. The new context emphasises one chain over another.

Most of the informants mention *'id al-adha* when they talk about Ibrahim. Hence, this important festival is an integral part of their annual memories.

---

[38] 'Ibn Jurayj: "The Ark left from Ayn Wardah on Friday after the tenth night of Rajab had passed. It came to Mount Judi on the Day of Ashura. It passed by the House, circumambulating it seven times. God lifted the House from drowning. Then the Ark went to Yemen and returned"', in ibid., p. 61.

[39] The Zakariya tradition to which I refer here is presented below.

[40] One tradition says that it is to be found in *Hazreti Yuşa Tepesi*, a hill located on the Asian shore of the Bosphorus in the Beykoz district of Istanbul, Turkey. See at http://en.wikipedia.org/wiki/Joshua%27s_Hill, last accessed 20 February 2014. A second place is in Jordan; see at http://www.usna.edu/Users/humss/bwheeler/joshua.html, last accessed 20 February 2014.

[41] Wheeler, *Prophets in the Quran*, p. 239.

However, some of the informants have experienced a calendar that extends the formal Islamic calendar due to local *mawlid*s – festivals in memory of one of the prophets or other holy persons. This is what a 40-year-old man living in Berlin told me about the prophet Zakariya:

> He was very important in our village in Iraq. When I was a child, we celebrated his *mawlid* with a procession and lit candles (*shama'*) in the evening. Then [probably in the late 1970s] it was forbidden by the *ulama*, and the processions were stopped. But my mother used to celebrate the memory of Zakariya secretly, marking his day by fasting and with special food at night. We all knew that it was because of his memory, and his meaning for our village. They stopped this practice because they wanted to purify our folk's habits.

This was told to me somewhat shamefacedly, as if it was not the right thing to say. He later mentioned that it is 'not good to visit the dead prophets. They worship them out of ignorance.' But still, he showed pride over his brave mother, who in secret had dared to oppose the new practice. Therefore, he seemed to enjoy the position of being at a critical distance to those who 'wanted to purify our folk's habits'. I interpret this distance to be in space as well as in opinion.

To the question about what prophet was the most impressive, a Muslim academic answered: 'I think, 'Isa ibn Maryam, because he made wonders and he healed the paralyzed ones.' To the question whether the prophets are a topic of discussion with non-Muslims, a Kurdish man answered that he had argued over this with a Christian friend in his home city. 'We discussed our respect towards Jesus, our common prophet, but his tradition is another direction. We were very good friends. 'Isa was at our common centre of orientation (*Mittelpunkt*). The exchange between the two of us was very good.' The wonders that 'Isa performed, referred to in the Qur'an [e.g. Q 5:110], were explicitly mentioned by one imam. ''Isa was created out of a wonder by God. Hence, all prophets have to do with *tawhid* [the teaching of one God].'

A Kurdish man said, however, that they avoided 'too much talk about 'Isa because of the Christians'. Coming to Germany, he concluded that 'one should talk more about 'Isa. We should see what a typical Muslim point of view is; that means that he is the son of Maryam and only a prophet.' Further, he continued, 'we should discuss what a typical Christian view is, which means that Jesus is the son of God.' When he referred to those who are not 'true believers', he added that they also need to hear who 'Isa was because 'they believe that he was just an ordinary man', nodding to me, a researcher in the field of religion, as if we were in agreement that Muslims and Christians alike hold 'Isa in high esteem as a sanctified man.

In the New Homeland

Those informants who have moved from their place of birth during their teens or as young adults to other countries like Germany or Norway are all part of reinforced waves of migration that have taken place during recent decades. Facts and stories connected directly to this journey were articulated by nobody. Still, on the one hand there is an apparent sense of pride in their home culture, with its religion, narratives and rituals, and on the other a feeling of having lost this same heritage, constantly mixed with an aspiration to explain and transmit these two contrary aspects of experience to themselves (an internal discussion) and to others who want to listen (an external discussion). Both types of discussion, for the Muslims I interviewed, seem as it were to negotiate and struggle to preserve certain religious and cultural continuities.

Seán McLoughlin writes that the establishment of new diasporas 'opens up the possibility for a new, more mobile, religious "homing desire" without the risk of losing all sense of continuity in a "chain of memory"'.[42] Migrant Muslims in Berlin and Stavanger create and cultivate their bits of pieces in *their* carpets of narratives, not necessarily the universal religion of Islam's central image of all the prophets' narratives, but at least bits and threads that are very vivid (like the memory of the *mawlid* of Zakariya), while other threads seem to be losing their colour. These Muslims negotiate in a religious system similar to what Hans Mol calls 'an island of meaning, tradition and belonging in the sea of anomie of modern industrial societies'.[43] The place to which some of the narratives are connected seems to be valued highly by some, but not to the extent so much that it becomes a place of pilgrimage. None of the informants admit that they participate in such visits (*ziyara*) when they return to their countries of origin. According to informants in Berlin and Stavanger there are tombs and places dedicated to the memory of Islamic prophets in Iraq, East Anatolia and Palestine, but for my informants the memory of these places has been leaching out over the years due to a decrease in the practices and rituals connected with them, but they are still not altogether forgotten.

---

[42]   Seán McLoughlin, 'Religion and Diaspora', in *The Routledge Companion to the Study of Religion*, 2nd ed. (London and New York, 2010), p. 572.

[43]   Cited in ibid., p. 569.

All the informants were eager to show that they knew many of the prophets by their names, but nobody seemed to know all the prophets appearing in the Qur'an; and I did not ask more questions when the less well-known prophets went unmentioned. Among believers who were not in active work in or for the mosques there was less exact knowledge about the prophets than I had expected. When I realised during an interview that the level of this knowledge was somewhat low, I added to the initial information which I had already given them: 'This is not a test – I only want to know how the prophets are significant to you.' Still, some of the informants, especially on email, became nervous about making mistakes in their answers.

Those not educated in Islamic theology and history do not seem to read collections which include histories of the prophets. However, the Iraqi Kurdish man mentioned a certain 'Abd al-Fatah 'Afif Tabara and his book *With the Prophets in the Qur'an* which he had read 15–20 years ago. He also mentioned Ibn Kathir's *Qisas al-anbiya'*, which I thought would have been referred to much more frequently given the many copies one can find in bookstores in the Middle East and Europe.

Those working in mosques undoubtedly wanted to transmit the stories orally. They were mostly well trained, and underlined the importance of transmitting the prophet stories as part of general education in Islamic topics and lifestyle. Thus the significance of the prophets seemed more important for teachers in the mosques than for Muslims more distant from Qur'anic narratives. 'The prophets belong to our heritage that I want to convey to our children,' said two female teachers, one in Berlin and one in Stavanger. An imam argued, as if parents were not clever enough to fulfil this duty, that 'it is important that the narratives are found in our books and that our teachers tell them in class.'

Most Muslims regretted that the stories about the prophets were no longer told face to face, as in their childhood's mosques and schools. Those among my informants who did not work in mosques were especially sad about this negative development. They wished to transmit the stories to their own children, but did not know how to do it; the narrative frame appears to have been lost along with the appearance of television sets in every home. One man said: 'I miss the atmosphere of telling narratives.' Another stated: 'Something has been lost on the way. In the past there were no media but we had more time. What else could we do but read and tell stories? Now it is different.'

Still, regret and pragmatism seem to co-exist: there were some who stated: 'It is a new time. There is now modernity with television and films.' Another added: 'The children will know the prophets through these new forms of media, and I think we do not need books for it.' Modernity offers new forms of transmission, and Muslims in Berlin and Stavanger realise that new media – CDs, films, the internet – have taken over.

For some, books are an alternative, but few know actual titles and nobody mentions publishers, or internet pages where such books might be purchased. Still, some books – and videos – are, according to my observations, circulated within families that are close to the mosques. 'These books must transmit the role and the goals of the Prophets,' said one Kurdish man. 'Their lives were not without purpose; this is a very important transmission.'

When I asked about the transmission of stories to children, their own or their pupils, one lady in Stavanger said, 'I have not yet started to tell the stories to my children [still in preparatory school]. But it is not because I regard them as unimportant. But I have no time. I want to put more emphasis on this matter as time goes by.' Obviously, she regretted her rare attendance in the mosque. She belongs to an active mosque where the women attend prayers, especially on Saturdays. In her case, her job and many responsibilities outside the mosque have left little time for teaching her children about the prophets. 'Maybe the stories are told and still will be told [in the mosque],' she added, as if in the near future she would have time to send her children there.

Many informants mention personal names as an aid for remembering the prophets and their ethical characteristics. 'Often names in pairs like Yahya and Zakariya, Musa and Harun, or Yunus and Hud are used for children in many families. Naming after grandparents is possible but also after the prophets. That seems to bring a good omen,' an imam in Berlin told me. This was confirmed by several other Muslims.

Five different sayings were mentioned: *sabr Ayub*, meaning utter patience; 'he is like Musa'; being brave or strong; 'he is like Nuh', he will live a long life; and 'the beauty of Yusuf'. Since patience was linked to several prophets this virtue seems to be a highly valued moral quality. Interestingly, however, the expression 'like Yusuf' pointed also to a bad attitude and to a so-called 'light' person. The fact that these negative characteristics are probably misinterpreted as having been said about the nobleman's wife (Q 12:30) was not in my mind when my informant mentioned Yusuf. Otherwise, it might well be that such characteristics have indeed been connected to Yusuf in the transmission of his life story.

The strongest witness to the role of Islamic faith and the prophets was uttered by a knowledgeable imam in Berlin: 'The *umma* means belonging, and the unity of all Muslims. We have been believers in one God since the very beginning, since Adam. And we are linked to all the prophets and to the message of Prophet

Muhammad.' This coincides with many statements during my informal talks with Muslims in both cities.

'The prophets are moral examples' is an assertion which many of the informants seemed to honour. 'They teach us with their lives,' said a well-educated mother of three children who was also showing them videos about the prophets' lives. A teacher of Arabic added: 'Children nowadays are very clever!' and continued, 'The prophets did have a difficult life, but they were the best. We have to make efforts, like them. There is no gift without suffering.'

Hence, my informants consider that moral aspects of Islam need to be transmitted, which means that education is an issue. 'But some stories should be adjusted for children. When children are said to be killed in the narrative, this should only be told at a later age,' a responsible person for a *madrasa* said. The narrative about Yusuf should be postponed till they are older, given the problematic behaviour of his (or the nobleman's) wife, which one informant connected to prostitution and weak morals.

The courage to be 'non-liberal' in theological issues was obviously something Muslims in Stavanger and Berlin were occupied with when I asked them about the role of the prophets. 'Things that seem illogical to us are logical to God. Some liberals attack us, but we know that these things come from God and the Holy Scripture. Hence, we must go on and tell these things,' an imam stated. He continued: 'It is not right to question sacred truths. One must risk being called "antediluvian".' He gave three examples, first mentioning the issue of homosexuality, defending the rights and freedom of homosexuals and the need to talk together and not persecute them, but 'it does not belong to our religion'. Secondly, he referred to the life of Ibrahim and his son being put at risk; and thirdly, to people's fasting and feeling pain during Ramadan. 'Is it right that Allah causes anguish?' He did not reach a conclusion, but again gave Allah the right to exercise His will. This imam showed how he is reinforcing one chain of memory by going back to the prime Islamic source, and finding strength in that foundation.

One informant who had lived in another German city for some years vehemently regretted that Muslims were not living up to Islamic standards for an ethical life. The characteristic of a person that 'he is on the way [Kurdish *re*] of Muhammad' means that 'you say the truth'. Hence, he continued, 'We are role models for our children. We have to show the outstanding qualities of the prophets.'

In all my informants' lives there seems to be an inner struggle between adjustments and changes, on the one hand, and obeying Islam's moral precepts

230 Islamic Myths and Memories

(represented by the prophets in this context), on the other. The stress of being forced to explain to the non-Muslim world what these moral qualities are, is clearly also a difficulty.

However, for all informants the aspect of living moral lives goes in the same direction as suggested by the young men between 16 and 30 years old whom Nikola Tietze interviewed in Germany and France in 2001. Tietze states:

> The religious memory and its melting together with other memories and the exchange between forgetting, repugnance and a new start means flexibility and discontinuity. In this matter the believer in the post-industrial modernity is different from the traditional Muslim. In the religiosity of the latter there is a merged unity of ideology, ethics, culture and utopia. One dimension does not mean anything on its own; only the link between them justifies the religious identification. The religious memory is a unified totality. The continuity of the *lignée croyante* overcomes the discontinuity which happens in the life of the believers; and they are bleaching these dissonances.[44]

Concluding Reflections

The histories of the prophets belong to two active *chains of memory*: first, the main *religious* narrative chain; and second the minor *national* or *regional* chain, that for Kurds is the Nuh story, for some Iraqi and Jordanian Muslims the Zakariya and Joshua stories, and for Palestinians the Khalil–Ibrahim story. According to Hervieu-Léger and Tietze, cultural, national and religious threads are intertwined and often difficult to separate.[45] For my informants the memory of the prophets and the faded rituals around their tombs seem to have been merged with childhood memories and moral examples that Islamic texts, and some oral sources found in the European context, are reinforcing.

While the Muhammad narratives are obviously emphasised at the expense of the other prophet narratives, this does not mean that the latter are actively ignored or suppressed. On the contrary, the stories are kept in mind even when an extended family is reduced to its nuclear core in the new surroundings, but all my informants confirm that the attention paid to the stories is noticeably reduced. Moral, ethical or political elements and implications interact, and go

---

[44]   Nikola Tietze, *Islamische Identitäten. Formen muslimer Religiösität junger Männer in Deutschland und Frankreich* (Hamburg, 2001), pp. 159–60, my translation.

[45]   Hervieu-Léger, *Religion as a Chain of Religion*, pp. 109–11.

together with *tarbiya* – the formation of children's religious upbringing. Hence the mosques emphasise their role in conducting and transmitting the prophet stories, but realise that they do not fully succeed.

I have discovered that these narratives have faded, but most of them have not changed from those they remember being told by family members or by teachers in schools and mosques. Aleida Assmann underlines the element of construction and reconstruction when she writes: '[Memory's] general function was conceived as the steering through time and change by retaining elements of the past and reconstructing them in such a way that they serve as a means of identification and orientation for the future.'[46] This coincides with the strong element of *order* – the prevention of chaos – that religious memory seems to give believers.[47]

I have not discovered whether the narratives told in Berlin are different from or have other emphases from those told in Stavanger. In order to be able to answer this, more research must be undertaken. But it is certain that Muslims in both cities feel that this part of their heritage is at risk. They undertake different strategies to keep up with what they feel is the right thing to do, like sending their children to *madrasa*s and to some extent teaching them at home. Thus the question of whether the interviewees consider *religious* narratives as something which they want to preserve for the next generations has been positively answered. It is also noticeable that some of these cherished narratives have a more *national* or *regional* character – for instance linked to Kurdish or Palestinian history and identity.

I have shown that the answers given to such detailed questions about personal, family and neighbouring issues concerning transmission of the stories about the prophets are related to childhood experiences as well as to societal, geographical and ethical issues. The process is one of negotiation with the new environment in Europe, to some extent with the Christian-majority churches. As Jan Knappert has pointed out, the narratives may be slightly altered due to exchanges with and the influence of the narratives in the majority society. It is also a matter of authority and influence to decide what narratives are to be transmitted, by whom and to whom. However, all families and individuals seem very confident that they will discover what is the best thing to do for their children. With the help of *madrasa*s and new media they hope and assume that their children will succeed in living moral lives – this is the purpose of the prophets' heritage.

---

[46]   Assmann, 'The Religious Roots', p. 271.

[47]   Hervieu-Léger, *Religion as Chain of Religion*, pp. 84–5.

These aspects of continuity and change in two different environments for Muslim minorities in Berlin and in Norway are interesting with respect to the continuity of their spirituality and the support of their religious identity. To some extent, the information provided by my informants, together with my own observations over a long period of time, confirm that these Muslims want the memory (of transmission in their past) to be continued for their pupils and their own children. Still, they are aware that something has been forgotten, especially due to change of context. There is, in other words, no conscious forgetting or depreciation of the narratives, but the metaphor 'bleaching of a former colourful carpet of narratives' seems to be an adequate description of the current state of affairs with regard to the reception of the prophet stories among my informants and in their communities.

Select Bibliography

Abdel-Fadil, Mona, 'The Islam-Online Crisis: A Battle of Wasatiyya vs. Salafi Ideologies?', *CyberOrient*, 5/1 (2011), available at http://www.cyberorient. net/article.do?articleId=6239, last accessed 20 February 2014.

Abu-Manneh, Butrus, *Studies on Islam and the Ottoman Empire in the 19th Century (1826–1876)* (Istanbul: ISIS, 2001).

Agnew, John and Duncan James, *The Power of Place: Bringing Together Geographical and Sociological Imaginations* (Boston, MA: Allen & Unwin, 1989).

Ahmed, Mohammed Shahab, *The Satanic Verses Incident in the Memory of the Early Muslim Community: An Analysis of the Early Riwâyas and their Isnâds.* Unpublished PhD dissertation, Department of Middle East Studies, Princeton University, 1999.

Akhtar, Shabbir, 'Art or Literary Terrorism?', in Dan Cohn-Sherbok (ed.), *The Salman Rushdie Controversy in Interreligious Perspective* (Lampeter: Mellen, 1990): 1–23.

Alexander, Scott C., 'Trust and Patience', in Jane Dammen McAuliffe (ed.), *Encyclopaedia of the Qur'an*, available at http://referenceworks.brillonline. com/entries/encyclopaedia-of-the-quran/trust-and-patience-COM_00 209, last accessed 20 February 2014.

Algar, Hamid, 'A Brief History of the Naqshbandi Order', in Marc Gaborieau, Alexandre Popovic and Thierry Zarcone (eds), *Naqshbandis: cheminements et situation actuelle d'un ordre mystique musulman* (Istanbul and Paris: Isis, 1990): 9–49.

Altınyıldız, Nur, 'İmperatorlukle Cumhuriyet arasındaki eşikte siyaset ve mimarlık: Eskiyi muhafaza/yeniyi inşa', in Ahmet Çiğdem (ed.), *Muhafazakârlık* (Istanbul: İletişim, 2003): 179–86.

Anderson, Benedict, *Imagined Communities: Reflections on the Origin and Spread of Nationalism* (London: Verso, 1983).

Antoun, Richard, *Muslim Preachers in the Modern World* (Princeton, NJ: Princeton University Press, 1989).

Appignanesi, Lisa and Sara Maitland (eds), *The Rushdie File* (London: Fourth Estate, 1989).

Armanios, Febe, 'The Islamic Traditions of Wahhabism and Salafiyya' (December 2003), Congressional Research Service Reports, available at http://fas.org/irp/crs/RS21695.pdf, last accessed 20 February 2014.

Arnold, Thomas, *The Preaching of Islam: A History of the Propagation of the Muslim Faith* (Lahore: Ashraf, 1961).

Ashtiany, Julia, '*Isnamads* and Models of Heroes', *Arabic and Middle Eastern Literature* 1/1 (1998).

Assmann, Aleida, 'The Religious Roots of Cultural Memory', *Norsk Teologisk Tidsskrift*, 4 (2008): 270–92.

Assmann, Jan, *Das kulturelle Gedächtnis: Schrift, Erinnerung und politische Identität in frühen Hochkulturen* (Munich: Beck, 1992/2005).

_____ *Religion and Cultural Memory: Ten Studies* (Stanford, CA: Stanford University Press, 2000/2006).

Atay, Tayfun, *Naqshbandi Sufis in a Western Setting*. Unpublished DPhil thesis, School of Oriental and African Studies, University of London, 1995.

'Athamina, Khalil, 'Al-Qasas: Its Emergence, Religious Origin and Its Socio-Political Impact on Early Muslim Society', *Studia Islamica*, 76 (1992): 53–74.

Atılgan, Gökhan, *Yön-Devrim hareketi: Kemalizm ile Marksizm arasında geleneksel aydınlar* (Istanbul: Türkiye Sosyal Tarih Araştırma Vakfı, 2002).

Atwan, Abdel Bari, *The Secret History of al-Qa'ida* (London: Saqi, 2006).

Ayvazoğlu, Beşir, 'Türk Muhâfazakärlığın kültürel kuruluşu', in Ahmet Çiğdem (ed.), *Muhâfazakârlık* (Istanbul: İletişim, 2003): 509–32.

_____ 'Ekrem Hakkı Ayverdi', in ibid.: 238–41.

Ayverdi, Sâmiha, *İstanbul Geceleri* (Istanbul: Kubbealtı, 1971).

_____ *Mesihpaşa İmamı* (Istanbul: Kubbealtı, 1974).

_____ *Kaybolan Anahtar* (Istanbul: Kubbealtı, 2008).

Azak, Umut, 'Sâmiha Ayverdi', in Ahmet Çiğdem (ed.), *Muhafazakârlık* (Istanbul: İletişim, 2003): 248–55.

Ådna, Gerd Marie, '*O Son of the Two Sacrifices': Muhammad and the Formation of Sacrifice in Early Islam*. Unpublished Dr.art. thesis, University of Bergen, 2007.

Ådna, Gerd Marie, *Muhammad and the Formation of Sacrifice* (Frankfurt a.M: Peter Lang, 2014).

Bahadıroğlu, Yavuz, *Biz Osmanlıyız* (Istanbul: Nesil, 2007).

Baker, Raymond, 'Invidious Comparisons: Realism, Postmodern Globalism, and Centrist Islamic Movements in Egypt', in John Esposito (ed.), *Political Islam: Revolution, Radicalism or Reform?* (Cairo: American University in Cairo Press, 1997): 115–34.

Bale, Jeffrey M., 'Islamism and Totalitarianism', *Totalitarian Movements & Political Religions*, 10/2 (2009): 73–96.

al-Banna, Hasan, 'Nahwa'l-nûr', published in *Al-Rasa'il al-thalatha* (Cairo: Dar al-Tiba'a wa'l-nashr al-Islamiyya, 1977): 74–116.

_____ *Mudhakarat al-da'wa wal-da'iya* (Cairo: Dar al-Kitab, n.d.).

_____ *Majmu'at risalat al-imam al-shahid Hasan al-Banna* (Beirut: Dar al-Andalus, 1965).

Barak, Oren, 'Commemorating Malikiyya: Political Myth, Multi-ethnic Identity and the Making of the Lebanese Army', *History and Memory*, 13/1 (2001): 60–84.

Barthes, Roland, *Mythologies* (London: Vintage, 1993).

Bauman, Zygmunt, *Globalization: The Human Consequences* (Cambridge: Polity, 1999).

Becker, Carl Heinrich, 'Die Kanzel im Kultus des alten Islam', in Carl Bezold (ed.), *Orientalische Studien Theodor Nöldeke ... gewidmet* (Giessen, 1906): 331–51.

Bell, Joseph Norment, '"Say it Again and Make Me Your Slave": Notes on al-Daylami's Seventh Sign of Man's Love for God', in Farhad Daftary and Joseph W. Meri (eds), *Culture and Memory in Medieval Islam: Essays in Honour of Wilferd Madelung* (London and New York: Tauris and Institute of Ismaili Studies, 2003): 190–209.

Berkes, Niyazi, *The Development of Secularism in Turkey* (Montreal: McGill University Press, 1964).

Berkey, Jonathan Porter, *Popular Preaching and Religious Authority in the Medieval Islamic Near East* (Seattle, WA: University of Washington Press, 2001).

Berkovits, Samuel, *The Battle for the Holy Places: The Struggle over Jerusalem and the Holy Sites in Israel, Judea, Samaria and the Gaza Districts* (Or Yehuda: Hed Arzi, 2000).

Bergen, Peter L., *The Osama bin Laden I Know: An Oral History of al Qaeda's Leader* (New York: Free Press, 2006).

Berger, Lutz, 'Religionsbehörde und Millî Görüş: Zwei Varianten eines traditionalistischen Islam in der Türkei', in Rüdiger Lohlker (ed.), *Hadithstudien – Die Überlieferungen des Propheten im Gespräch. Festschrift für Prof. Dr. Tilman Nagel* (Hamburg: Kovač, 2009): 41–76.

Berk, Bekir, *Doğu olaylar ve tehlikenin kaynağı* (Istanbul: Yeni Asya, 1991).

Berman, Marshal, *All That Is Solid Melts into Air* (New York: Simon and Schuster, 1982).

Beyer, Peter, *Religions in Global Society* (London: Routledge, 2006).

Bin Laden, Osama, and Randall B. Hamud, *Osama bin Laden: America's Enemy in His Own Words* (San Diego, CA: Nadeem, 2005).

_____ and Bruce Lawrence, *Messages to the World: The Statements of Osama Bin Laden* (London: Verso, 2005).

Bora, Tanıl and Burak Onaran, 'Nostalji ve Muhafazakârlık', in Ahmet Çiğdem (ed.), *Muhafazakârlık* (Istanbul: İletişim, 2003): 234–60.

Bouguenaya-Mermer, Yamina and Ali Mermer, *Risale-i nur'dan toplumsal barış önerisi* (Istanbul: Nesil, 1997).

Bourdieu, Pierre, 'Genesis and Structure of the Religious Field', *Comparative Social Research*, 53 (1991): 1–44.

Bozdağ, Muhammet, *İstemenin Esrarı* (Istanbul: Nesil, 2007).

Brenner, Neil, 'The Limits to Scale? Methodological Reflections on Scalar Structuration', *Progress in Human Geography*, 25/4 (2001): 591–614.

Brinner, William M., *The History of al-Tabari*, Vol. 2: *Prophets and Patriarchs* (Albany, NY: State University of New York Press, 1987).

_____ 'Noah', in Jane Dammen McAuliffe (ed.), *Encyclopaedia of the Qur'an* (Georgetown University, Washington, DC: Brill, 2009), available at http://referenceworks.brillonline.com/entries/encyclopaedia-of-the-quran/noah-COM_00134, last accessed 20 February 2014.

Butler, Jean, 'Tidlig islamsk historie i mnemohistorisk belysning – Et case-study af sûrat al-kâfirûn', *Religionsvidenskabeligt Tidsskrift*, 52 (2008): 53–67.

Çağapatay, Suna and Soner Çağapatay, 'Ottomania All the Rage in Turkey', *Today's Zaman*, 1 April 2012, available at http://www.todayszaman.com/news-275971-ottomania-all-the-rage-in-turkey.html, last accessed 20 February 2014.

Cânan, İbrahim, *Oturanların açışışdan Atatürk Üniversitesi lojmanları veya taklitçili-ğimizin muha-sebesi* (Ankara: Ayyıldız, 1979).

Çangaoğlu, Abdullah, 'Osmanlı devleti'nde devşirme sistemi', *Sızıntı*, 16 (1994): 160–2.

Cao, Shuji, *Zhongguo renko shi* ('A history of Chinese population') (Shanghai: udan daxue chubanshe, 2001).

Carter, Erica, Judith Donald and James Squires (eds), *Space and Place: Theories of Identity and Location* (London: Lawrence & Wishart, 1993).

Castells, Manuel, *The Information Age: Economy, Society and Culture*, Vol. 1: *The Rise of the Network Society* (Oxford: Blackwell, 1996).

_____ *The Information Age: Economy, Society and Culture*, Vol. II: *The Power of Identity* (Oxford: Blackwell, 1997).

Çetinsaya, Gökhan, 'Cumhuriyet Türkiyesin'de Osmancılık', in Ahmet Çiğdem (ed.), *Muhafazakârlık* (Istanbul: İletişim, 2003): 361–80.

Cheikho, Louis, 'Quelques légendes islamiques apocryphes', *Mélanges de la faculté Orientale, Université Saint-Joseph*, 4 (1910): 5–56.

Chidester, David and Linenthal, Edward (eds), *American Sacred Space* (Bloomington, IN: Indiana University Press, 1995).

Chivallon, Christine, 'Religion as Space for the Expression of Caribbean Identity in the United Kingdom', *Environment & Planning D: Society & Space*, 19/4 (2001): 461–84.

Çırpçı, Filiz, 'Amerikan usulü lâiklik', *Köprü*, 81 (February 1984): 7–8.

Çolak, Yılmaz, 'Ottomanism vs. Kemalism: Collective Memory and Cultural Pluralism in 1990s Turkey', *Middle Eastern Studies*, 42 (2006): 587–602.

Confino, Alon, 'Collective Memory and Cultural History: Problems of Method', *American Historical Review*, 102 (1997), 1386–403.

Cook, David, *Studies in Muslim Apocalyptic* (Princeton, NJ: Princeton University Press, 2002).

———— *Contemporary Muslim Apocalyptic Literature* (Syracuse, NY: Syracuse University Press, 2005).

Copeaux, Étienne, *Espaces et temps de la nation turque: Analyse d'une historiographie nationaliste 1931–1993* (Paris: Éditions CNRS, 1997).

Creswell, Keppel, *Early Muslim Architecture* (Oxford: Oxford University Press, 1969).

Damrel, David, 'A Sufi Apocalypse', *ISIM Newsletter*, 4 (1999): 1–4.

———— 'Aspects of the Naqshbandi-Haqqani Order in North America', in Jamal Malik and John Hinnels (eds), *Sufism in the West* (London and New York: Routledge, 2006): 115–26.

Dayf, Shawqi, *al-Fann wa-madhaahibihi fi al-adab al-jahili* (Cairo: Matba'at Muhammad biMisr, 1960).

Debus, Esther, *Sebilürreşad: Eine vergleichende Untersuchung zur islamischen Opposition der vor- und nach-kemalistischen Ära* (Frankfurt-am-Main: Lang, 1991).

Demirhan, Talip, 'Hollanda aynasında "Türk demokrasisi"', *Köprü*, 140 (November 1989): 29–32.

Determann, Matthias, 'The Crusades in Arab School Textbooks', *Islam and Christian-Muslim Relations*, 19/2 (2008): 199–214.

Deutz-Schroeder, Monika and Klaus Schroeder, 'Das DDR-Bild von Schülern in Bayern', *Einsichten und Perspektiven: Bayerische Zeitschrift für Politik und Geschichte*, 1 (2008). Available at http://www.km.bayern.de/blz/eup/01_08/3.asp, last accessed 20 February 2014.

Devji, Faisal, *Landscapes of the Jihad: Militancy, Morality, Modernity* (Ithaca, NY: Cornell University Press, 2005).

Draper, Ian K.B., 'From Celts to Kaaba: Sufism in Glastonbury', in David Westerlund (ed.), *Sufism in Europe and North America* (London and New York: Routledge, 2004): 144–56.

Duri, Abd al-Aziz, 'Fikrat al-quds fi'l-islam', *Qadaya Arabiyya* (1981): 7–28.

Durkheim, Émile, *The Elementary Forms of the Religious Life* (New York: Free Press, 1912/1995).

Dörler, Elisabeth, *Verständigung leben und lernen am Beispiel von türkischen Muslimen und Vorarlberger Christen* (Feldkirch: Quelle, 2003).

Eade, John and Michael Sallnow (eds), *Contesting the Sacred: The Anthropology of Christian Pilgrimage* (London and New York: Routledge, 1991).

Eickelman, Dale F. and James Piscatori (eds), *Muslim Travellers: Pilgrimage, Migration and the Religious Imagination* (London: Routledge, 1990).

_____ and Jon Anderson, 'Redefining Muslim Publics', in Dale Eickelman and Jon Anderson (eds), *New Media in the Muslim World: The Emerging Public Sphere* (Bloomington, IN: Indiana University Press, 1999): 1–18.

Eisenstadt, Samuel N., *Fundamentalism, Sectarianism and Revolution: The Jacobin Dimension of Modernity* (Cambridge: Cambridge University Press, 1999).

Elad, Amikam, *Medieval Jerusalem and Islamic Worship: Holy Places, Ceremonies, Pilgrimage* (Leiden, Köln and New York: Brill, 1995).

_____ 'The Status of Jerusalem During the Umayyad Period', *Hamizrach Hachasah*, 44 (2004): 17–68.

El-Haj, Nadia, *Facts on the Ground: Archaeological Practice and Territorial Self-fashioning in Israeli Society* (Chicago, IL: University of Chicago Press, 2001).

Eliade, Mircea, *The Myth of Eternal Return: Or, Cosmos and History* (Princeton, NJ: Princeton University Press, 1954).

_____ *The Sacred and The Profane: The Nature of Religion* (San Diego, CA: Harcourt Brace, 1959).

van Engeland, Anicée, 'Le droit international des droits de l'homme et la République Islamique d'Iran: Respect des obligations internationales par un gouvernement islamique', *European University Institute Working Papers*, Max Weber Program (August 2008).

Escobar, Arturo, 'Culture Sits in Places: Reflections on Globalism and Subaltern Strategies of Localization', *Political Geography*, 20/2 (2001): 139–74.

Esposito, John L., *The Islamic Threat: Myth or Reality?* (3rd edn, New York: Oxford University Press, 1999).

Fletcher, Joseph, *Studies on Chinese and Islamic Inner Asia*, ed. Beatrice Forbes Manz (Aldershot: Ashgate, 1995).

Flood, Finnbar, 'Between Cult and Culture: Bamiyan, Islamic Iconoclasm, and the Museum', *Art Bulletin*, 84/4 (2002): 641–60.

Foucault, Michel, *Power/Knowledge: Selected Interviews and Other Writings, 1972–1977*, ed. Colin Gordon (New York: Harvester, 1980).

Friedland, Roger and Richard Hecht, *To Rule Jerusalem* (Cambridge: Cambridge University Press, 1996).

Frisch, Michael, 'American History and the Structures of Collective Memory: A Modest Exercise in Empirical Iconography', *Journal of American History*, 75 (1989): 1130–55.

Fu, Shuhua, 'Xinlin de mikuang' ('The bewildered heart'), *Hainan shifan xueyuan xuebao*, 5 (2005): 50–62.

Fu, Tongxian, *Zhongguo huijiaoshi* ('A history of Islam in China') (Beijing: shangwu yinshuguan, 1940).

Furnish, Timothy R., *Holiest Wars: Islamic Mahdis, Their Jihads, and Osama bin Laden* (Westport, CT: Praeger, 2005).

Gaffney, Patrick, *The Prophet's Pulpit: Islamic Preaching in Contemporary Egypt* (Berkeley, CA: University of California Press, 1994).

Galal, Ehab, 'Yusuf al-Qaradawi and the New Islamic TV', in Bettina Gräf and Jakob Skovgaard-Petersen (eds), *Global Mufti: The Phenomenon of Yusuf al-Qaradawi* (London: Hurst, 2009): 49–180.

Gammer, Moshe, *Muslim Resistance to the Tsar: Shamil and the Conquest of Chechnia and Daghestan* (London: Frank Cass, 1994).

Geaves, Ron, 'The Haqqani Naqshbandis: A Study of Apocalyptic Millennialism within Islam', in Stanley E. Porter, Michael A. Hayes and David Tombs (eds), *Faith in the Millennium* (Sheffield: Sheffield Academic Press, 2001): 215–31.

Germanus, Julius, 'Legacy of Ancient Arabia', *Islamic Culture*, 37 (1963): 261–9.

Giddens, Anthony, *The Consequences of Modernity* (Cambridge: Polity, 1990).

Gil, Moshe, *A History of Palestine, 634–1099* (Cambridge: Cambridge University Press, 1992).

Gilliot, Claude, *Exégèse, langue et théologie en Islam: L'Exégèse coranique de Tabari (m. 311/923)* (Paris: Vrin, 1990).

Gladney, Dru C., *Dislocating China: Muslims, Minorities, and Other Subaltern Subjects* (Chicago, IL: University of Chicago Press, 2004).

Glaßen, Erika, "'Huzur'": Trägheit, Seelenruhe, soziale Harmonie. Zur osmanischen Mentalitätsgeschichte', in Jean-Louis Bacqué-Grammont (ed.), *Türkische Miszellen: Robert Anhegger Festschrift/armağanı/mélanges* (Istanbul: Divit, 1987): 145–66.

Goldziher, Ignaz, *Muslim Studies*, ed. Samuel Miklos Stern (London: Allen & Unwin, 1971).

Gören, Selda, 'Eski Türk evleri ve özellikleri', *Yeni Nesil* (19 July 1991).

Gräf, Bettina, 'IslamOnline.net: Independent, Interactive, Popular', *Arab Media & Society* (January 2008), available at http://arabmediasociety.sqgd. co.uk/articles/downloads/20080115032719_AMS4_Bettina_Graf.pdf, last accessed 20 February 2014.

_____ and Jakob Skovgaard-Petersen (eds), *Global Mufti: The Phenomenon of Yusuf al-Qaradawi* (London: Hurst, 2009).

Gülen, Fethullah, *Zamanın Altın Dilimi* (Istanbul: Işık, 2003).

_____ *Asrın getirdiği tereddütler* (3 vols, Istanbul: Işık, 2003).

_____ *Çağ ve Nesil* (Istanbul: Işık, 2003).

Gürbüz, Nedim, 'Vah Turizm!', *Köprü*, 62 (July 1982): 5–7.

Habibis, Daphne, 'Millenarianism and Mahdism in Lebanon', *Archives Européenes de Sociologie*, 30 (1989): 221–40.

_____ 'Change and Continuity: A Sufi Order in Contemporary Lebanon', *Social Analysis*, 31 (1992): 44–78.

Haenni, Patrick, 'Islamisme, management et vidéoclips', *L'Expansion* (1 April 2005), available at http://lexpansion.lexpress.fr/actualite-economique/ islamisme-management-et-videoclips_1400372.html, last accessed 23 February 2014.

Hajj, The [*sic*], Smadar Lavie and Forest Rouse, 'Notes on the Fantastic Journey of the Hajj, His Anthropologist, and Her American Passport', *American Ethnologist*, 20/2 (May 1993), 363–84.

al-Hakim, Umar 'Abd, 'Da'wat al-muqawama al-islamiyya al-'alamiyya' ('The Call for Global Islamic Resistance'), (2005), available at http://archive.org/ stream/The-call-for-a-global-Islamic-resistance#page/n13/mode/2up, last accessed 20 February 2014.

Halbwachs, Maurice, *On Collective Memory*, ed., transl., and with an introduction by Lewis A. Coser (Chicago: Chicago University Press, 1941/1952/1992).

_____ *Les cadres sociaux de la mémoire* (Paris: Albin Michel, 1994).

Halliday, Fred, *100 Myths about the Middle East* (London: Saqi Books, 2005).

Hamori, Andras, 'Exemplum, Anecdote and the Gentle Heart in the Text of al-Gahshiyari', *Asiatische Studien*, 50/2 (1996): 363–70.

Hamzah, Dyala, 'Is There an Arab Public Sphere? The Palestinian Intifada, a Saudi Fatwa, and the Egyptian Press', in Armando Salvatore and Mark LeVine (eds), *Religion, Social Practice, and Contested Hegemonies: Reconstructing the Public Sphere in Muslim Majority Societies* (New York: Palgrave, 2005): 181–206.

Hanioğlu, Şükrü, *Atatürk: An Intellectual Biography* (Princeton, NJ and Oxford: Princeton University Press, 2011).

Hansen, Hendrik and Peter Kainz, 'Radical Islamism and Totalitarian Ideology: A Comparison of Sayyid Qutb's Islamism with Marxism and National Socialism', *Totalitarian Movements & Political Religions*, 8/1 (2007): 55–76.

al-Haqqani al-Naqshbandi, Muhammad Nazim Adil, *Mercy Ocean: The Teachings of Mevlana Sheikh Abdullah Ad-Daghistani* (Bk 2, n.p., 1980).

_____ *Mystical Secrets of the Last Days* (Los Altos CA: The Haqqani Islamic Trust for New Muslims, 1994).

al-Haqqani, Nazim, *Secret Desires* (London: Zero Publications, 1996).

Hastings, Adrian, 'Holy Lands and their Political Consequences', *Nations and Nationalism*, 9/1 (2003): 29–54.

Hegghammer, Thomas, *Al-Qaida Statements 2003–2004 – A Compilation of Translated Texts by Usama bin Ladin and Ayman al-Zawahiri*, FFI/RAPPORT-2005/01428, Forsvarets Forskningsinstitutt, 2005.

Helfont, Samuel, *Yusuf al-Qaradawi: Islam and Modernity* (Tel Aviv: Moshe Dayan Center, 2009).

Hervieu-Léger, Danièle, *Religion as a Chain of Memory* (Cambridge: Polity, 1993/2000).

Heyd, Uriel, 'The Ottoman Ulemā and Westernization in the Time of Selim III and Mahmud II', in Uriel Heyd (ed.), *Studies in Islamic History and Civilization* (Jerusalem: Hebrew University, 1961): 63–96.

Hill, Andrew, 'The bin Laden Tapes', *Journal for Cultural Research*, 10/1 (2006): 35–46.

Hjarvard, Stig, 'News Media and the Globalization of the Public Sphere', in Stig Hjarvard (ed.), *News in a Globalized Society* (Gothenburg: Nordicom, 2001): 17–39.

Hobsbawm, Eric and Terence Ranger (eds), *The Invention of Tradition* (Cambridge: Cambridge University Press, 1983).

Ibn Hazm, Abu Muhammad 'Ali ibn Ahmad ibn Sa'id, *al-Fasl fi'l-milal wa'l-ahwâ wa'l-nihal*, Vol. I (Beirut: Dar al-Ma'rifa, 1975).

Ibn al-Jawzi, *Mirat al-zaman fi tarikh al-a'yan* (Haydarabad: Dairatu'l-Maarifil-Osmania, 1951–52).

_____ *al-Muntazam fi tarikh al-muluk wa-al-umam* (Haydarabad: n.p., 1359h).

_____ *Laftat al-kabid* (Beirut, 1987).

Ibn Jubayr, *Rihlat ibn Jubayr* (Beirut, 1974).

Ibrahim, Raymond and Victor Davis Hanson (eds), *The Al Qaeda Reader* (New York: Doubleday, 2007).

Ibrahim, Saad Eddin, 'The Causes of Muslim Countries' Poor Record of Human Rights', in Shireen T. Hunter (ed.) with Huma Malik, *Islam and Human Rights: Advancing a US–Muslim Dialogue* (Washington, DC: Center for Strategic and International Studies, 2005): 70–76.

Idris, Ja'far Shaykh, 'al-Da'wa wasa'il al-ittisal al-haditha', *al-Bayan*, 148, available at http://www.jaafaridris.com/Arabic/aarticles/dawa.htm, last accessed 10 April 2006.

Ihsanoglu, Ekmeleddin, *The Islamic World in the New Century: The Organisation of the Islamic Conference, 1969–2009* (London: Hurst, 2010).

Imam, Imam Muhammad, 'Khidmat al-islam 'ibr al-intarnat ... jihad hadha al-'asr' (interview with Yusuf al-Qaradawi), *al-Sharq al-Awsat*, 12 November 1999, 18.

Inglehart, Ronald, 'How Solid Is Mass Support for Democracy – and How Can We Measure It?', *Political Science and Politics*, 36 (2003): 51–7.

Işın, Ekrem, 'Tanzimat ailesi ve modern âdâb-ı muâşeret', in Halit İnalcık and Mehmet Seyitdanlıoğlu (eds), *Tanzimat. Değişim sürecinde Osmanlı İmparatorluğu*, (Istanbul: Phoenix, 2006): 387–400.

İsmail, Hekimoğlu, *100 Soruda Bediüzzaman Said Nursi, Risale-i Nur Külliyatı ve Risale-i Nur Talebeleri* (Istanbul: Nesil, 1994).

_____ *Müslüman ve para* (Istanbul: Timaş, 2004).

Ismail, Wael, 'The Construction of a National Identity in Exile: Palestinians in Egypt'. Unpublished MA thesis, American University in Cairo, 2007.

Israeli, Raphael, *Islam in China: A Critical Bibliography* (Westport, CT: Greenwood, 1994).

_____ *Muslims in China: Religion, Ethnicity, Culture, and Politics* (Lanham, MD: Lexington Books, 2007).

Ivakhiv, Adrian, 'Toward a Geography of "Religion": Mapping the Distribution of an Unstable Signifier', *Annals of the Association of American Geographers*, 96/1 (2006): 169–75.

Izutsu, Toshihiko, *Ethico-Religious Concepts in the Qur'an* (Montreal: McGill University Press 1962/2002).

Jbara, Taysir, *Palestinian Leader, Hajj Amin al-Husayni, Mufti of Jerusalem* (Princeton, NJ: Kingston, 1985).

Jonas, Andrew, 'The Scale Politics of Spatiality', *Environment and Planning D*, 12 (1994): 257–64.

Jung, Christine, *Islamische Fernsehsender in der Türkei. Zur Entwicklung des türkischen Fernsehens zwischen Staat, Markt und Religion* (Berlin: Schwarz, 2003).

Kabbani, Hisham, *The Approach of Armageddon? An Islamic Perspective* (Washington, DC: Islamic Supreme Council of America, 2002).

Kabbani, Muhammad Hisham, *The Naqshbandi Sufi Way: History and Guidebook of the Saints of the Golden Chain* (Chicago, IL: Kazi Publications, 1995).

el-Kadi, Ahmet, 'Bir ders daha', *Zafer* 96 (December 1984): 4–8.

Kaner, Nazlı, *Sâmiha Ayverdi (1905–1993) und die osmanische Gesellschaft. Zur Soziogenese eines ideologischen Begriffs: osmanlı* (Würzburg: Ergon, 1998).

Kansteiner, Wulf, 'Finding Meaning in Memory: A Methodological Critique of Collective Memory Studies', *History and Theory*, 41 (May 2002): 179–97.

_____ 'Nazis, Viewers and Statistics: Television History, Television Audience Research and Collective Memory in West Germany', *Journal of Contemporary History*, 39 (2004): 575–98.

Kaplan, Mustafa, 'Bâb-ı Âli baskını', *Yeni Nesil*, 27 November 1985.

_____ 'Yahudilerin emellerine sed çeken Osmanlı', *Yeni Nesil*, 31 January 1986.

Kara, İsmail, *İslâmcıların siyasi görüşleri* (Istanbul: İz, 1994).

_____ 'Turban and Fez: Ulema as Opposition', in Elisabeth Özdalga (ed.), *Late Ottoman Society: The Intellectual Legacy* (London and New York: Routledge Curzon, 2005): 162–200.

Karabaşoğlu, Metin, 'Said Nursi', in Yasin Aktay (ed.), *İslâmcılık*, (Istanbul: İletişim, 2004): 270–87.

Kassab, Akram, *al-Manhaj al-da'wi 'inda'l-Qaradawi* (Cairo: Maktabat Wahba, 2006).

al-Kaylani, Shamsuddin, 'Concepts of Human Rights in Islamic Doctrines (Sunnis, Shi'ites, Isma'ilis, Qarmatians, Mu'tazilis, Sufiss, Wahhabis)', in Salma K. Jayyusi (ed.), *Human Rights in Arab Thought: A Reader* (New York: I.B. Tauris, 2009): 181–9.

Kemper, Michael, 'The Changing Images of Jihad Leaders: Shamil and Abd al-Qadir in Daghestani and Algerian Historical Writing', *Nova Religio*, 11/2 (November 2007): 28–58.

Kepel, Gilles, *The Prophet and Pharaoh: Muslim Extremism in Egypt* (London: Al Saqi Books, 1985).

_____ *The War for Muslim Minds: Islam and the West* (Cambridge, MA: Belknap Press of Harvard University Press, 2004).

Khalidi, Tarif, *Arabic Historical Thought in the Classical Period* (Cambridge: Cambridge University Press, 1994).

_____ *The Muslim Jesus: Sayings and Stories in Islamic Literature* (London and Cambridge, MA: Harvard University Press, 2001).

Kim, Hodong, *Holy War in China: The Muslim Rebellion and State in Chinese Central Asia, 1864–1877* (Stanford, CA: Stanford University Press, 2004).

Kırkıncı, Mehmed, *İslamda birlik*, (Istanbul: Timaş, 1998).

_____ *Nasıl bir maârif? Nasıl bir eğitim?* (Erzurum: Ekev, 2001).

al-Kisa'i, Sahib, *The Tales of the Prophets of al-Kisa'i*, trans. Wheeler M. Thackston, Jr. (Boston, MA: Twayne, 1978).

Kısakürek, Necip Fazıl, 'Ve tarihçe', *Büyük Doğu*, 2/30 (24 May 1946): 11.

_____ 'Abdülhamîd ve Avrupalı', *Büyük Doğu* (29 September 1965): 10–11.

_____ *Son devrin din mazlumları* (Istanbul: Büyük Doğu, 1974).

Kister, Meir, 'You Shall Only Set Out for Three Mosques: A Study of an Early Tradition', *Le Museon*, 82 (1969): 173–96.

Klass, Dennis and Robert Goss, 'The Politics of Grief and Continuing Bonds with the Dead: The Cases of Maoist China and Wahhabi Islam', *Death Studies*, 27/9 (2003): 787–811.

Klausen, Jytte, *The Cartoons that Shook the World* (New Haven, CT: Yale University Press, 2009).

Knappert, Jan, *Islamic Legends: Histories of the Heroes, Saints and Prophets of Islam* (Leiden: Brill, 1985).

Knysh, Alexander, '"Irfan" Revisited: Khomeini and the Legacy of Islamic Mystical Philosophy', *Middle East Journal*, 46/4 (1992): 631–53.

Kong, Lily, 'Negotiating Conceptions of Sacred Space: A Case Study of Religious Buildings in Singapore', *Transactions of the Institute of British Geographers*, 18 (1993): 342–58.

_____ 'Ideological Hegemony and the Political Symbolism of Religious Buildings in Singapore', *Environment and Planning D*, 11 (1993): 23–45.

Köse, Ali, *Conversion to Islam: A Study of Native British Converts* (London and New York: Kegan Paul International, 1996).

Köse, Elifhan, 'Muhafazakar bir kadın portresi olarak Semiha Ayverdi: Muhafazakarlık Düşüncesinde Kadınlara İlişkin Bir Hat Çizebilmek', *Fe Dergi-feminist eleştiri*, 1.1 (2009): 11–20, available at http://cins.ankara.edu.tr/kose.html, last accessed 20 February 2014.

Kreiser, Klaus, 'Die neue Türkei (1920–2002)', in Klaus Kreiser and Andreas Neumann (eds), *Kleine Geschichte der Türkei* (Stuttgart: Reclam, 2003): 383–475.

Latour, Bruno, *We Have Never Been Modern*, trans. Catherine Porter (Cambridge, MA: Harvard University Press, 1993).

Leder, Stefan, 'Conventions of Fictional Narration', in Stefan Leder (ed.), *Story-telling in the Framework of Non-Fictional Arabic Literature* (Wiesbaden: Harrassowitz, 1998): 41–55.

Lefebvre, Henri, *The Production of Space*, trans. Donald Nicholson-Smith (Oxford: Blackwell, 1991).

Ley, David and Olds, Kris, 'Landscape as Spectacle: World's Fairs and the Culture of Heroic Consumption', *Environment and Planning D: Society and Space*, 6 (1988): 191–212.

Li, Shujiang, *Mythology and Folklore of the Hui, a Muslim Chinese People* (Albany, NY: State University of New York Press, 1994).

Lia, Brynjar, *The Society of the Muslim Brothers in Egypt: The Rise of an Islamic Mass-movement, 1928–1942* (Reading: Ithaca, 1998).

_____ *Architect of Global Jihad: The Life of al-Qaida Strategist Abu Mus'ab al-Suri* (New York: Columbia University Press, 2008).

Lincoln, Bruce, 'Notes toward a Theory of Religion and Revolution', in Bruce Lincoln (ed.), *Religion, Rebellion, Revolution: An Interdisciplinary and Cross-cultural Collection of Essays* (New York: Palgrave Macmillan, 1985): 270–9.

_____ *Myth, Cosmos, and Society: Indo-European Themes of Creation and Destruction* (Cambridge, MA: Harvard University Press, 1986).

_____ *Discourse and the Construction of Society: Comparative Studies of Myth, Ritual, and Classification* (Oxford: Oxford University Press, 1989).

_____ *Death, War, and Sacrifice: Studies in Ideology and Practice* (Chicago: University of Chicago Press, 1991).

_____ 'Conflict', in Mark C. Taylor (ed.), *Critical Terms for Religious Studies* (Chicago: University of Chicago Press, 1998): 55–8.

_____ *Theorizing Myth* (Chicago: University of Chicago Press, 1999).

_____ *Holy Terrors: Thinking about Religion after September 11* (Chicago: University of Chicago Press, 2003).

_____ *Religion, Empire, and Torture: The Case of Achaemenian Persia, with a Postscript on Abu Ghraib* (Chicago: University of Chicago Press, 2007).

Lipman, Jonathan N., *Familiar Strangers: A History of Muslims in Northwest China* (Seattle, WA: University of Washington Press, 1998).

Liu, Xinmin, 'A Marginal Return? – The Problematic in Zhang Chengzhi's Reinvention of Ethnic Identity', *Journal of Contemporary China*, 6/16 (1997): 567–80.

Livne-Kafri, Ofer (ed.), *Abu al-Ma'ali al-Musharraf b. al-Murajja b. Ibrahim al-Maqdisi, Kitab fada'il bayt al-maqdis wa-al-khalil wa-fada'il al-sham* (Shfaram: n.s., 1995).

Lowenthal, David, *The Past Is a Foreign Country* (Cambridge: Cambridge University Press, 1985).

Lyons, Malcolm Cameron, *The Arabian Epic and Oral Story-telling* (Cambridge: Cambridge University Press, 1995).

Ma, Tong, *Zhongguo yisilan jiaopai yu menhuan zhidu shilue* ('A short history of Chinese Islamic sects and the Menhuan system') (Lanzhou: ningxia renmin chubanshe, 1999).

Maalouf, Amin, *The Crusades through Arab Eyes* (Cairo: American University in Cairo Press, 1983).

Malik, Jamal and John Hinnels (eds), *Sufism in the West* (London and New York: Routledge, 2006).

Malik, Kenan, *From Fatwa to Jihad: The Rushdie Affair and Its Legacy* (London: Atlantic Books, 2009).

Massey, Doreen, 'Power-Geometry and a Progressive Sense of Place', in Jon Bird, Barry Curtis, Tim Putnam, George Robertson and Lisa Tickner (eds), *Mapping the Futures: Local Cultures, Global Change* (New York: Routledge, 1993): 59–69.

_____ 'Places and their Past', *History Workshop Journal*, 39 (1995): 182–92.

McAuliffe, Jane Dammen, 'Assessing the *Israiliyyat*: An Exegetical Conundrum', in S. Leder (ed.), *Story-telling in the Framework of Non-Fictional Arabic Literature* (Wiesbaden: Harrassowitz, 1998): 345–64.

McLoughlin, Seán, 'Religion and Diaspora', in *The Routledge Companion to the Study of Religion* (2nd ed.), (London and New York: Routledge, 2010): 558–80.

Meijer, Roel (ed.), *Global Salafism: Islam's New Religious Movement* (London: Hurst, 2009).

Meital, Yoram, 'Sadat's Grave and the Commemoration of the 1973 War in Egypt', in Michael E. Geisler (ed.), *Symbols, Fractured Identities: Contesting the National Narrative* (Lebanon, NH: Middlebury College Press, 2005): 222–40.

Menzies, Gavin, *1421: The Year China Discovered the World* (New York: Transworld, 2008).

Mitchell, Richard P., *The Society of the Muslim Brothers* (Oxford: Oxford University Press, 1993).

Mittwoch, Eugen, 'Zur Enstehungsgeschichte des islamischen Gebets und Kultus', *Abhandlungen der Königlich-Preussischen Akademie der Wissenschaften* (1913): 1–42.

Monroe, James, 'Oral Composition in Pre-Islamic Poetry', *Journal of Arabic Literature*, 3 (1972): 1–52.

Monshipouri, Mahmood, *Muslims in Global Politics: Identities, Interests, and Human Rights* (Philadelphia, PA: University of Pennsylvania Press, 2009).

Mozaffari, Mehdi, *Fatwa: Violence and Discourtesy* (Aarhus: Aarhus University Press, 1998).

Mubarak, Zaki, *al-Nathr al-fanni fi l-qarn al-rabi'* (Cairo, 1934).

Murata, Sachiko and William C. Chittick, *The Vision of Islam* (St Paul, MN: Paragon House, 2006).

Murphy, Caryle, *Passion for Islam: Shaping the Modern Middle East: The Egyptian Experience* (New York: Scribner, 2002).

Mürsel, Safa, 'Türkiye'de anayasa dâvâsı', *Köprü*, 54 (November 1981): 6–8.

Mårtensson, Ulrika, 'Discourse and Historical Analysis: The Case of al-Tabari's History of the Messengers and the Kings', *Journal of Islamic Studies*, 16/3 (2005): 287–331.

_____ *Tabari*, in Farhan A. Nizami (ed.), *Makers of Islamic Civilization* (Oxford: Oxford University Press, 2009).

Naipaul, V.S., *Among the Believers: An Islamic Journey* (New York: Picador, 2003).

Na'na'a, Ramzi, *al-Israiliyyat wa-atharuha fi kutub al-tafsir* (Damascus, 1970).

Nash, Kate, *Contemporary Political Sociology: Globalization, Politics and Power* (Oxford: Blackwell, 2000).

Nathan, Andrew J., *China's Transition* (New York: Columbia University Press, 1997).

Naylor, Simon and James Ryan, 'The Mosque in the Suburbs: Negotiating Religion and Ethnicity in South London', *Social & Cultural Geography*, 3/1 (2002): 39–59.

Neuwirth, Angelika, 'Quranic Literary Structure Revisited: *Surat al-Rahman* between Mythic Account and Decodation Myth', in Stefan Leder (ed.), *Storytelling in the Framework of Non-Fictional Arabic Literature* (Wiesbaden: Harrassowitz, 1998): 407–15.

Nielsen, Jørgen S., Mustafa Draper and Galina Yemelianova, 'Transnational Sufism: The Haqqaniyya', in Jamal Malik and John Hinnels (eds), *Sufism in the West* (London and New York: Routledge, 2006).

Nilsen, Anne Birgitta, 'Osama bin Ladens skjulte slagkraft', *Norsk Medietidsskrift*, 4 (2007): 298–312.

_____ 'Osama bin Ladens slagkraft', *Babylon Nordisk Tidsskrift for Midtøstenstudier*, 2 (2008): 40–9.

_____ 'Osama bin Ladens retorikk', *Rhetorica Scandinavica*, 51 (2009): 6–24.

Nora, Pierre, 'Between Memory and History: Les lieux de mémoire', *Representations*, 26 (Spring 1989): 7–24.

Nordbruch, Götz, *Nazism in Syria and Lebanon: The Ambivalence of the German Option, 1933–1945* (London: Routledge, 2008).

Noth, Albrecht, *The Early Arabic Historical Tradition: A Source-Critical Study* (Princeton, NJ: Darwin, 1994).

Nursi, Said, *Münâzarat* (Istanbul: Sinan, 1958).

_____ *Kastamonu Lâhıkası* (Istanbul: Yeni Asya, 2000).

Oğuz, Necmeddin, 'Dualı açılış', *Yeni Nesil*, 5 October 1987.

_____ 'Cami inşaatına devlet desteği', *Yeni Nesil*, 14 May 1988.

_____ '"Amsterdam" da 22 cami her an ibadete açık: Dinî hizmetlere devlet yardımı', *Yeni Nesil*, 16 May 1988.

_____ '"Holanda" da ilkokul', *Yeni Nesil*, 7 April 1991.

Osama, Muhammad Fathi, 'Islam, Terrorism, and Western Misapprehensions', in Ibrahim M. Abu-Rabi' (ed.), *The Blackwell Companion to Contemporary Islamic Thought* (Malden, MA: Blackwell Publishing, 2006): 375–87.

Otto, Rudolph, *The Idea of the Holy: An Inquiry into the Non-rational Factor in the Idea of the Divine and Its Relation to the Natural*, trans. James. W. Harvey (Harmondsworth: Pelican Books, 1959).

Öz, Sema, 'İslâmî geleneklerimiz yaşatılmalı', *Yeni Nesil*, 2 July 1991.

Özyürek, Esra, *Nostalgia for the Modern: State Secularism and Everyday Politics in Turkey* (Durham, NC and London: Duke University Press, 2006).

Pargeter, Alison, *The Muslim Brotherhood: The Burden of Tradition* (London: Saqi, 2010).

Parry, V.J., 'Enderun', *Encyclopaedia of Islam*, Second Edition, Brill Online, 2013, 25 March 2013, available at http://www.paulyonline.brill.nl/entries/encyclopaedia-of-islam-2/enderun-SIM_2189, last accessed 20 February 2014.

Pedersen, Johannes, 'The Islamic Preacher', *Goldziher Memorial*, 1 (1948): 232–40.

_____ 'The Criticism of the Islamic Preacher', *Die Welt des Islams*, 2 (1953): 216–31.

_____ 'Khatib', *Encyclopaedia of Islam 2*, Vol. IV: 1109–11.

Peskes, Esther, 'Die Wahhābīya als innerislamisches Feindbild. Zum Hintergrund anti-wahhabitischer Publikationen in der zeitgenössischen Türkei', *Welt des Islams*, 40 (2000): 344–74.

Polka, Sagi, 'The Centrist Stream in Egypt and its Role in the Public Discourse Surrounding the Shaping of the Country's Cultural Identity', *Middle Eastern Studies*, 39/3 (July 2003): 39–64.

Porath, Yoram, *The Emergence of the Palestinian-Arab National Movement, 1918–1929* (London: Cass, 1974).

Pred, Allen, 'Place as Historically Contingent Process: Structuration and the Time-Geography of Becoming Places', *Annals of the Association of American Geographers*, 74/2 (1984): 279–97.

al-Qabbani, 'Adnan Muhammad, *al-Futuhat al-haqqaniyya fi manaqib ajilla', al-Silsila al-dhahabiyya li'l-tariqa al-naqshbandiyya al-'aliyya* (n.p., n.d.).

al-Qaradawi, Yusuf, *Durus al-nakba al-thaniyya: limadha inhazamna … wa kayfa nantasiru* (n.p., n.d., second printing 1969).

_____ *Al-hulul al-mustawrada wa kayfa janat 'ala ummatina* (Beirut: Mu'asasat al-Risala, 1971).

_____ *Al-Halal wal-haram fi al-islam* (Beirut: Al-Maktab al-Islami, 1973).

_____ *Min fiqh al-dawla al-muslima* (Cairo: Dar al-Shuruq, 1997).

_____ *Thaqafatuna bayna al-infitah wal-inghilaq* (Cairo: Dar al-Shuruq, 2000).

_____ *Ummatuna bayna al-qarnayn* (Cairo: Dar al-Shuruq, 2000).

_____ *Ibn al-qarya wa'l-kuttab* (Cairo: Dar al-Shuruq, 2002).

_____ 'Taqdim', in *Qararat wa-fatawa al-majlis al-urubbi lil-ifta' wal-buhuth* (Cairo: Dar al-tawjih wa'l-nashr al-islamiyya, 2002): 5–10.

_____ *Hajat al-bashriyya ila al-risala al-hadariyya li-ummatina* (Cairo: Maktabat wahhaba, 2004).

_____ *Nahnu wal-gharb: as'ila sha'ika wa ajwiba hasima* (Cairo: Dar al-tawzi' wa'l-nashr al-islamiyya, 2006).

_____ *Fi fiqh al-aqalliyyat al-muslima* (Cairo: Dar al-shuruq, 2007).

Rappaport, Joanne, *Cumbe Reborn: Andean Ethnography of History* (Chicago, IL: University of Chicago Press, 1994).

Rappaport, Roy A., *Ritual and Religion in the Making of Humanity* (Cambridge: Cambridge University Press, 1999).

Rawlinson, Andrew, 'A History of Western Sufism', *Diskus*, 1 (1993): 63.

Refik, İbrahim, 'Tacın incisindeki Osmanlı'nın yetimleri', *Sızıntı*, 15 (1993): 397–401, 446–50.

Reinkowski, Maurus, *Filastin, Filistin und Eretz Israel. Die späte osmanische Herrschaft über Palästina in der arabischen, türkischen und israelischen Historiographie* (Berlin: Schwarz, 1995).

Reiter, Yitzhak, '"Third in Holiness, First in Politics": Al-Haram al-Sharif in Muslim Eyes', in Yitzhak Reiter (ed.), *Sovereignty of God and Man: Sanctity and Political Centrality on the Temple Mount* (Jerusalem: Jerusalem Institute for Israel Studies and Teddy Kollek Center for Jerusalem Studies, 2001): 155–80.

_____ *Jerusalem and Its Role in Islamic Solidarity* (New York: Palgrave Macmillan, 2008).

Rekhess, Elie, 'The Arabs of Israel After Oslo: Localization of the National Struggle', *Israel Studies*, 7/3 (2002): 1–44.

Riexinger, Martin, '"Turkey, Completely Independent!": Contemporary Turkish Left-wing Nationalism (*ulusal sol/ulusalcılık*): Its Predecessors, Objectives and Enemies', *Oriente Moderno*, 90/2 (2011): 353–96.

_____ 'Islamic Opposition to the Darwinian Theory of Evolution', in Lewis R. James and Olav Hammer (eds), *Handbook of Religion and the Authority of Science* (Leiden: Brill, 2011): 484–509.

Riley-Smith, Jonathan, *The Crusades, Christianity, and Islam* (New York: Columbia University Press, 2008).

Ritivoi, Andreea Deciu, *Paul Ricoeur: Tradition and Innovation in Rhetorical Theory* (Albany, NY: State University of New York Press, 2006).

Rosenthal, Franz, *The History of al-Tabari*, Vol. 1: *General Introduction and From the Creation to the Flood* (New York: State University of New York Press, 1989).

Rubin, Uri, 'Prophets and Prophethood', in Andrew Rippin (ed.), *The Blackwell Companion to the Qur'an* (Malden, MA, Oxford and Chichester: Wiley-Blackwell, 2009): 234–47.

Rushdie, Salman, *The Satanic Verses* (London: Viking Penguin, 1988).

Ruthven, Malise, *A Satanic Affair: Salman Rushdie and the Rage of Islam* (London: Chatto & Windus, 1990).

al-Saggaf, Yeslam, 'The Online Public Sphere in the Arab World: The War in Iraq on the Al Arabiya Website', *Journal of Computer-Mediated Communication*, 12 (2006): 311–34.

Sağlam, Vedat, *Köy enstitülerinden imam-hatip okullarına eğitim ve kültür* (İstanbul: Nesil Yayınları, 2003).

Salvatore, Armando, '"Public Islam" and the Nation-State in Egypt', *ISIM Newsletter*, 8 (September, 2001): 20.

al-Samman, Muhammad, 'Abd Allah, 'al-Ma'ani al-hayya fi'l-islam', *Rasa'il al-fikra al-islamiyya*, 3 (Cairo, 1953): 1–75.

al-Saqqaf, Hasan b. Ali, *al-Salafiyya al-wahhabiyya* (Beirut: Dar al-Mizan, 2005).

_____ *The New Imagined Community: Advanced Media Technologies and the Construction of National and Muslim Identities of Migrants* (Brighton, Portland, OR and Vancouver: Sussex Academic Press, 2009).

Scheuer, Michael, *Through Our Enemies' Eyes: Osama bin Laden, Radical Islam, and the Future of America* (rev. edn, Washington, DC: Potomac Books, 2006).

Schimmel, Annemarie, 'Samiha Ayverdi – eine istanbuler Schriftstellerin', in Wilhelm Hoenerbach (ed.), *Der Orient in der Forschung. Festschrift für Otto Spies* (Wiesbaden: Harrassowitz, 1967): 569–85.

Schleifer, 'Abdallah S., 'Interview with Sheikh Yusuf al-Qaradawi', *Transnational Broadcasting Studies*, 13 (autumn/winter 2005), available at http://www.tbsjournal.com/Archives/Fall04/interviewyusufqaradawi.htm, last accessed 20 February 2014.

Scott, James, *Seeing Like a State: How Certain Schemes to Improve the Human Condition Have Failed* (New Haven, CT: Yale University Press, 1998).

Sells, Michael A., 'Memory', in Jane Dammen McAuliffe (ed.), *Encyclopaedia of the Qur'an* (Georgetown University, Washington DC: Brill, 2011); Brill Online, 28 June 2011, available at http://referenceworks.brillonline.com/entries/encyclopaedia-of-the-quran/memory-SIM_00276, last accessed 20 February 2014.

Seufert, Günter, *Islam in der Türkei: Islamismus als symbolische Repräsentation einer sich modernisierenden muslimischen Gesellschaft* (Stuttgart: Steiner, 1997).

Shavit, Uriya, 'Should Muslims Integrate into the West?' *Middle East Quarterly*, 14/4 (autumn 2007): 13–21.

Sivan, Emmanuel, 'The Beginnings of the Fada'il al-Quds Literature', *Israel Oriental Studies*, 1 (1971): 262–71.

_____ *Arab Political Myths* (Tel Aviv: Am Oved, 1988).

Skovgaard-Petersen, Jakob, 'Yusuf al-Qaradawi and al-Azhar', in Bettina Gräf and Jakob Skovgaard-Petersen (eds), *Global Mufti: The Phenomenon of Yusuf al-Qaradawi* (London: Hurst, 2009): 27–53.

Smith, Andrea L., 'Heteroglossia, "Common Sense", and Social Memory', *American Ethnologist*, 31 (2004): 251–69.

Smith, Anthony, 'National Identity and Myths of Ethnic Descent', in *idem* (ed.), *Myths and Memories of the Nation* (Oxford: Oxford University Press, 1999).

Smith, Neil, 'Homeless/Global: Scaling Places', in Jon Bird, Barry Curtis, Tim Putnam, George Robertson, and Lisa Tickner (eds), *Mapping the Futures: Local Cultures, Global Change* (London and New York: Routledge, 1993): 87–119.

Smooha, Sami, *Index of Arab-Jewish Relations in Israel, 2004* (Haifa: University of Haifa Press, 2005).

Soage, Ana Belén, 'Shaykh Yusuf al-Qaradawi: Portrait of a Leading Islamist Cleric', *Middle East Review of International Affairs*, 12/1 (March 2008): 51–68.

Stemmann, Juan José, 'Middle East Salafism's Influence and the Radicalization of Muslim Communities in Europe', *Middle East Review of International Affairs*, 10/3 (September 2005): 1–14.

Stewart, John, *Nestorian Missionary Enterprise: The Story of a Church on Fire* (Piscataway, NJ: Gorgias, 1928/2007).

Suleiman, Yasir, *A War of Words: Language and Conflict in the Middle East*, Cambridge Middle East Studies (Cambridge: Cambridge University Press, 2004).

Swyngedouw, Eric, 'The Mammon Quest; "Glocalization", Interspatial Competition and the Monetary Order: The Construction of New Scales', in Mick Dunford and Giorgis Kafkalas (eds), *Cities and Regions in the New Europe* (London: Belhaven, 1992): 39–67.

_____ 'Territorial Organization and the Space/Technology Nexus', *Transactions of the Institute of British Geographers*, 17 (1992b: 417–33.

_____ 'Neither Global nor Local: "Glocalization" and the Politics of Scale', in Kevin Cox (ed.), *Spaces of Globalisation: Reasserting the Power of the Local* (New York and London: Guilford, 1997): 137–66.

_____ 'Globalisation or "Glocalisation"? Networks, Territories and Rescaling', *Cambridge Review of International Affairs*, 17/1 (2004): 25–48.

al-Tabarî, Muhammad b. Jarîr, *Jami' al-bayan 'an ta'wiy al-Qur'an* (Beirut: Dar al-Fikr, 1995).

al-Tahhan, Mustafa, *Sifat al-da'iya al-muslima* (Kuwait: al-Kuwait University Press, 2000).

Talattof, Kamran, 'Comrade Akbar: Islam, Marxism, and Modernity', *Comparative Studies of South Asia, Africa and the Middle East*, 25/3 (2005): 634–49.

Talhami, Ghada, 'The Modern History of Islamic Jerusalem: Academic Myths and Propaganda', *Middle East Policy*, 7/2 (2000): 113–29.

Tammam, Husam, 'Yusuf Qaradawi and the Muslim Brothers: The Nature of a Special Relationship', in Bettina Gräf and Jakob Skovgaard-Petersen (eds), *Global Mufti: The Phenomenon of Yusuf al-Qaradawi* (London: Hurst, 2009): 55–83.

Tatham, Steve, *Losing Arab Hearts and Minds: The Coalition, Al-Jazeera and Muslim Public Opinion* (London: Hurst, 2006).

Tezcan, Levent, *Religiöse Strategien der 'machbaren' Gesellschaft. Verwaltete Religion und islamistische Utopie in der Türkei* (Bielefeld: Transcript, 2003).

Tietze, Nikola, *Islamische Identitäten. Formen muslimischer Religiösität junger Männer in Deutschland und Frankreich* (Hamburg: Hamburger Edition, 2001).

Toledano, Ehud, *Slavery and its Abolition in the Ottoman Middle East* (Seattle, WA: Washington University Press, 1998).

Toprak, Binnaz, *Islamist Intellectuals of the 1980s in Turkey* (Istanbul: Redhouse, 1987).

Tottoli, Roberto, 'Origin and Use of the Term *Israiliyyat* in Muslim Literature', *Arabica* 46 (1999): 193–221.

Tripp, Charles, *Islam and the Moral Economy: The Challenge of Capitalism* (Cambridge: Cambridge University Press, 2006).

Tu, Weiming, 'Destructive Will and Ideological Holocaust: Maoism as a Source of Social Suffering in China', *Daedalus*, 125/1 (1996): 149–80.

Turner, Victor, 'Pilgrimages as Social Processes', in Victor Turner (ed.), *Drama, Fields, and Metaphors: Symbolic Action in Human Society* (Ithaca, NY: Cornell University Press, 1974): 166–230.

_____ 'Liminal to Liminoid, in Play, Flow, and Ritual: An Essay in Comparative Symbology', *Rice University Studies*, 60/3 (1974): 53–92.

Vajda, G. 'Isra'iliyyat', *Encyclopaedia of Islam*, Second Edition, Brill Online, 2013, available at http://referenceworks.brillonline.com/entries/encyclopaedia-of-islam-2/israiliyyat-SIM_3670, last accessed 20 February 2014.

Vakkasoğlu, Vehbi, *Bozgun (bir devrin çöküşü)* (Istanbul: Yeni Asya, 1977).

_____ *İslâm Dünya gündeminde* (Istanbul: Yeni Asya, 1984).

_____ *Osmanlı insanı* (Istanbul: Nesil, 2004).

Van der Leeuw, Gerardus, *Religion in Essence and Manifestation*, trans. James Turner (New York: Macmillan, 1938/1986).

Van der Veer, Peter, 'Writing Violence', in David Ludden (ed.), *Contesting the Nation: Religion, Community, and the Politics of Democracy in India* (Philadelphia, PA: University of Pennsylvania Press, 1996): 250–69.

_____ 'Riots and Rituals: The Construction of Violence and Public Space in Hindu Nationalism', in Paul Brass (ed.), *Riots and Pogroms* (New York: New York University Press, 1996): 154–76.

Waardenburg, Jacques, *Muslims as Actors: Islamic Meanings and Muslim Interpretations in the Perspective of the Study of Religions* (Berlin and New York: de Gruyter, 2007): 359–76.

Wa'il, Lutfi, *Dawlat al-du'a al-judud* (Cairo, 2005).

Walker, Paul, *Exploring an Islamic Empire: Fatimid History and Its Sources* (London: I.B. Tauris, 2002).

Wang, Jianping, *Concord and Conflict: The Hui Communities of Yunnan Society* (Philadelphia, PA: Coronet Books, 1996).

Wang, Weizhou, 'The Green Flag Instead of the Red Flag', *Duping*, 36/37 (2007).

Watt, W. Montgomery and M.V. McDonald, *The History of al-Tabari*, Vol. VI: *Muhammad at Mecca* (New York: State University of New York Press, 1988).

Weismann, Itzchak, 'The Politics of Popular Islam: Sufis, Salafis, and Muslim Brothers in Twentieth-Century Hamah', *International Journal of Middle East Studies*, 37 (2005): 39–58.

_____ *The Naqshbandiyya: Orthodoxy and Activism in a Worldwide Sufi Tradition* (London and New York: Routledge, 2007).

Wheeler, Brannon M., *Prophets in the Quran: An Introduction to the Quran and Muslim Exegesis*, sel. and trans. Brannon M. Wheeler (London and New York: Continuum, 2002).

Wielandt, Rotraud, *Das Bild der Europäer in der modernen arabischen Erzähl- und Theaterliteratur* (Wiesbaden: Harrassowitz, 1980).

Wien, Peter, *Iraqi Arab Nationalism: Authoritarian, Totalitarian and Pro-Fascist Inclinations, 1932–1941* (London: Routledge, 2008).

Wild, Stefan, 'National Socialism in the Arab Near East between 1933 and 1939', *Welt des Islams*, 25/4 (1985): 126–73.

Wise, Lindsay, '*Words from the Heart': New Forms of Islamic Preaching in Egypt.* Unpublished MPhil thesis in Modern Middle Eastern Studies, Oxford University, 2003.

_____ 'Amr Khaled vs. Yusuf al Qaradawi: The Danish Cartoon Controversy and the Clash of Two Islamic TV Titans', *Transnational Broadcasting Studies*, 16 (2006), available at www.tbsjournal.com/wise.htm, last accessed 23 February 2014.

Wright, Lawrence, *The Looming Tower: Al-Qaeda and the Road to 9/11* (New York: Vintage Books, 2006).

Xu, Jian, 'Radical Ethnicity and Apocryphal History: Reading the Sublime Object of Humanism in Zhang Chengzhi's Late Fictions', *Positions*, 10/3 (2002): 525–47.

Xu, Jilin, 'Piping de daode yu daode de piping' ('The ethics of critique and moralized critiques'), *Wenyililun*, 8 (1996): 23–33.

al-Ya'qubi, Ahmad ibn Abu Ya'qub, *Ta'rikh al-Ya'qubi*. 2 vols (Beirut: Dar Sadir and Dar Bayrut, 1960).

Yavuz, Hakan, *Islamic Political Identity in Turkey* (Oxford: University Press, 2003).

Young, L.C. and S.R. Ford, 'God Is Society: The Religious Dimension of Maoism', *Sociological Inquiry*, 47/2 (1977): 89–97.

Zelkina, Anna, *In Quest of God and Freedom: The Sufi Response to the Russian Advance in the North Caucasus* (London: Hurst, 2000).

Zhang, Chengzhi, *Xinlingshi* ('History of the soul') (Guangzhou: Huacheng chubanshe, 1991).

——— *Zhang Chengzhi wenxue zuopin xuanji: xinlingshi juan* ('Collected literary works of Zhang Chengzhi: History of the soul') (Haiko: hainan chubanshe, 1996).

——— *Zhonghua sanwen zhencangben: zhang chengzhi juan* ('The collector's edition of Chinese prose: collected essays of Zhang Chengzhi') (Beijing: renmin wenxue chubanshe, 1997).

——— *Jin muchang* ('Golden pasture') (Beijing: renmin wenxue chubanshe, 2007).

———*Wusedeyiduan* ('Colorful heresy') (Hongkong: daofeng chubanshe, 2007).

———*Xianhua de feixu* ('Flowers on ruins') (Beijing: xinshijie chubanshe, 2008).

Zhang, Yiwu, 'Cong daode xunhuan dao shenxue xunhuan – wenhua maoxian zhuyi de xingtai fenxi' ('From moral rules to theological rules – an analysis of cultural adventurist mentality'), *Shanghai wenhua*, 6 (1995): 90–9.

Index

Page numbers in *italics* refer to figures and tables.